DESERT WILDLIFE

Desert Wildlife

EDMUND C. JAEGER

STANFORD UNIVERSITY PRESS
Stanford, California

Stanford University Press
Stanford, California
Copyright © 1950, 1961, by the Board of Trustees of the
Leland Stanford Junior University
Printed in the United States of America
Cloth ISBN 0-8047-0123-7
Paper ISBN 0-8047-0124-5
First published in 1950 as *Our Desert Neighbors*
This edition first published in 1961
Last figure below indicates year of this printing:
81

Preface

Desert Wildlife is a series of intimate and authentic sketches depicting the lives of native animals of our Southwestern deserts, from mammals to birds and reptiles, as well as many of the lesser desert denizens such as land snails, scorpions, millepedes, and common insects of special interest. The mammals and birds have been given specially full treatment. Although the approach is basically scientific, this book is designed for readers of all ages who wish to learn of the ways of the wild animal neighbors met on desert travels.

It is a revision of the author's popular *Our Desert Neighbors* (Stanford University Press, 1950) with additional chapters, many new field notes, photographs, and sketches.

A number of the added chapters appeared in somewhat abridged form in past numbers of *The Desert Magazine,* and the author wishes to thank Mr. Charles E. Shelton, publisher, for permission to use this material. Certain portions of other chapters appeared much earlier in *St. Nicholas Magazine* and in the author's two now out-of-print books, *Denizens of the Desert* (Houghton Mifflin Company, 1922) and *Denizens of the Mountains* (Charles C Thomas, 1929). No book of this nature can be written without help from biologists whose writings appear in many professional journals and monographs: to these the author wishes to express his gratitude.

Credit for the art work must be given to Merle Gish, to Charles Papp, and to the numerous camera artists and institutions whose names appear below the many unusual and excellent photographs. Photographic illustrations without personal names below them record some of the author's moments of pleasure in desert wilderness places.

EDMUND C. JAEGER

Riverside, California
July 10, 1961

Contents

Illustrations

DESERT WILDLIFE

I. The Magic Circle

The desert road we were following skirted a low rise, carried us across a broad, bumpy cross wash, and divided abruptly. We chose the fainter of the two trails and continued on our way, cutting across a flat valley. This was typical Mohave Desert country: Joshua trees, creosote bushes, and scattered deerhorn cactus, all interspersed with low shrubs. There was nothing spectacular here in the way of scenery; apparently nothing to distinguish this sandy, gravelly area from hundreds of others just like it. But at that moment we chanced to glance to our left, and what we saw caused us to stop the car to look more closely.

There, a few yards from the winding road, stood a Joshua tree. In that little, almost flat-bottomed valley there were dozens of other "Joshuas," both taller and greater in size than this one. Our first look, however, made us realize that here was a tree yucca truly unique. It could easily bear the distinction of having the tallest straight trunk of any Joshua tree in the world. For twenty-two feet it shot straight upward like a telephone pole, and then, at the very top, as if aware of its error in departing from the normal ways of its kind, it suddenly branched out, not into the usual two, but into four distinct upward-curving spiny arms, each about four feet in length. These arms were so situated that they formed a perfect round-bottomed cradle. An enterprising pair of red-tailed hawks had evidently recognized in this high arboreal basket the perfect nesting site, and there in its center had constructed a large bulky nest of creosote twigs. Its great height from the ground made it unusually safe from the molestations of wandering predators.

Such a tall-stemmed Joshua tree is a rarity. Seldom is one seen that rises more than six or eight feet in height before branching; one that has failed to branch for over twenty feet is an exceptional find. It was evident that for a full thirty or forty years this lone yucca, while leading a sort of charmed, unmolested life, had grown only upward; and never in all that time had it thrown out a panicle of flowers, nor had its terminal bud ever been damaged by wind or had insects bored within its woody tissue. This we knew, because this particular subspecies of Joshua tree branches only under one of those three conditions. This long freedom from injury or mishap, this long-delayed attempt to flower, were in themselves very singular and strange records among the tree yuccas of our deserts.

We walked around to view the tree from many angles and to learn what curious desert wonders could be found near it. We were soon rewarded with so many sights of unusual interest that we decided to draw an imaginary circle, with the Joshua tree as its center and with a radius of a hundred feet, and then to list all the things we saw within what we decided to call our "Magic Circle." Let those who think that desert areas are places of desolation and just so much gray-green brush, sand, and gravel read now an account of our census.

One of the first things we jotted down on our list was neither animal nor vegetable, but mineral. It was lying beside a scrubby creosote bush among rain- and wind-worn pebbles—a black meteoric stone over an inch and a half long and weighing several ounces. Once part of a flaming molten mass, shooting through the air at a speed so fast that it almost burned itself up, this small, irregular chunk of metal now looked cold and lifeless. We speculated as to how many millions of miles it must have traveled before entering our atmosphere.

We moved farther within the Magic Circle. Only a few feet from our tree were two cactus wrens' nests, one a male's flimsily built roosting quarters and the other a female's better-constructed nest. Both nests were set in spiny cactus about three feet off the ground; most secure, for the yellow-sheathed spines of the cactus would deter even the hungriest enemy from climbing up to molest the bird inhabitants. The incubation nest had been built on top of a former nest, and perhaps even by the same pair of birds. True to cactus wren custom, it was made of the stems of wild buckwheat and vinegarweed, and decorated and lined with bits of woolly filago.

One of the cholla cacti nearby now attracted our attention, for because of recent heavy rains it had grown several new joints. Plainly visible on these fresh shoots were some seldom-seen fleshy, ephemeral leaves, no doubt vestiges of organs much better developed in some ancestral cacti.

Just beyond, another Joshua tree caught our eye. It was unbranched and stood about seven feet high. What attracted our attention to it was the peculiar shape of most of its long, spine-tipped leaves. Nearly every one was twisted into a Turkish scimitar or into a corkscrew. What strange shivering fits and nightmares had influenced this plant's centers of cell organization we may never know, nor do we ever again expect to see another tree yucca with leaves quite like that one.

On a creosote bush we next found the small, dark-brown nest of a potter bee, with its water-proof protective cover of bits of gravel set in hardened wax to form an intricate mosaic. A question that has always puzzled naturalists is, how does a potter bee know how to make such a durable nest?

GIANT TREE YUCCA—CENTER OF THE MAGIC CIRCLE

Our inspection was diverted momentarily to the ground when we noted a little *Trombidium* crawling over the sand. This is a handsome, harmless harvest mite that looks like an animated squarish bit of scarlet plush. As he walked busily about in search of food, his fine colors flashed in the afternoon sun. His scientific name, *Trombidium*, means "the little timid one." The Mexicans long ago gave him the musical name *angelito*, little angel.

Penetrating some of the more barren sandy spaces between shrubs were a number of small holes, each surrounded by largish, soft, earth pellets, each the size of a tapioca ball. From the size of these earth balls, it was clear that they were not fashioned by ants. We set to work with a digging tool and soon turned up a plump, brown millepede. It had doubtless gone underground just after a rain had moistened the earth.

Speaking of holes in the ground, one often wonders what creatures make those openings of varied size and shape so often seen in the desert soils. Within our Magic Circle we saw many such holes: here were the entrances to the subterranean homes of white-footed mice, kangaroo rats, and antelope ground squirrels; the slanting, ovoid burrow entrances made by scorpions; and the gravel-rimmed "wells" made by ground spiders. Several kinds of holes were, of course, made by ants which inhabited the area. The most common species were the harvesters and the honey ants. The formicaries, or homes, of the harvester ants can be recognized by the craterlets of alfilaria seeds about the entrance; those made by the honey ants by the broad marginal mounds of loose gravel. The honey ant might be called the ghost ant of this desert, its almost transparent amber-colored body being very difficult to see against the background of grayish sands. It makes small living honey bottles out of certain members of its colony.

A few feet beyond, we spotted a brush rabbit's shallow

burrow. There, about three feet down its length, sat the gray proprietor all hunched up, head facing down the tunnel, his pomponlike white tail toward us. He probably was fully confident that he was securely hidden, though we could have caught him easily by merely reaching in at arm's length. Several minutes later we found the place where a large desert jack rabbit had been flushed from its "form." The jack rabbit is, of course, really a hare, not a rabbit, and in the typical manner of the hares, he fashions a form for himself by nibbling out a hollow within a dense brush thicket or a clump of grass, never digging himself a burrow as a true rabbit does. Such a form provides a place where the owner may sit in hiding or bed down when not foraging.

In lifting a prostrate, dead Joshua tree trunk, we discovered a four-inch *Xantusia,* or desert night lizard, one of the most unusual of all lizards inhabiting the Mohave region. Evidently it had been feeding upon termites, which were plentiful among the rotting wood fibers, and as we uncovered this saurian it scuttled to safety, seeking refuge under another decumbent limb. This was the only form of reptilian life we noted within our Magic Circle.

Seeing the termites inside the log gave us the idea of searching elsewhere for them. Sure enough, almost at the base of our unbranched tree giant, we found the somewhat clayish, sandy soil crisscrossed with many peculiar long mud cylinders about a third of an inch in diameter. When touched, these collapsed as though made of powder, revealing within a crawling mass of termites. They were soon moving for cover. Termites detest sunlight, and in order to feed in the security of darkness, this species constructs thin earthen cases or covers the vegetation upon which they have chosen to feed.

Under adjacent creosote bushes we spied numbers of what appeared to be flattish lumps of dried, white froth, each shaped like a fried egg, with the bloated "yolk" made up, as was revealed by further examination, of millions of microscopic gray-black spores. It was one of those odd plant-animals known as slime molds or Mycetozoa. In the now dry state it was covered with an ashy-white coating; but at one time it was a living, slow-creeping jellylike object, created by Nature, as it were, in a moment of fancy after a warm summer shower. The untrained observer may easily mistake one of these dried organisms for the droppings of some large bird of prey.

The only evidence of any large carnivore within our area was an abandoned badger's den. It had been long in disuse, for it was partially filled with earth and across its wide mouth had been spun the typically scraggly, tough, irregular, and untidy web of a black widow spider.

Close by were found the leaf-covered, cigar-shaped cocoons of a case-bearer moth, as well as the "robin's pin-cushion" or fuzzy creosote gall caused by the activities of a cynipid wasp. In a wild buckwheat bush was suspended the beautiful dome-shaped web of a metepeirid spider.

All was silent, except for the occasional droning of a fly and the intermittent wispy sound created by a small green creosote grasshopper, with its intricate silver markings. Once a thrasher at a distance burst into song; at another time a distant cactus wren voiced a brief protest. The still air was heavy with the pungent scent of creosote bush.

All these things and more we saw or heard within our Magic Circle of a hundred-foot radius. And in the center stood our tall, long-trunked Joshua tree with its crown of four branches and its basketlike hawk's nest of creosote twigs.

In the evening, against the silhouette of the rocky hills surrounding the valley and the colorful clouds, small pipistrellid bats darted overhead. The last notes of the thrasher were heard far away. As the sky grew darker, bringing out the stars, we looked beyond our Magic Circle to that larger circle, the rim of the horizon.

2. The Desert Kit Fox

Up in the land of the Cosos, near the southern end of the Argus Mountains, lies an ancient lake bed whose bottom is populated today by numerous huge, bizarre forms of limestone spires known as the Pinnacles. No one is sure of their origin, but it is believed that these grotesque columns of lime, huddled in bunches or standing apart in isolation, are mammoth deposits of white minerals built up around underwater vents of hot springs.

They are an impressive sight at any time, but under the "white-shadow light" of the full moon they present a spectacle of awe and beauty. On summer nights when the silence of the great desert and the brilliant moon make for philosophic musings and reminiscence, I like to walk on the dry sands of the saltbush-edged washes that run down among the Pinnacles toward Searles Dry Lake and think of the history of this strange land, its faunal and floral past, its long geological pageant of days and nights.

On one such warm evening in September as I walked with two companions, for the most part silent, over the hummocks of sand between the Pinnacles and along one of the dry courseways of cloudburst waters, I was surprised to find that a fourth companion had joined us—a small cat-sized creature, almost a phantom, that now we saw faintly, and then not at all. Like a shadowy something, it seemed to float ghostlike before us, then fade into the half-darkness before coming alongside or following behind. So careful was it not to come too near, so close was its color to that of the silver sand, so silent was it of foot, that although we strained our eyes and ears we could not fully make out its outline or decide upon its true nature.

Only when I struck a match did the light apprise us of the animal's identity. Then we saw that our phantom creature was none other than *Vulpes velox,* the desert kit fox. Filled with curiosity and finding himself unmolested, he tried to play hide-and-seek with us, running before, alongside, and behind us for more than an hour like an affectionate little dog. He remained with us so long that we adopted him as our mascot. On returning to the camp where our bedrolls were lying on the sand, we put out food for the little ghost of the night and had the satisfaction of seeing next morning that he had taken it. Numerous dainty, almost cat-sized tracks had been left about us on the clean sand, showing that as we slept he had gone about making further inspection of his new neighbors.

On other occasions kit foxes have come about in the dim light of my small campfire and made themselves familiar, and once, while I slept up among the rocks of a Chuckawalla Mountain hillside, I was awakened near daybreak by a slight noise and found myself looking squarely into the face of a kit fox. There he was, right beside me, cautiously and curiously peering into my face. Fortunately, I had my wits about me; I was careful to be very quiet, hardly daring to wink my eyes; and so for a moment he stood there in what seemed wild fascination and foolish curiosity combined. Then he turned and faded away into the half-darkness.

The kit fox, or desert swift, as it is sometimes called, is unquestionably one of America's most handsome carnivores. Dainty, gentle, and keen of sight, he wanders about us almost unknown and seldom seen. He is considerably smaller than his distant cousin the gray fox. His body length from nose tip to tail is only twenty inches, and the bushy, black-tipped tail* is not more than half that long. The fur is unusually full, soft, and dense, and in color a beautiful grizzled white and light-yellowish buff with scattered, long, black-tipped overhairs. This paleness of coloration is a protective feature of no small importance, since it enables the animal to slip about on the gray or yellowish sands at early dawn and dusk, and even on moonlight nights, with little fear of detection; even in the full light of early morning it does not stand out conspicuously against the gray of its environment.

The kit fox has short, stout limbs, which make it stand relatively lower than the gray fox. The short, well-muscled legs help it to break into quick pace when getting away on the run, but they do not aid the animal in maintaining an enduring speed. The kit fox, in spite of a reputation to that effect, is not an animal of unusual fleetness even when pursued. What it lacks in speed, however, it makes up by an extraordinary ability to make quick turns and take advantage of any scant cover of brush or rocks. The soles of the feet are covered with long fur, only the small toepads being bare, which makes for better traction on the open, level sands over which it so often runs. The ears are comparatively short, well pointed, and heavily furred, both without and within.

---

* The desert fox (*Canis leucopus*) of southwestern Asia has a white-tipped tail. This desert hunting species lives largely on jerboalike rodents or gerbils, very common in sandy regions there.

YOUNG KIT FOX

The hearing is keen, and at the slightest sound or movement the animal is immediately alert.

Like many of the foxes, the kit fox is, as a rule, solitary, rarely, if ever, associating in numbers as the other Canidae do. Early in the spring, however, they may be seen in pairs, and the burrows are then prepared for the young. The ordinary retreat is a burrow appropriated from some rodent and then enlarged to suit current needs. If kit foxes must dig their own holes, they usually choose to work in loose, sandy soil upon which plants are growing, since the roots help to keep the sand coherent and thus make it easier to burrow in without danger of caving. As a protection from being flooded out, the animals often excavate in the sides of small embankments. Frequently, however, the dens are found in perfectly flat ground, their presence being easily detected by the heap of sand or earth which has been thrown up about the entrance. As a general rule, there are several openings, a safety measure in case of danger. The burrow may be six or even eight feet long and descend from four to six feet before the nest cavity is reached. The diameter varies from eight to ten inches. If it is occupied, there is usually fresh earth at the entrance and fox tracks in numbers leading into and out of it. In these burrows the animals repose during the day and in them the young are born.

The average number of kittens in a litter is thought to be four or five. The vixen has but six teats. The young stay with the parents until April or early May.

The best place to go to find the burrows of the kit fox is open, sandy desert where kangaroo rat colonies are abundant. Both foxes and coyotes eagerly seek out these small rodents for food. In dune areas where kangaroo rats are found, the sand is always covered with countless impressions of kit fox feet. In many places we see where the animals made attempts, often successful, to dig the rodents from their numerous tunnels. Dr. Joseph Grinnell, late director of the Museum of Vertebrate Zoology of the University of California, was so impressed with the part the kangaroo rats played in furnishing food for the kit fox that he spoke of them as the "staff of life" of this animal. Other food consists of lizards, insects, and an occasional rabbit or bird. Animals such as rodents which are not dug from their underground retreats are stalked, catlike, on the spot, but are usually carried to the den to be eaten.

3. The Gray Fox

I long ago took the advice of an early-rising prospector-naturalist that one should get up at dawn and be on the trail before all the nocturnal wild creatures have gone to their lairs for the day. During the night hours most of the wild animals are out and active, and if we would see them we must get up at least an hour or two before sunrise. Among the first tracks I come upon in my morning wanderings are those of the gray fox. The catlike marks are so plentiful along the sandy wash that runs alongside my desert camp that almost instinctively I call the place Fox Alley. The country all about is very rocky, and the foxes, to save their feet, have chosen the sandy canyon bottom for their principal highway. "Here," said I one day, "I will sit down beside the trail to see what comes by."

I watched there beside the trail a good many early mornings and several moonlit evenings before I saw my fox. But the sight I eventually had of it well repaid my days of waiting, for under the conditions I saw an animal not running away from me in fright but acting wholly naturally. It was a female bound for the home lair with a wood rat in her jaws; there must be young foxes at home. Gracefully she trotted along with her head well up and her eyes gleaming. I watched her as she disappeared up the canyon and into the brush. This was one of the red-letter experiences of my days in the wild.

Many days I searched for the lair, but I always came home from my hunt baffled and unsatisfied. If I did not find the den soon, the young foxes would grow up and leave the burrow and I would never see them. One day, after a long ramble, I saw two baby foxes playing about the entrance of a small hole in the side of a gully. I approached them so cautiously that they manifested little more than curiosity when at last they caught sight of me. I kept a fine screen of brush between them and myself and I don't think that they had any realization of danger. I remained at a fair distance and then sat down to watch them. One of them ran playfully into the den and soon came out dragging a bunch of feathers. This he pawed over, took into his mouth, and shook thoroughly, and then he rolled gleefully over and over in the dust. The other pup all the time looked on with amusing curiosity. Finally he came up and pulled the bird skin away from his playmate. Thus the fun went on. The vixen, or mother fox, was probably inside the den, for it was not yet time for her to go out to hunt; but since it was fully my intention to come back and see more at another time I did not think it wise to disturb the family to find out. So when both of the little foxes went into the hole, I slipped away.

I told an old prospector friend of my find. He surprised me the next morning by bringing in one of the babies for a camp pet. "Got it in a box trap," he said, "and almost had both of them." The young fox soon overcame his fears, and he proved unusually playful and created a great deal of amusement among the men at our camp. So mischievous was he that nothing within reach was safe from mauling. Old shoes, the corners of blankets that hung down from the beds, sticks of wood from the wood box—everything had to be pulled and chewed. As it grew older, the animal wandered from time to time out into the brush, to be gone for several days at a time, but always it returned and manifested the greatest satisfaction at being back again.

The west coast of the United States is a fox paradise. No fewer than eight different races of the gray fox are found in California. Each of the coastal islands of southern California gives a home to a distinct race. The Lower and Upper Sonoran Life Zones of the southeastern deserts are inhabited by the Arizona gray fox. The humid coast belt of central California claims its redwood fox, and the region included between the interior of Humboldt County and Mount Shasta is inhabited by the Townsend gray fox. It is a curious fact that the fox found in the famous Rancho La Brea fossil beds of Los Angeles is apparently identical with these foxes now living in the far-western mountains and valleys. "This probably represents one of the few if not the only carnivorous mammal," said Frank S. Daggett, "that passed unaltered in form through conditions that brought extinction or great modification to the fauna of southern California generally."

The Western gray foxes exhibit little of the cunning and crafty intelligence shown by the red foxes of Europe and eastern United States. Indeed, they are so persistently and unsuspiciously foolish that they seem to be the dunces of the wild, and trappers find them among the easiest of our larger mammals to catch. They seem never to have been intended by nature to live in a man-infested land. Neither their wits nor their cleverness is of the kind to help them out in the presence of man's trapping devices.

When left alone, the gray fox manages to get along very well. He is a rustler in the matter of supplying himself with food. He never lies around waiting for something to turn up, but goes out on the hunt as soon as the long shadows of evening have crept over the mountain. On cloudy days I have seen him out hunting, but I am inclined to think that this is not usual.

Almost all of his food is alive, on the move, and ready to speed away from him at his approach. Often, because of the adeptness in flight of his intended prey, he must find himself without a meal just when he is most hungry.

Competition between foxes and other animals for food in times of fair abundance must be small. Foxes subsist largely on rodents, of which the supply is generally plentiful, small birds which roost near the ground, wild fruits, and insects. Indeed, much of the food of the fox is such as is generally ignored by the larger Canidae. In relation to the destruction of rodents, the fox's economic record is good, for he is a tireless destroyer of mice, ground squirrels, pack rats, and gophers. To sick and crippled birds he proves a blessing, for he gobbles them up and puts a quick end to their misery; to strong and healthy ones he is a constant menace. This carnivorous night prowler, with his sharp eyes, keen ears, and quick, snapping jaws, makes sad end of many a bird, her eggs, and young. It is an easy trick for him to take the birds that nest or roost near the ground or in low bushes. A fox can climb into a small bush with ease, and even up onto the branches of a good-sized tree if the trunk leans at a fair angle away from the vertical. This animal is so sly, secretive, and owl-like in his silence of movement that roosting birds have little chance to evade him.

The female has entire charge in rearing the young. She must do all the hunting for her pups, and in time of need it is she who is called upon to defend her offspring. Generally shy, she shows absolute self-abnegation after the appearance of the young, and offers a most threatening front to any creature that disturbs the peace of her family. The number of pups is three to five; they are born in April, May, or June. The illustration at the head of this chapter is of a gray fox pup.

The gray fox shows no unusual ability as a songster. He saves himself the cursing bestowed on the noisy coyotes. A fox can hardly be said to bark in the true sense of the word, for his voice is little more than a coarse, croaking yelp, given, not in series like the coyote's "song," but singly and infrequently. I hear it most often at dusk, when the foxes are just beginning to come out for the night's prowl.

The natural enemies other than man are few. The meat of canines, like the meat of birds of prey, is generally distasteful to other carnivores. I have known prospectors who tried to save on rations by cooking up fox and coyote meat for their dogs. Though they had attempted to disguise the flavor by seasoning the meat with onions, pepper, and vinegar, their beasts would have none of it.

4. The Coyote

One may be in desert country thick with coyotes* for days and nights without hearing their wild cry or without seeing a single animal. Every morning the numerous new tracks seen in the clean gray sand of arroyos or in the sun-baked dust of winding roads indicate that the wily, untamed dogs are about. You may even see where they have been in your camp. Silent and sagacious, they stalk about at night, in early morning, or in the late afternoon, and

---

* Several desert races of the coyote (*Canis latrans*) have been described (*C. l. estor, C. l. mearnsi*). They are not only paler and grayer in coloration than the neighboring coastal and mountain coyotes but also smaller. The Mearns coyote (named after Dr. Edgar A. Mearns of the United States Boundary Survey), which dwells in the hot southern deserts of California and Arizona and the arid regions of contiguous Sonora, is very small owing to its meager diet, high summer temperatures, and occasional long periods of severe drought when most of the small rodents and insects upon which it feeds perish.

The word *coyote* is an American-Spanish appellation, a corruption of the Aztec *coyotl*. It is properly pronounced koy-o-tay.

find out all that is going on about them; but never once do they let you have a look at them, even though you make studied effort. During the day they hide in places so secreted that it is only on rare occasions that you discover the hideout. Sometimes they lie under cover of bushes, for several times when, for amusement, I have rolled huge stones down steep canyon sides studded with low bushes, coyotes have jumped out and run away. I recently saw a large stone tossed into a low juniper on a hillside and a big coyote bolted from hiding. I do not believe he took pleasantly to this rude disturbance of his diurnal siesta.

At other times, and often for no explained reason, the chorus of coyote cries, the high-pitched ringing serenades that so delight the ear of the desert camper, are heard night after night. Now and then one even sees and hears a coyote during the day. Once in late June, while out wandering in search of rare plants in the dry Inyo Mountains, I saw a wildly barking coyote out at midday, but so occupied was he with his doleful howlings that he seemed wholly uncautious and completely unsuspicious of danger. He was coming along a ridge at a galloping gait, every now and then stopping and yapping a while. He turned directly toward me and, although I was in plain sight, continued to approach me until within about fifty feet. Then suddenly he noticed me, and with a great start of surprise he abruptly stopped barking and dashed for the cover of some near-by bushes.

A similar thing happened recently along the north base of the Chuckawalla Mountains of the Colorado Desert. Here, just at sunup, a coyote was heard boldly serenading. The loudness of his barking indicated that he must be very near, so my companions and I rushed out from our camp behind an ironwood tree to see what he was up to. He was, in fact, about a quarter of a mile away, approaching us. He was loping along in the broad, open spaces between creosote bushes and was evidently preoccupied. Although here again the animal could easily have seen us, he came right on, barking loudly every little while, and was surprised and alarmed only when he came to within ten yards of us. It is quite possible that neither of these coyotes had ever seen a human being before.

The time of most frequent short barks and serenades of ringing cries is after dusk or early in the morning just before dawn, as the coyotes go out to hunt or when they are about to return to cover. Often shortly after sundown one hears in the distance a series of short yaps and broken high-pitched barks and cries, followed by others after a brief interval of silence; if the animal is far away, only the terminal notes may be heard. Soon this call is answered by another animal, perhaps indicating that it is a call to get together on the hunt. Says Dr. Vernon Bailey, in his article on the mammals of Oregon, "Their *yap, yap, yap, yi, yi, yi* followed by a long shrill *on, on, on, on, on* rings far in a still night, so fast and jumbled that the voice of one often sounds like two, and two in a chorus like six in a real call of the wild, and a neighboring cliff sometimes doubles or quadruples these sounds."*

I once saw two coyotes in eager pursuit of a jack rabbit. The more they gained on the fleeing hare the noisier they became. When the rabbit finally eluded them by dashing over a steep bank and into a thicket, the excited calls ceased abruptly. The coyotes stood still a moment on the edge of the bank, apparently in amazed disappointment. After circling the dense growth a few times, they trotted off in what appeared to be a state of unconcern. Just before and during the early moments of a vigorous thunderstorm, and again after the deep rumblings have ceased, these gray-coated dogs

---

* "The Mammals and Life Zones of Oregon," *N. A. Fauna*, No. 55, p. 277.

of the desert demonstrate their vocal abilities to best advantage. If the animals are quite near, the penetrating quality of the high-pitched cries may almost make one shudder with fear.

One of the most obvious evidences of the relative local abundance of coyotes is the presence of many much-used "scent posts," where there are accumulations of feces together with white urine-stained spots. These places occur most often on ridges, and the amount of fecal material may be considerable. The posts, barren of all vegetation, are regularly used as the animals pass over the lookout trails so common on ridges or along the edges of cliffs which afford a commanding view. Toenail scratches on the ground made after defecation and urination are prevalent evidence that the odor of excreta invokes in them responses similar to those produced among domestic dogs.

In rocky desert, coyotes confine their trails very much to the soft sand, brush- or tree-bordered washes, and gullies. There they probably find their best hunting and also a surface less wearing on their feet. They strongly dislike little rocks on their trail and will break step rather than tread on one. Observing their trails, I have noticed this time and again. Domestic dogs out in the wild are not always so wise and cautious about stepping on stones, and when abroad, perhaps out with their master on the hunt, turn up after a few days with sore and bleeding feet.

The coyote is a wide and restless wanderer. Good evidence of this may be found in the Little San Bernardino Mountains to the north of the Coachella Valley in California. From the piñon-covered crest of the range, where I frequently camp, to the nearest date orchards in the valley below is a distance of fifteen miles; yet quite frequently I find in the high mountain gullies near my camp coyote dung made up almost wholly of date seeds. This means that the animals make the trip down to the desert floor, eat their fill

DESERT COYOTE

of dates, and get back again to their mountain retreats in a single night—a remarkable accomplishment.

In an arid land where the density of animal populations is never great, it is only by keeping continually on the hunt during the silent night hours that coyotes can come upon sufficient food to satisfy their hunger. If you see a coyote out on the hunt during the day, it is because he is a very hungry animal and his night rambles have failed to yield a normal quota of food. Freshly caught rodents, such as ground squirrels, kangaroo rats, white-footed mice dug from their burrows among rocks or in the wastes of blown sand, and rabbits run down in the open, constitute their principal fare. Birds are not often eaten. During times of lean pickings, juniper seeds, the curiously coiled pods of the screw bean, gourd seeds, and even dry grass may help them eke out a scant living until better days are at hand. Around the larger groves of Washingtonia palms north of Indio, coyote trails are abundant. Examination of the feces will show that these adaptable beasts have been feeding almost exclusively on the rounded, sugary-meated berries of the palms. On open desert, such as on the Mohave's creosote-bush flats, rabbit hair and kangaroo rat fur are among the commonest fecal constituents. Around almost every sandy flat where kangaroo rats are abundant, one comes upon numerous evidences that coyotes regularly dig into the burrows.

I know of several rock-lined *tinajas,* or tanks, in the Chuckawalla Mountains where water is found the year round. During the spring and summer these pools are often populated with swarms of tadpoles, small frogs, and fairy shrimps. Once during the first days of May I came upon an adult coyote fishing in the waters of one of these tanks. It was early morning, and the animal was so interested and preoccupied that he never noticed my approach. It seemed almost like a matter of play for him as he dashed, now here, now there, along the water's edge, snapping into the water and gobbling up the small swimming creatures. From the many tracks I saw in the sands of the wash both above and below the pools, I concluded that such frog and prawn hunts were frequent. I watched this coyote for fully ten minutes before a slight motion on my part, made to relieve a cramped muscle, caused a crackling sound that alerted him to his danger and sent him sneaking off in haste up the gully. It was in all a very rare experience—a look into a coyote's private life I had hardly expected.

In general, I think it may be said that a coyote, especially when gaunt with hunger, snatches up about everything edible, from insects, especially grasshoppers, to carrion, with preference always, of course, for fresh meat and sweet fruits. Adaptability in the matter of diet is an important factor influencing the survival of this seemingly ever hungry dog of the desert. In most of the areas in which he lives he is almost always the most frequently seen carnivore. His abundance and persistence appear very secure.

To those desert settlers who have encroached upon the coyote's domain and who complain of his depredations upon their hen flocks, I say this: It is surely proper once in a while to put oneself into sympathetic relation with the desert's wild animals that often wander about in your midst half-starved or starving. Such mental transfer will help you better to understand the acts of desperation they engage in to get at supplies of food. It is always a wrongheaded attitude to assume that only man has rights; the wild animals have some, too.

Even a coyote has some good deeds to his credit: he is a most valuable check on harmful rodents and also on sick rodents which harbor dangerous plagues such as tularemia and the dread bubonic plague, diseases which are transmissible to man. He thus proves himself a valuable health officer, benefiting and protecting not only game and other animals but also man. By taking the weaklings and diseased among quail and deer and other game animals, he doubtless assists in improving the vigor of the species as well as negating the chance for the spread of wildlife epidemics such as coccidial diseases. The coyote is always a useful scavenger and perhaps not such a bad neighbor as one might think.

Frank C. Craighead, Jr., wildlife biologist writing for the New York Zoological Society and the Conservation Foundation, well sums up the valuable status of the coyote when he says:

"Coyotes are a desirable and indispensable part of a collective predator population which serves to regulate prey populations on wildlife lands. They perform a useful function as scavengers and they do more good as rodent destroyers than harm as killers of livestock."

On domestic sheep ranges coyotes may prove to be a problem when overgrazing makes it impossible for rodents to exist in any numbers, owing to lack of food and cover. Then of course the coyotes must rely on larger animals for sustenance. The sensible remedy is not to get rid of the coyotes but to stop misusing the land, in other words, to practice better range management.

In a land where, even in years of good rainfall, surface waters are scarce and scattered far, a dreadful toll of wildlife is taken in years of light precipitation. With no berries to feed on and few insects, starvation and thirst bring misery to many an animal's final days. A series of years of drought and famine may just about clean out most of the small rodents, and years are required to bring their numbers back to normal. During these drought times the coyote becomes at the same time good friend and worst foe of our animal life, particularly of the birds—good friend because he becomes a digger of wells where diurnal animals may come to drink; worst foe because at these same wells he gobbles up the small creatures that come to drink at night or at daybreak.

The coyote wells are coyote-made excavations in water-laden sands. Generally, they are found at the foot of high, dry waterfalls. Here the debris-laden waters of successive summer cloudbursts, having rushed over the falls, hollow out deep cuplike pits in which water long persists in the interstices of the coarse sands and gravels that fill them. As from day to day the water level drops, the coyotes dig deeper and deeper. Sometimes they even tunnel in diagonally several feet. Wild bees as well as birds flock to these watering places by day and wild animals at night. Many are the trails that lead to them: they evidently are known to the wild beasts and birds over a wide area.

The period of mating among coyotes extends from near the first of the year in the low, warm deserts to March and April in the piñon mountains of higher altitudes. "It may be said that in general," says G. W. D. Hamlett, of the Bureau of Biological Survey, "the male is sterile during at least eight months of the year; the female during at least ten."* Gestation is about sixty-three days, and a single litter is raised each year.

Coyotes seldom excavate dens for themselves. They generally obtain them by ejecting squirrels or badgers or by utilizing those abandoned by some previous fossorial occupant. Such burrows, once appropriated, are enlarged to suit the coyote's caprice and needs. One which I saw dug out by a trapper so he could take the young ran underground fully seventeen feet. It was a somewhat meandering tunnel, going under earth in one place four feet. There were several short side tunnels. The den near the end where the young hid was, however, not more than two feet below the surface. It was a rounded "room" almost three feet in diameter, with only dust on the floor for bedding: perhaps the coyote realizes that bedding materials harbor parasites. The entrance was a hole in the dry bank of an arroyo about a foot in diame-

---

* *Technical Bulletin No. 616*, U.S.D.A. (1938), p. 11.

ter and screened from direct view by cat's-claw bushes in which a tangle of Brandegea vines grew to conceal still further the dark entrance hole.

When the five or six young are born, they are dark brown or dark gray-black. This is doubtless a valuable protective adaptation, since it makes them difficult to detect in the dark recesses of the den. By the time they are able to make their clumsy way out of the burrow, this dark color has given way to a clay or gray-yellow, which is in color harmony with their new surroundings.

Coyote pups are alert and playful, full of inquisitiveness and intelligence. On pleasant days they are, for the most part, out in the open, playing in the sunshine and learning to exercise their jaws on rabbit skins and bones, which often lie about in the dust of the den entrance. In the wilds, one does not too often have opportunity to see the rollicking soft-furred youngsters of a coyote family enjoying their natural life of freedom. One day in mid-April it was my good fortune to come upon a mother and five third-grown young just as I ascended along a brush-bordered trail to the brow of a hill. For some moments they were so preoccupied with their frolic that they did not detect me. They were in a little clearing. The pups were chasing one another and tumbling about, playing much like puppies of the domestic dog, uttering barks and yaps. Once they heard just above them the sharp scream of a red-tailed hawk; they gave it a moment of alert attention, then went back to their play. The mother was lying at one side, sleepily looking on and occasionally pawing at large green-black flies that sometimes annoyed her. Suddenly she noticed me; a sharp little bark was all that was needed to break up the play. A quick look about, and the whole bunch dashed into the thicket. I never saw them again.

While the young are in the den, the parents prey upon rabbits and small rodents to a much greater extent than usual. In inhabited country they may then commit extensive ravages upon lambs and poultry. Sometimes they seem to kill merely to gratify their propensity for destruction, especially when in reach of abundant and easy prey.

Notwithstanding the proverbial shyness, cowardice, and trickery of the adult coyote in its wild state, instances are well known of animals which, taken when quite young, became perfectly tame and attached to the person who reared them. They exhibited lack of trust only to strangers. This may be said to a certain extent also of the wildcat. In either case, the secret of successful domestication seems to be in getting the animal away from its parents before its eyes are open.

For a number of years there have been persistent reports coming to me of real wolves having been seen near Twenty-nine Palms, California. The chances are a thousand to one that the animals are nothing more than stray timber-dwelling mountain coyotes. These would appear very large to persons used to seeing only the desert species. This is particularly true if the animals were seen only at a distance. As Dr. Joseph Grinnell said in his *Fur-Bearing Mammals of California,* "Any wolf seen in California is likely to be a coyote." The only authenticated account of a true wolf ever being seen in southern California came from the Providence Mountains. The skull finally came into possession of the Museum of Vertebrate Zoology of the University of California and was examined by Dr. Grinnell, so the evidence is complete and convincing.

5. The Desert Lynx

Desert wildcats or desert lynxes, as they are more properly called, are such sly and secretive creatures that, were it not for their occasional ravages upon the poultry yards of desert settlers or their getting caught in traps, they would scarcely be known. They prefer the foothill brush country but are fairly abundant over much of the open, barren, rocky areas of the arid Southwest. They are bold, cunning hunters and range widely at night, taking toll of ground- or brush-roosting birds, mice, rabbits, and other game. When restless or pressed by hunger they hunt in the daytime. They often spend the daylight hours sunning themselves on rocks or lying under bushes and in rock fissures and caves, sleeping while digesting the food taken during the previous night.

From time to time while on my desert rambles I come upon a wildcat at rest and have opportunity to watch it bound away to safety. I cannot say that they are good runners. Their retreat gait is a series of successive bounds, like the bobbing, leaping motion of a madly fleeing jack rabbit.

Since they have comparatively small lungs they get easily winded and when pressed by a pursuer soon seek cover. One that I surprised in the arrowweed thickets along the Colorado River took to the water and proved itself an adept swimmer, going right across a lagoon, although the distance was almost two hundred feet. As a rule, lynxes are not lovers of water any more than are tame cats.

Some years ago, while camping during late April among some mesquite thickets, I had a chance to learn firsthand of the extraordinary behavior of this wild carnivore at mating time. I was awakened near midnight by an interrupted series of ferocious hisses, shrill screams, harsh squalls, and deep-toned yowls. No alley strays could ever have half-equaled this cat concert of the desert wilds. Luckily, it was moonlight and I was able to see the animals almost perfectly. The female most of the time lay crouched upon the ground while the big male, which must have weighed twenty pounds, walked menacingly about her. Sometimes they both sat upright, facing each other. The loud and ludicrous serenade was kept up for almost half an hour, and it ended with a dual climax of discordant, frightening squalls as mating took place.

Wildcat kittens are born any time during the early or late spring and occasionally in summer. There are generally three or four of them and they look quite like domestic kittens. However, they have a stocky build, with large heads and enormous padded paws that no tame kitten ever had. The tail is only a queer hairy stump. On the jaws are heavy tufts of hair and on the ear tips fine pencils of long black hairs. Bobcat kittens may seem to be innocent, tame-tempered creatures, but when suddenly surprised they spit and hiss in evident distrust. When very young they may make interesting pets, but soon, and often suddenly, they become vicious, showing all the wild attributes of their kind.

These animals show the greatest antipathy toward their domestic cousins and also toward dogs. A homesteader whom

I once met in the desert brush country said he found it necessary to keep close watch on his tame cat, especially at night. To ensure her a safe retreat he had cut a hole in the back door of his shanty just large enough for the cat to pass through, and too small for the wildcats. A crude stairlike incline on the outside of the house led to a somewhat larger hole in the attic, and up this his small dog scrambled at the first sight of a wildcat. He had had several "quick caresses" from wildcats' paws and needed no more inducement than the sight or sound of a bobcat to send him hurriedly out of sight.

Bobcats have an exemplary record as destroyers of harmful, disease-carrying rodents, such as ground squirrels, wood rats, white-footed mice, and rabbits. "The few quail a bobcat is able to catch," says Dr. Lloyd Ingles, "are more likely to be the cripples, weaklings, or those having coccidiosis—a disease which may decimate an entire covey."*

The ground color of the desert wildcat's fur is usually gray, dappled with brown and black. The belly is white spotted with black. The short tail has a black tip and from one to six black bars.

One September a man came to my door with the report that he had a genuine Canadian lynx at his desert hide-out in the rocky, brush-covered hills. He begged me to come out and see it for myself.

It was about six in the evening when we hid out in a blind behind some sumac bushes. Shortly after, I raised my binoculars, and one careful look confirmed my belief that we had before us no Canadian lynx but only a good-sized male desert bobcat. He had tufts of hair on his ears, to be sure, but not nearly long enough to be those of the northern lynx. Moreover, when the animal turned to walk away, I could see that the five-inch stubby tail was black only on the top of the

* Lloyd Glenn Ingles, *Mammals of California and Its Coastal Waters* (Stanford: Stanford University Press, 1954), p. 130.

tip. If it had been one of the forest-dwelling cats of the far-north country, its tail would have shown a tip that was circled black. In addition, a lynx would have had much larger paws and stockier legs.

The desert regions of the southwestern United States and northern Mexico are occupied by a bobcat of paler coloration than that of the more humid areas of the Pacific coast. It is often called Bailey's Bobcat by the serious students of mammals because of its scientific name, *Lynx rufus baileyi*. The specific name *rufus* means reddish and was given because of the reddish-brown tinge of certain parts of the upper pelt of the animal originally described. *Baileyi* honors the able explorer and student of mammals, Vernon Bailey, for many years field naturalist for the U.S. Biological Survey and author of many publications on birds and mammals. The frequently used name, wildcat, is well deserved, for this animal is not capable of being truly tamed. Bobcat is a name given because of the animal's short tail.

Every now and then I find people who think that bobcats and wildcats are quite different animals. According to them, bobcats live in the low hills; but when they live in the mountains they are called wildcats. Such talk reminds me of an old desert man who declared that when "a certain grass" grows along the edge of water it should be called Bermuda grass, but when occurring out in the open it should be spoken of as devil grass.

There are other common errors about bobcats: One is that bobcats are crosses between the big northern lynxes and domestic cats; the other is that the males should be called bobcats whereas the females should be called wildcats. Most of my knowledge of wildcats has been acquired, not from reading books on wildlife or listening to the tales of hunters, but from personal observations of these crafty hunters.

I once watched for some weeks the development of a

family of three bobcat kittens. I first saw them shortly after they had opened their eyes. When their eyes were open, the mother brought them out of the rock-covered den each evening at dusk, and I watched as they played with one another or lay upon a large flat rock and fed at her teats.

Once I saw her leave and return 20 minutes later with a freshly killed squirrel. This she dropped before them and soon they were sniffing and pulling it about. The rodent was eventually eaten by the mother, the kittens being yet too young to eat flesh. As the days passed, I could see steady development of the play instinct along with evidence of gaining body strength. Before I left the vicinity, both mother and kittens were going out together on the evening hunts.

One early morning I witnessed the exciting spectacle of the mother cat catching a gopher as I walked along one of the well-established animal trails. I first saw her some distance ahead lying prone on a slight rise of ground. I stopped and noted that she was looking intently at a pile of loose earth before her. Not long afterward she rose in an expectant and tense springing position. It was evident that she saw the gopher coming up to the entrance of its hole with a load of loose earth. A moment later she leaped forward, thrust her right paw into the burrow and adroitly brought out and pounced upon her prize. Then she bit it several times and carried it off, probably to her kittens.

Occasionally these animals are real problems to farmers who find them raiding their poultry pens and killing chickens and other fowl in unusual numbers, seemingly for the mere love of slaying. The thirst for blood sometimes leads them to kill lambs too. Under such circumstances, doing away with the animals is justifiable.

The wildcat population is declining, owing to constant trapping and hunting. Some day Americans may become aware, as the Scandinavians and some other European nations have, of the fact that they must protect the wildcat as a valuable and interesting animal, one to observe and admire. The late student of mammals, Joseph Grinnell, said: "The value of the wildcat in maintaining a proper check upon certain smaller animals and birds is sufficient to justify intentional preservation of it in uncultivated territory."

6. *The Desert Bighorn*

A day of high excitement and one always remembered is the day on which we see our first desert bighorn. These animals are now so few in number and generally so well secluded in their rocky habitat that they are seldom seen, even by those who travel most often over the desert's rocky, byway trails. Signs of desert sheep in the form of hoofprints and numerous brown fecal pellets are quite frequently observed, but so wary are the animals during daylight hours, so nearly does their coat of gray-brown hair match the rocky, brush-dotted terrain, that at a distance the animals are usually wholly unobvious.

It is most pleasing to catch sight of a fine, big ram, particularly if he is seen in silhouette atop a huge rock or on the edge of a high escarpment, for then his regalness of form is best displayed, showing the massive curved horns adorning the head, the gracefully lined face, and the stocky but smoothly formed body. If the animal turns and stands with head pointing away, we may see prominently displayed the remarkable white rump patch. A large male will measure at least five feet in length from nose tip to the root of the small black tail, and will be three and one-half feet high. The average weight for a well-matured ram is 250 to 300 pounds.

There is much reliable testimony indicating the former uninterrupted occurrence of desert sheep throughout almost all the wild arid mountain ranges, from Sonora northward to mid-Nevada. The present paucity of animals is due first of all to the great destruction wrought by scabies, introduced, in the later 1800's, when tame sheep were brought in to the Far West to graze. With the domesticated sheep came also the dreaded anthrax. Then came the influx of settlers, miners, and travelers, and consequent unscrupulous hunting. Bighorn have been on the protected list since 1883, but poaching has been constant. As human population density increases, the number of sheep will decrease in all areas outside the game refuges and the national and state parks and monuments. At present, the greatest concentration of desert bighorn is in the isolated ranges of southern Nevada. There, through the practice of wise management methods and constant vigil on the part of the rangers of the Desert Game Refuge, not only have the sheep appreciably increased in number, but a reservoir has been created from which the depleted ranges can be gradually restocked. This refuge should be kept inviolate from hunters for all time to come.

Bighorn find their most ideal conditions for existence in the almost waterless, desolate, rocky ranges which jut up from the low desert plains. Their wonderful powers of leaping and climbing and their ability to go for long periods without resort to watering places especially adapt them to such situations. I have seen them climb rocky slopes which the average man can scarcely get over, with almost the speed of a deer. They make no mistakes in their footing and adeptly descend precipitous escarpments which defy the hardiest mountaineers. Except for a short period during the hottest

DESERT BIGHORN
SHEEP MOUNTAINS, NEVADA

portion of the year, they are able to get most of their water from the wide variety of plants on which they subsist.

Sometimes in winter we find their tracks out in the open desert, but these for the most part mark their occasional journeys from one mountain range to another. During this season they often bed down at night on rocky spurs or ridges close to the desert floor, but they begin to ascend the steep slopes in the very early morning to do their feeding. At dusk they again work their way back to the low bedding grounds. These are easy to identify, as each sheep paws out a platter-like depression in loose soil. Very often these depressions are made with a north and south axis so the sheep can get the full benefit of the early sun's rays on their bodies. Before lying down they paw the earth, then go down first on the front limbs; in rising, the hind limbs are used first. Sheep urinate and defecate immediately after rising. In summer, they seek the crests of the ranges and bed correspondingly high. There, green food is available and the supplies of water are more dependable.

Copulation takes place in September and October. When the lambing season comes, in March or early April, the ewes, unaccompanied by the males, seek the roughest and steepest areas available—country so difficult to climb over that few animals other than sheep can get into it. In the Sheep Mountains of Nevada the principal lambing grounds are on the rugged, almost perpendicular, southern sunny exposures. One lamb is born at a time. The lambs are soon able to follow the parents over the feeding grounds and engage in lively gambols and other play activities. By mid-August they are half-grown. If they are taken captive early, they do well and become very tame and affectionate. Attempts to subject older animals to captivity have generally proved failures. Removed from their natural wild home, they become broken in spirit and sullen, refuse to eat, and in a short time die.

In June, July, and August the sexes mingle freely, and

one may see several ewes consorting with a ram. During this time they wander rather widely, but as a rule they have regular sleeping quarters.

When grazing, the animals move with great deliberation. They are dainty feeders, but a great variety of food—thistles, grasses, annual flowers, and leafy brush—is eaten. In the southern deserts where barrel cacti grow, the sheep sometimes open these natural barrels of water with their strong horns, then eat out the succulent pulp.

The length of a sheep's life is almost wholly dependent on the rate of tooth wear, and that in turn on the nature of the food eaten. An animal may be in fine physical condition up to the time when the teeth begin to wear unduly, and then suddenly go into a decline. I well remember a fine ram in the Panamint Mountains who for years frequented one of the springs. The last time I visited the area a great change had come over him. Although still young in years, he was in exceedingly poor condition, with every rib showing. Slow starvation through inability to bite and chew properly was to be his lot.

The growth of the boldly coiled, massive horns of wild sheep is a strange phenomenon which has long attracted the interest of naturalists. The bony horn cone or *os cornu*, as it is sometimes called, is borne on the frontal bone. It remains throughout life, and its covering consists of a series of sheaths of cornified epidermis. The new cone of horn is formed on the surface of the bony core, and as it thickens the growth of the preceding season is pushed upward and outward toward the end of the horn. This horny covering is not shed regularly, as among pronghorn antelopes, but slowly splits off or wears away through almost constant contact with the brush and rocks. The remains of many seasons of horn growth can always be found, each marked by a ring showing when the new horn core broke loose at the base as it was pushed outward toward the apex of the horn. Older sheep are seldom seen without their dark, umber-brown horns broken at the tips. This is due to the hard use they give the horns in prying up rocks and digging in stony ground for bulbs and deeply placed succulent roots and stems of plants during seasons of drought.

The female sheep have horns, too, but they are much smaller. Instead of curling boldly round to the front and beside the head as in the male, they are only slightly curved and project backward. During the rutting season the heavy-headed, massive-horned males literally become battering-rams, using the horns as weapons of offense as they rush head-on in combat with their rivals. Full of feverish passion, they may even rush headlong to butt their heads against the trunks of trees. I have seen them at this season go up to a young pine tree and swing the head from side to side, scratching the head and heavy horns against the branches.

A colossal and absurd untruth is told that wild sheep, especially the large-horned rams, when hotly pursued, leap over cliffs, landing and rolling over on their bulky horns and turning a kind of mid-air somersault. The story is, of course, another instance of a fertile imaginative faculty flowering at its best.

When suddenly alarmed at close range, a bighorn ram will often mount a rocky eminence and give vent to occasional snorts or blowing sounds as a sign of uneasiness. If the observer is cautious, he may have the animal before him for up to ten or fifteen minutes at a time, giving unusual opportunities for photographic work and close observation. The females seem much more timid. The upper picture on page 38 was taken while a ram stood chewing his cud not more than fifteen feet from my breakfast table. For some reason, this animal was unafraid and grazed by day and bedded down at night within a hundred-yard radius of my camp. Such an experience is unusual.

The wild burros, which are descendants of animals abandoned by old-time miners, are among the worst enemies of desert sheep. Bighorn are annoyed by the mere presence of burros and will seldom drink where burros have preceded them. The burros not only muddy and befoul the waters at the springs but also severely reduce the scarce forage on which the sheep live. As the burros increase, and that increase is often rapid, the sheep decrease. In some areas the burros have brought the entire sheep population almost to the point of extinction. The few deer which are found in sheep country offer no serious competition for food or water, and the two kinds of animals live side by side.

The bighorn rely mainly on their keen sense of sight to apprise them of the presence of enemies. The hearing, originally acute, is dulled by the numerous ticks which usually completely fill the ear passages.

7. *Desert Deer*

Deer on the desert is a strange idea to most people, even to permanent desert dwellers, who, like so many, take it for granted that deer are animals only of the brush-covered or pine-clad mountains. But the deserts—at least certain ones—have their deer, some all the time, others at least temporarily. The desert trough known as Owens Valley, which lies between the High Sierra and the precipitous, somewhat lower and much drier Inyo Range, has visitations of California mule deer during late autumn when they leave the cold, storm-swept Sierra and move eastward in considerable numbers to find a temporary home in the warmer brush-covered Inyos. The migrations may last several days. In the spring there is a spectacular return mass migration. But these deer are only desert visitants, and can hardly be called desert denizens since their actual home is in the high mountains to the west.

But the variety of the California mule deer (*Odocoileus hemionus eremicus*) known, because of its bigger ears and heavier, larger body, as the burro deer (*cuervo* to the Mexicans) is quite a different animal. It is a year-round desert resident. The deserts of Pima and Yuma counties along the lower Colorado River in mid-western Arizona and far-eastern Imperial and Riverside counties in California, where the heat of summer is often long-lasting and intense, are local dwelling places for this imposing pale-colored animal. In northeastern Baja California and on the dry cactus-covered flats of the western Sonoran plains, small herds of burro deer are yet found. It was from northwestern Sonora, just to the east of Tiburón Island, that the type specimen was taken and brought to the attention of scientists long ago. The first valid description of this animal was made by Dr. Alexander Mearns of the U.S. Mexican Boundary Survey in 1897. The type specimen was killed in the barren Sierra Seri by Dr. W. J. McGee of the Bureau of Ethnology while making a study of the very primitive Seri Indians who lived on Tiburón Island and the mainland along the Gulf of California. He found that these people occasionally hunted deer for food and for the hide.

The California mule deer range touches on the margin of burro deer country along the edge of the Colorado Desert in the United States and Lower California, where the great difference in size and color between the two is at once apparent.

Clavijero, the Mexican historian (1731–87), long ago mentioned the stalking of desert deer by Lower California aborigines of the mid-peninsula with the aid of an antler and head disguise, and Consag, in his diary of his Baja California 1751 expedition, reports the natives driving these deer with grass fires, a method probably not often used, since grasses and woody perennial vegetation are generally too sparse in this country to support running fires.

That these large antlered animals were already scarce in the early 1900's in Papagoland near the Pinacate Mountains of Sonora is attested by the fact that neither Carl Lumholtz

(*New Trails in Mexico*) nor William T. Hornaday (*Camp-Fires on Desert and Lava*), who explored this area well in 1905 and 1906, mentions seeing them. Joseph Grinnell in *An Account of the Mammals and Birds of the Lower Colorado Valley* says that he saw very few burro deer at the time he made his studies in 1910. Since those days there seems to have been some resurgence in numbers, but these are still comparatively scarce animals. When burro deer are seen in California or Arizona, they are generally found as individuals or in small herds of six to ten in the willow and cottonwood thickets along the Colorado River bottom or in the nearby arid mountains, creosote-bush desert flats, or ironwood washes. They feed on willow twigs, on the tender shoots of palo verde trees, and on the nutritious leaves of ironwood trees, among other things. The time of browsing is mostly at night or evening, but on several occasions I have seen burro deer feeding in the daytime.

Except when frightened, each deer herd stays pretty much in a restricted home area, seldom roaming about aimlessly. When out on the desert proper they hide during the day in the small side washes, concealing themselves under brush or the small trees that grow there. Because of their small numbers, their tracks and trails (except near waterholes) are seldom noticed. I remember on a number of occasions seeing their large tracks, along with the smaller spore of javelinas, in the mud near several springs in the Gila-Mohawk Mountain area of Arizona. Progression, except when walking, is generally by a series of graceful bounds, all four feet leaving the ground simultaneously. Over short distances this pace is very rapid.

In dry months the animals like to drink daily (mostly at night) at the seepages and springs. When succulent green food is plentiful, they may drink only every third day.

During pairing time in January the bucks are exceedingly pugnacious and quarrel fiercely over the few does. The stronger, older animals are of course the successful breeders, and this tends to keep the stock strong.

The ordinarily large antlers of the males usually are dropped in late March or April. Quite soon new ones begin to form, hidden, of course, by the velvet. When the seasons are exceedingly dry, the antlers are smaller than usual. Older bucks (five to eight years) have smaller antlers, which continue to decline in size and total pound-weight as years go on. According to Dr. A. Starker Leopold of the University of California Museum of Vertebrate Zoology, the full rack of 10 points is achieved in the third or fourth year.

The fawns are not dropped until the summer rains, in July and August, when there is a new crop of grasses and annuals as well as new tender twigs on which the animals can feed and make extra supplies of milk. This is somewhat later than when mountain-dwelling mule deer give birth to fawns.

If winter and spring feed has been plentiful, the does may have twin fawns, but usually only one is born. The young stay with the mother throughout the first year. The spots so characteristic of young deer are said to be retained only until late September or October.

At somewhat higher elevations, feeding on chaparral of the piñon-juniper woodlands, arid desert flats, or rocky hills of southern New Mexico, the Big Bend area of Texas, and adjacent similar areas in the states of Chihuahua, Coahuila, and Durango of Mexico, is another kind of pale-coated mule deer known as the desert mule deer, Crook's mule deer, or gray mule deer (*Odocoileus hemionus crooki*). Its general habits are much like those of the burro deer.

About the only animal the burro and Crook's desert deer must fear is man. The coyotes kill very few, and then it is mostly the diseased or starving animals that fall prey to them. My friend Gale Monson of the Fish and Wildlife Service writes me from Yuma that in southwestern Arizona the mountain lion is just about absent from desert mule deer country.

"We have only one record of a lion killing a deer on the Kofa Game Range—and this was an old tom who was trapped in 1944 after killing a number of bighorn sheep as well as deer. I don't think they come anywhere near Laguna Prieta, and I suspect lions are now extinct in the Colorado Delta.

"There is no doubt," Monson continues, "that deer are preyed upon by bobcats, as we have at least two eye-witness experiences; but I doubt that either bobcats or coyotes have much effect on their numbers." He goes on to say that observers have seen deer chase coyotes away from waterholes, striking at them with their forefeet.

One of Monson's men had an experience with deer worthy of note. This Fish and Wildlife Service man was taking a dawn-to-dusk waterhole count at Hoodoo Well in the Kofa Mountains, and for several days the tally averaged about 20 deer per day. On the eve of his final day, knowing that a number of deer were watering at night, he closed the corral gates so animals could not get to the waterhole. Next morning at daybreak, when he went again to his station to resume the count, he found 65 deer outside the fence waiting to drink. When he went to open the gate, the animals scarcely got out of his way, and they almost ran over him when the gate was finally opened.

The two great enemies of this desert deer are hunters and the overgrazing of the range by the stockmen's herds. "Overshooting," says A. Starker Leopold in *Wildlife of Mexico,* "was begun at an early date." He mentions how in 1884–85 in the Bolsón de Mapimi of northeastern Durango, Don Donaciano Montera, a professional hunter, killed 400 desert-dwelling mule deer, including both bucks and does.

Unfortunately, some states still permit and encourage the killing of these fine deer, even though their numbers are so small; few Mexicans pay any attention to regulatory laws and shoot deer whenever and wherever chance affords the opportunity. Dr. Alexander Mearns in his *Mammals of the*

Mexican Boundary of the United States wrote in 1907 that burro deer occurred "in large herds in Lower California during the winter season." No such numbers are found today.

A few of the animals are killed at night by automobiles. I recently saw such a fatality on the highway between Yuma and Quartzsite, Arizona. The animal must have weighed close to 130 pounds and gave the impression of being a very strongly built creature. I could see that it had had the usual number of ectoparasites, from ticks to fleas. Hitting such a large animal had been costly to the fast-driving motorist; the front end of his car must have been much damaged by the impact. Later in the day just after sunset I saw three burro deer crossing the road in front of us, not appearing unduly alarmed at our approach. One was an antlered buck, the other two were yearling does.

8. The Pronghorn Antelope

No more sleek-appearing, intelligent animal ever graced the American West than the fleet-footed pronghorn antelope or prongbuck (*Antilocapra americana*). Said Washington Irving: "Nothing can surpass the delicate and elegant finish of their limbs in which lightness, elasticity and strength are wonderfully combined. All the attitudes and movements of this wonderful animal are graceful and picturesque; and it is altogether a fit subject for the fanciful uses of the poet."

About the size of a small deer but with proportionately longer legs, it has a general color of soft buff, with parts of the face, sides, underparts, and rump white. A black mask occurs on the foreface of the buck; also a distinctive large black spot on either side of the upper neck just below the level of the eye. Two broad white bars adorn the tawny neck. This disruptive color pattern serves well to keep the animal from being too readily seen, especially at a distance. Large black eyes set in deep protruding sockets on the sides of the head are a marked feature of the handsome face. Both males and females carry black, flattened horns, which rise from the skull just above the eyes. These have backward- and inward-pointed tips and a hooked process or prong about two-thirds the distance to the end. Ordinarily the females' horns are considerably shorter, being less than the length of the erect, pointed ears. These curved horns are peculiar among mammals in having a living bony core over which a deciduous rough-surfaced sheath is grown. This is made of agglutinated hairs and develops from the tip downward. The does shed their horn sheaths a little later than the males.

One of the most unique features of the pronghorn is the large, glistening-white rump patch, which can be spread at will when the animal is alarmed. Then it forms a great rosette of long white radiating hairs startling to behold and easy to see from afar. Even very young animals are able to flash the white rump patch.

There is little doubt that this mammal is of American origin, as evidenced by fossil remains of this and related forms. Some of these fossil animals show close relationship to African types of antelopes of today. These interesting ruminants, the sole remaining representative of a wholly American family, the *Antilocapridae,* at one time probably exceeded the buffalo in numbers, 30 to 40 million or perhaps even more of them roaming the grassland plains and broad valleys from the Mississippi River almost to the Pacific Coast.

Although briefly mentioned in the writings of Spanish travelers, the pronghorn or prongbuck was first made known to modern science on the return of Lewis and Clark (1806) from their famous journeys of exploration to the upper reaches of the Missouri River.

This mammal is a timid, gregarious creature of fleet gait, being able to maintain speeds of 30 to 40 miles an hour for long distances. They have very sensitive noses and the keenest eyesight of any of the ruminants, and much superior to

ANTELOPE

MALHEUR NATIONAL WILDLIFE REFUGE, OREGON

that of man. They are particularly adept at detecting small movements at great distances. Because of this, they readily become aware of approaching predators such as coyotes and are able to give the alarm. At first signs of danger they come from all directions, says Helmut Karl Buechner, of the State College of Washington, to join into a compact group, and then, stringing out in single file, they flee. A mature doe is generally seen leading the herd, while a buck, as master of the herd, brings up the rear.

When lying down, the members of a band usually face in different directions, and when one antelope senses danger it immediately sounds an explosive snort or nudges its neighbor. Soon all spring up and are ready to flee, with rump patches flashing. The first show of fear is the raising of the longer hairs on the back of the neck and immediately above the short tail. If they take shelter behind a hill to avoid a cold breeze they usually face upward to give their acute ears and noses every chance to pick up a strange sound or scent.

Upon seeing any motion, they first stand and watch; they then cautiously approach and circle about the moving object. Always social and generally friendly, they may come very near. They trust their speed to carry them to safety. Their great curiousity often leads them toward man with his rifle. In the old days of antelope abundance, hunters often found the curiosity-bent creatures walking almost into camp to inspect it. As M. P. Skinner of the American Museum of Natural History says: "Pronghorns do not seek to elude observation; all they care about is to be able to see for themselves."

Because of the unique structure of their hair, pronghorns are able to thrive in a wide variety of climates, and this accounts for their one-time broad distribution from mid-Mexico to southwestern Canada. The hair is "pithy," containing a great number of air cells, and so makes the animal's coat a protection against extremes of heat and cold. Moreover, because of special skin muscles these hairs can be erected to permit free circulation of air next to the skin: this is the antelope's efficient cooling device. In winter the hair lies flat, forming an insulating coat. The short, loose underfur gives only a small amount of added protection. The hair is very brittle, loosely attached, and constantly being shed; hence the hide is never used for rugs, as is the skin of the deer. The entire pelage is shed twice a year.

Although they are typical animals of the grassland plains, the antelopes' principal food over the entire range of distribution is not grass but weeds of many kinds (some of them poisonous to sheep and cattle), tender herbs, and the leaves and tender shoots of various shrubs. Almost all of the bitter wormwoods (*Artemisia*), especially the three-toothed sagebrush, rabbitbrushes (*Chrysothamnus*), and twigs of juniper and bitterbrush (*Purshia*) seem to be their favorite browse. Grasses ordinarily are only sparingly cropped. At times wild flowers are chosen. On the whole, they are careful choosers of food. Unlike cattle, they browse at night as well as by day. Their hours of feeding are very irregular and often interspersed by periods of lying down and cud-chewing.

Writing in 1917 of the foods of the antelope of the Lower California deserts, Robert C. Murphy says:

Although desert bunch-grass, called by the Mexicans "guayeta" was common in scattered patches . . . I looked in vain for evidence that the animals fed on it. . . . The foliage of the trailing lavender-flowered four o'clock, *Abronia villosa*, which grew in sandy parts of the Creosote Association, was a favorite forage. Another plant that they crushed and mouthed, apparently for the moisture it contained, was the desert broom-rape, *Orobanche multiflora*, a parasite on the roots of other species. We found many of its flowering heads uprooted and chewed in the wake of browsing antelope. Captain Funcke informed me that he had also seen the animals eating leaves of the ironwood (*Olneya tesota*).

Although pronghorns are known to be able to drink bitter alkaline water, and are said to repair periodically to regular watering places, those of the Pattie Basin do not drink at all during the greater part of the year . . . there is certainly no water between the mountain tinajas and the Tres Pozos, and the tracks of antelopes have never been observed to lead to either source.

In the southern deserts the antelope herds wander rather widely, but there is no definite migration as there is in their northern habitat, where there is a well-defined movement of large herds from winter to summer range. The winter range is generally in the arid plain country, where warmer conditions prevail and where food is less likely to be hidden under a blanket of snow. The summer range of herds living near the mountains includes brush and tree zones up to 8,000 feet. Since these animals prefer the open plains where distant views are possible, the mixed bands of does, bucks, and fawns graze mostly on the flats and meadows and drink at the water holes found among the scattered growths of pines and aspens.

In late February the does separate and begin to hunt areas where they can drop their young, while the old bucks go off alone. The time of fawning generally approximates the time of best feeding conditions. In the high mesas the young may be born in June, while on the low hot deserts it may be in February or early March. Twins are normal, but single young are frequent.

The best kidding sites are in low brush-covered basins surrounded by low hills. The low bushes form effective cover and make it possible for the mother to scan the area for wildcats and coyotes. This is particularly true if she is standing apart on a rise shortly after the birth. The young remain hidden for about two weeks, spending much of their time lying on the ground except at feeding time, when they stand up. If alarmed, they extend the head flat to the earth and remain in one spot practically motionless for extended periods. Because of their grayish-brown furry coat they are difficult to spot, so well do they blend with the color of the earth and rocks and surrounding vegetation. The precocious babies are born with open eyes and carry no scent. At the age of ten days they can outrun the average dog. However, they may fall prey to coyotes and bobcats.

Mr. Arthur S. Einarson in his book *The Pronghorn Antelope* tells us that sometimes one mother will look out for several kids while the others go off to graze.

Up to several months old, the antelope kids are very playful. They run together in circles, jump on and off their mothers' backs, and play the old game of "king of the mountain" on a rock. They may butt heads, or jump a few feet in the air with a playful twisting of the hind parts.

Young pronghorns often show great affection for their keepers, especially children who are willing to romp with them or scratch the tops of their heads. They will even play a bit with the family dog, which they can always outrun.

At ten months the young are almost full grown and to the novice can scarcely be distinguished from prime adults.

At the time the young are born, most of the bucks go off in "bachelor herds" and often do not return until autumn, when the does are collected in harems for mating.

The pronghorn has been hunted almost to the point of extermination. Its numbers have also been reduced by loss of its habitat through plowing of the land and by fencing for cattle and sheep.

Had it not been for a few conservationists (I do not refer to those who, while calling themselves conservationists, would perpetuate wildlife only to have something to shoot at), this splendid animal would doubtless have gone the way of the great auk, the passenger pigeon, and the heath hen.

Before it was too late, there were a few far-seeing private landowners who protected the small remaining herds, and good antelope range was purchased in Oregon and Nevada by the Boone and Crockett Club and the Audubon Society. The Sheldon National Antelope Refuge and the Hart Mountain Antelope Refuge were established where a nucleus of antelope herds could be perpetuated. The authorities in charge of these refuges have done an excellent job in providing for the needs of the pronghorn and for their increase in other areas. Now in California, Arizona, Utah, New Mexico, Texas, Colorado, Wyoming, North and South Dakota, Saskatchewan, and Alberta, where transplants have been made, small protected private land areas and public refuges are in operation. The plight of the pronghorns in Mexico, where enforcement of the hunting laws is poor, is extremely precarious. The Mexicans still have small herds, perhaps 700 or 800 antelopes, in Chihuahua, Coahuila, and Sonora, and perhaps a very few in the midpeninsula of Lower California. At last a few weak efforts are being made to put a stop to the illegal hunting, by people on both sides of the border, who hunt the animals with jeeps and even airplanes.

I have just been going over some of the old pronghorn country in Baja California where 75 years ago there were vast numbers of these hardy animals. Most of these herds were completely shot out even before 1915. About all that is left to indicate their former abundance are their trails on the barren, volcanic hills—trails, in spite of all the intervening years of weathering, still very plain. They are mostly five to 20 feet above the level, rock-covered plains.

In California a few antelopes still feed on the plains of Modoc and eastern Lassen counties. The Kern County herds and those of the Mohave and Colorado deserts are gone. The last of the Colorado Desert antelopes were wiped out by military personnel during World War II.

Pronghorns once found ideal habitat over much of Nevada's wastelands, but even before the end of World War II most had disappeared except in the Sheldon National Antelope Refuge.

In New Mexico most of the animals range on the eastern plains. Most of them are on privately owned lands, but federal lands, unfortunately now open to hunting, also have small bands. Fencing definitely limits the movements of antelope, since they hesitate, although they are able, to go through or under barbed wire fences; sheep fences are real barriers, since they cannot go through and will not jump over them. This hesitancy or inability to leap over any high or large object is attributed to the fact that in their ancestral natural habitat, the open plain, they rarely met obstructions of appreciable height.

Arizona still has antelope, perhaps as many as 5,000 or 6,000. Climatic conditions are particularly favorable there, and in former days they lived in great numbers both on grassy plains and in sunny parklike openings among the scattered junipers, piñons and yuccas. Gentle as cattle of the range, they were easily shot, little skill being required by the hunters. Many cattlemen, who still hold the mistaken idea that antelope compete with cattle for food, do not take kindly to them. Near the Mexican border, in the Cabeza Prieta Game Refuge, there are about 40 pronghorns of the subspecies *sonoriensis*. They are the last remnant of the pale-haired race found in the United States, and should be carefully protected. In their wanderings they sometimes move over into the Organ-Pipe Cactus National Monument and into adjacent wild country in Mexico.

9. The Desert Hare

No animal is more familiar to the desert traveler than the black-tailed hare, popularly known as the desert jack rabbit. On nearly every walk abroad, one sees him several times as he bounds away from his hiding in the brush. The motorist repeatedly sees him leap and run across or along the highway, and the hunters are out in search of him almost daily, flushing him from his form in a thicket of brush and watching as he bolts for safety in long zigzag leaps.

Yet despite this familiar association with the hare, few people really know what he does when he is not on the run. In spite of the hunting and persecution and the consequent dangers he faces, in spite of the cunning of his numerous canine and avian enemies, and in spite of the diseases that plague his life, the black-tailed hare has maintained his average-population number from year to year with remarkable constancy.

We know very little about this creature simply because few people have the patience to watch him often and over long periods of time. The hare is a most secretive animal, screening himself in every possible way from the gaze of his enemies. Any movement he sees, any molestations he experiences are, for him, signals to drop his ordinary activities immediately and to assume first the role of the alert watcher and next that of the racer; ever vigilant, he awaits, as it were, only the sound of the starting gun to get him under way. He is thus, in the eyes of most persons, the speedster par excellence and little more.

There is in popular usage now among bird students a term which has no counterpart or synonym among those who seek knowledge about mammals. That term is "bird watcher." The bird watcher is one who spends long hours of silence and inactivity in the field in front of a nest or feeding area, recording in the minutest detail with notebook and camera every movement, every mannerism of the birds he would know. We need to assume this same sort of attitude in observing our common mammals if we ever hope to know their real life fully. We should become "mammal watchers," taking time out to live with the animals unobtrusively, as Eugene Marais lived with a tribe of baboons in South Africa. Three full years, you may recall, he spent on the mountains of Doorhock, watching for days without interruption the baboons' behavior, finally recording his findings in that charming and enlightening volume, *My Friends, the Baboons.*

In our quest for information on the habits of the hare in its natural environment, we chose for extensive study an area on the west bank of the Mohave River, just north of Hesperia. This is a brush area supporting a large population of both jack and brush rabbits. Here the broad, sagebrush- and golden-bush-covered plain gradually slopes toward the river, with only a small barranca or drop-off just before it reaches the sandy river bed. There are many scattered Joshua trees, and in the stream bed itself are small seepages of water with green herbs about them, all constituting an environment which naturally attracts many smaller mammals and birds.

Tree Yucca Stripped of Leaves by Neotoma in a Drought Year

The whole upland area above the river we found to be crisscrossed with a surprising number of well-beaten narrow trails, some of them evidently very old. They came in from all directions, but all were headed ultimately for the river bed and its water. These runs much resemble the trails made by ground squirrels. They average about five inches in width and are clearly visible, since they are barren of all plant growth and their loosened gray sands are in sharp color contrast with the darker gray-blue borders of brush on the undisturbed soil. These are the trailways of the jack rabbit, shared occasionally by his little brother, the cottontail.

We followed a number of these well-beaten paths for nearly a mile back from the river. They seemed roughly to parallel one another. The only time they swerved from their almost straight courses was when they edged around a fallen Joshua tree that blocked the way, or when they bridged an intervening arroyo that cut across the routes.

Every fifty feet or so there were minor cross trails. Almost regularly along the main trails there were enlarged spaces where the topsoil had been converted into shallow platterlike hollows of fine gray dust. These dust bowls serve the rabbits well, both as resting sites and as dusting places to aid them in keeping down the numbers of parasitic insects and mites that attack their hides and fur. Combating lice and other annoying pests, such as fleas, must present quite a problem to wild creatures. As we see the great number of these dusting sites and note the ample evidence of their frequent use, we are led to believe that the jack rabbits successfully cope with this difficult problem of ridding themselves of lice and fleas and ticks.

Here and there along the trails we saw indications of feeding. At one spot, where a branch of a leaning Joshua tree was barely scraping the ground, the hungry rabbits had gnawed off all the tenderest leaves several inches back. Strewn about like chips were the remaining short sections of the dried and bleached spinelike leaves. We were sure that rabbits were responsible for these chips, because intermingled with the leaf remnants were many of the characteristic droppings. We had long suspected that the desert hare must at times utilize this ready source of spiny though nutritious food, but now there was little doubt. In a place near by, we found that woodcutters had felled many green tree yuccas for wood to use in the manufacture of commercial products, and there, too, we noticed that the black-tailed hares had eaten freely of the green, stiff, swordlike leaves found on or near the ground at the ends of the newly cut branches.

In their quest for nourishing food, the black-tailed hares eat a wide variety of greenstuffs. In the spring season, grasses and green herbs are the first choice, but later, when the vegetation has been seared by the intense summer heat, the somewhat dry yet tender stems and leaves of brush are taken. It is during this time that the desert hares engage in that curious habit of clipping eight- to ten-inch sprigs off the ends of the lower branches of the creosote bushes. The amount of such trimming is enormous in any widespread area, and it is easy, especially in late autumn, to find the circles of trimmings, either green or dried, under hundreds of *Larrea* bushes. No other bushes seem to be worked on in this manner; why, we cannot say. There is no evidence that either the cut twigs or the intensely bitter leaves are eaten, and it may be that this work of brush-cutting is an endeavor to sharpen the incisor teeth. The animals trim most of the bushes they work upon as high up as they can reach while standing on their haunches. The ends of the branches are diagonally cut off, so neatly that they almost appear to have been severed with a sharp jack-knife.

During most of the day, the desert hares lie about under brush or sit in forms—cleared places they have nibbled out in the brush or grass tussocks. As evening comes on, they and the cottontails, with whom they always seem to be at peace, venture out with great caution to feed, never hurrying, traveling slowly for fifteen or twenty short leaps at a time before pausing. In this leisurely manner they may sometimes go a mile or so in order to obtain their favorite foods. They are also much abroad at night, especially on moonlit nights, and in the very early morning.

The hare's appetite must be prodigious, for Arnold and Reynolds, writing in the *Journal of Wild Life Management,* tell us that the average number of fecal pellets dropped by jack rabbits in a day is 531 when eating native green forage materials. This is irrespective of age, sex, or species. Moreover, the character of the forage affects only the pellet weights, not the pellet counts. Some of these pellets consist wholly of undigested woody matter; in others almost half the bulk may be gravel, and rather coarse gravel at that. It is hard to explain how the gravel grains are picked up or why. Usually jack rabbits are rather careful feeders, foraging mostly from plant parts found well off the ground.

In the old books, rabbits and hares were classified, along with the many kinds of mice, squirrels, and other gnawers, as rodents. Recent studies, however, indicate sufficient peculiarities to warrant putting them and the hay-gathering cony of the high mountain rockslides in a separate group called the Lagomorpha—literally, animals of rabbitlike form. Unlike true rodents, lagomorphs have two pairs of upper incisor or front cutting teeth instead of the usual one pair. These two sets are arranged in two tiers or ranks, one behind the other, the inner ones backing up and acting as a sort of brace to strengthen the front ones. If you should find an old rabbit skull while on your desert rambles, notice this peculiar and interesting feature.

While we are speaking of skulls, there is one cranial feature of the desert races of the black-tailed hare that is most significant. On the rabbit's skull there are two very prominent bubblelike structures of thin bone just behind the openings of the ears. These are called audital *bullae* (Latin plural for bubble). These bullae, along with the ear pinnae, are found to be much larger in the rabbits of the southern deserts than in the rabbits of the same species inhabiting the more humid coastal area. This is probably because sound perception is more difficult in deserts, where humidity is low and temperatures are higher.

It occurred to us one day that it might be of interest to know just how long the ears of a full-grown male desert jack rabbit actually are. We asked several of our hunter friends, and the estimates and guesses we got were so varied that we decided to find out by measuring.

We found that the average length of the ears is about five and one-half inches. These were measurements taken on dead animals. Observations make us believe that the ears are even longer in the living rabbits.

Dr. Robert Orr says in his monograph on the rabbits of California:

Field observations have repeatedly shown that hearing is relied upon by rabbits to a greater extent than any of the other senses in detecting the presence of enemies. Individuals feeding in the open, where they are constantly in danger of attack by birds of prey and carnivorous animals, continually shift their ears about in an effort to detect any unusual sounds. The senses of sight and smell are of relatively little importance in this regard when compared with hearing. If one moves noiselessly, he may approach very close to a rabbit even in the open, without the latter showing awareness of the observer's presence."*

A hare is able to speedily lower those enormously long, nearly transparent, paper-thin ears when dashing through the brush at terrific speed; this is particularly true if the brush is thorny. Those great appendages are exceedingly tender and delicate structures; they are most essential to his well-being, and even to his existence.

* *The Rabbits of California,* Occasional Papers, California Academy of Sciences, No. XIX, p. 16.

Many are the times in a jack rabbit's life when he is aroused and must flee for his life as he is sighted and pursued by either a single coyote or a band of them. On several occasions we have seen the fear-stricken, bulging-eyed creatures pursued by these dogs of the desert, with savage coyote yelps and cries.

But the hare is not always the hapless victim of the chase. He possesses an instinctive ingenuity in eluding his enemies, and often his clever ruses for escape are successful. We once saw a hare pursued by a coyote while at the same time a big red-tailed hawk was maneuvering over him. All the cards seemed to be stacked against the hare, but he made his escape.

Besides the coyote, other enemies of the jack rabbit are the bobcat, the large birds of prey, man (especially along the highways), and the larger desert snakes, such as the gopher or bull snake and the rattlesnake. However, these reptiles are comparatively scarce on the open desert floor. It is the young hares that suffer most from snakes, since they are less suspicious and hence less wary. Gopher snakes wander widely, killing their victims by constriction. The rattlesnakes are not so active but are equally deadly. Once a rattlesnake has bitten an animal, it may allow the victim to move several yards away, seemingly without paying attention to it. Then it carefully tracks it down, following exactly along the path of the dying animal until it finds it. The so-called pits or sunken areas between the eye and nostril of the rattlesnake are delicate sensory organs enabling the snake to detect heat at considerable distances. Any warm-blooded animal gives off enough body heat to stimulate these peculiar but exceedingly sensitive organs. The rattler in this way can tell where a rabbit is hiding even though it cannot see it.

There are often several litters of jack rabbit young each year. If there is only one, it is almost always brought forth in April or May. The young are born full-furred, with open eyes and active bodies, quite in contrast with the young of cottontail and brush rabbits. These, when born, are almost naked and immature and are not able to take care of themselves for several days. The young of jack rabbits are born on the ground, but true rabbits are usually littered in underground burrows.

The Panamint Indians, who spent the winter and spring months around the waterholes and mesquite thickets on the barren floor of Death Valley, subsisted almost entirely throughout this period on food gathered during the preceding autumn. This fare consisted of insects, lizards, plant greens, the seeds of wild rice, mesquite beans, and piñon nuts gathered in the Grapevine Mountains. Autumn also was the time of the communal rabbit drives and antelope hunts.

The rabbit drives generally were held in October just after the pine-nut harvest. To find rabbits in numbers the men from all of the neighboring habitations gathered in mountainous brush-covered open areas such as Harrisburg Flats. Long two-foot-wide nets made from fibers of Indian hemp and milkweeds were stretched to form V-shaped barriers held upright by poles; then a few of the participants stationed themselves behind the nets. The others formed a circle, perhaps a mile in diameter, and then, yelling and beating the brush, began closing in toward the center, driving the rabbits before them at full speed into the nets, where they became enmeshed. They were then clubbed to death by the men standing by the nets. At the close of each day there was a great feast. The period of such hunts lasted about a month.

The skins of the rabbits were cured, cut into strips and twisted, then sewn together to make soft, warm blankets for winter use. The meat sometimes was dried, but most of it was eaten fresh-roasted. Rabbits thus formed an important temporary dietary element in the Indians' meager economy.

The animal most frequently driven into the nets was the familiar black-tailed, gray-sided California jack rabbit; in lesser numbers were the Black Hills cottontail.

SAGEBRUSH FLATS
HOME OF THE SAGEBRUSH CHIPMUNK, PYGMY RABBIT, AND
NUMEROUS WILD MICE

The most handsome of the jack rabbits is the large-eared, slender-legged antelope hare (called *el liebre* by the Mexicans) of the grassy plains of southwestern New Mexico, southern Arizona, the tableland of Mexico, and the arid coastal cactus-studded plains of Sonora, Sinaloa, and northern Tepic. This creature's ability to "flash" its undercoat of white hair has earned for it the name antelope, from the pronghorn antelope which also exhibits this phenomenon.

One evening in the tree deserts of west-central Sonora, one of these long-legged jacks darted with astonishing fleetness right through our camp, flashing the white of its otherwise black tail as it passed. Later I was able to see the peculiar phenomenon of "side flashing." While walking along a grass-bordered cattle track, I flushed from its form one of these hares. He seemed not particularly alarmed and moved off at moderate speed at an angle. Suddenly we saw a large flash of white from the side and rump. A few yards on, we saw it again. This sudden showing of white is accomplished by special muscles, which draw up the white area of the sides between shoulder and rump and at the same time shift the buffy or brown area of the back forward and together, to form only a rather inconspicuous narrow band.

When traveling in zigzag patterns, these rabbits sometimes draw up the white area to give a flash first on one side and then on the other. It is a good example of what animal behaviorists call directive coloration. Certainly it is a ready means of calling the attention of other hares during the rutting period; it may warn hares which are near by to be on the alert; it also may serve as a means of confusing a predatory enemy.

One of the greatest enemies of these speedy hares is the caracara, a large white-necked, black-capped hawklike bird of prey. It is a swift and bold hunter and strikes with cruel beak and talons. The hare's only safety lies in its great speed and in its ability to dash quickly into thick brush. The less alert, less suspicious young are especially vulnerable to the attack of caracaras, which hunt on the ground as well as from the air.

The ears of the antelope hare are amazingly long, often up to eight inches, or one-third the length of the animal's body. There is no black patch on the back of the ears at the tip, as shown by the California or desert jack rabbit.

When white-sided hares are sitting still or slowly moving about in the open, their ears are continually shifted about to catch the slightest sound. It is then that they show up to best advantage, being often fully erect, with the sun shining through the pink, translucent, thin-cartilaged pinnae. As a general rule the ears are only flattened back against the neck and shoulders when the animal is in full retreat or when it is feeding under low twiggy brush.

Drought has had a marked effect in diminishing the desert's rabbit population. One spring recently, I took a 1,200-mile trip through the mountains and valleys of the Death Valley area. Neither while driving nor while walking did I see more than two jack rabbits or cottontails. I fared as poorly on a 600-mile trip into Baja California. The number of rabbits often fluctuates in 10- to 12-year cycles corresponding roughly to the cycles of maximum sun spots. Whether there is a connection I do not know.

The scarcity of rabbits in turn affects the predators such as coyotes and bobcats, which largely feed upon them. As rabbits become scarce, these carnivores turn more and more to feeding on the smaller rodents and thus come into competition with the rodent-feeding foxes and snakes, making the times harder for all of them. This illustrates the great dependence of one group of animals on another; the slightest upset in the balance of nature can have wide-reaching effects on the lives of many of the smaller creatures.

10. *The Cottontail*

The only rabbit other than the black-tailed hare inhabiting the deserts of southern California, Nevada, Arizona, and Lower California, also much of arid and semiarid Mexico east of the Sierra Occidental, is the much smaller and surely less plentiful Arizona cottontail, *Sylvilagus auduboni.* These animals occupy much the same sort of brushy areas as the jack rabbit; but, by preference, they live in places with thicker brush cover, such as can be found along mountain borders, about the base of rocky canyon walls, the floors of dry washes, or along river beds. Arrowweed, mesquite, and cat's-claw thickets are especially sought. One seldom, if ever, sees cottontails on the great expanses of widely spaced creosote and burroweed brush in the broad, uninhabited basins of the mid-Mohave Desert. Their altitudinal range is from below sea level in Death Valley and the Salton Sink to as high as 7,500 feet in the desert mountains. Like so many desert animals, the cottontails are in general much paler in color than closely related subspecies inhabiting the coastal area, those from Death Valley being palest of all.

Their ear length, too, is greater, as we found among the desert jack rabbits.

The desert cottontail gaily sports his gray coat and white puffy tail as he runs to cover in the brush. I once brought into my camp cabin a young cottontail and reared him on milk and greenstuffs. He was almost as playful as a kitten, especially in the evening just after sundown. For an hour or more he would dash about in the greatest spirit of frolic, kicking his hind feet in the air, hiding behind the crude furniture, and rolling about on the floor. All sorts of surprise runs were made, generally ending up in a period of secretiveness. Nights, in part, he spent behind a bunch of pine cones I had piled in a corner, but hardly was it dawn before he was out playing again. For no apparent reason, my midget prankster suddenly ended up an evening of mad sport by dying in the night; thus ended a three weeks' period of enjoyable companionship.

When not out foraging in the open or playing, adult cottontails seek permanent diurnal shelter in holes in the ground. Some of these holes they may dig themselves, but it is more probable that, for the most part, they adapt to their needs the burrows previously dug by other animals such as ground squirrels. These holes they may enlarge or extend. Regardless of other alterations they may make in their newly acquired underground home, one change they almost always make is an extra outlet, sometimes even a third, especially if the burrow is made at the base of large-rooted shrubs. Such sites usually afford ample protection against digging predators such as coyotes and badgers. The additional outlets allow a means of ready exit when digging carnivores are working down the burrow from the other end.

The blind and almost hairless young are generally born in the burrow. The litter usually numbers from two to six, three probably being an average number. The peak of the breeding season is in March and April.

During the day, desert cottontails sometimes hide in forms (hollowed-out places) made in bushes or grass tussocks, as the jack rabbits do. They may sometimes make these "hides" themselves, but it is my belief that they more often adapt to their use the forms made by black-tailed hares. When startled by the approach of someone walking through the brush, they bolt out of their shelters in a short, zigzag dash, appearing to have come suddenly from nowhere. The clever rabbit often eludes pursuit, after popping out of his hidings, by suddenly disappearing within another clump of brush, generally readily at hand.

One of the most curious habits of the cottontail is its way, when alarmed at its feeding ground, of making queer thumping noises by striking the hind feet on the hard earth, a thud that is "often audible," says Dr. Orr, "one hundred feet away." It is thought to be a danger warning to other rabbits feeding nearby, although it may be, as is the case with trade rats, merely a fright reaction. The trade rats generally make their thumping noises with both hind feet held together and in series, but the cottontails seldom make more than a single thump at a time.

II. Wild Mice

Among the desert's small wild crea-
tures there are none more secretive and plentiful than the
many species of wild mice, which are exceedingly important
in the economy of the wild.

Although they are very abundant, few people see them,
since they are strictly creatures of the night and, on the whole,
most quiet in their activities. There is scarcely a square foot
of either brush-covered, open desert or rocky hillside that is
not almost nightly visited by these diligent harvesters as they
search for food.

WHITE-FOOTED MICE

The most common of these wild mice are the white-footed
or deer mice belonging to the genus *Peromyscus*. Their large
ears, bright eyes, and soft furry bodies (dark smoky-gray
above and white below) make them among the most beautiful small creatures we see. In summer they frequent the
open country, but in winter they seek, when possible, the
shelter of settlers' cabins, stealing, for use in building their

winter nests, wads of cotton from unprotected mattresses and
getting into supply cans left open. A mess of shredded papers, tattered bags, chewed rags, and numerous black fecal
"seeds" is left as evidence of their winter occupancy.

On a recent cold winter evening, I placed my small campfire of ironwood next to a steep embankment in order to get
shelter from the breeze and extra warmth from the reflected
heat. Soon, from under the litter of dead branches of a palo
verde tree which stood just above the clay embankment, two
white-footed mice came out and, like black, beady-eyed
gnomes, peeked over the edge at the bright fire below. It did
not take them long to come down and begin to stuff their
furry cheek pouches with the crumbs and oatmeal which my
companion and I had purposely thrown on the sand at sup-
pertime to attract just such rodent visitors. The forepaws
worked at almost shuttle speed to stuff full the furry cheek
pouches; then the mice went back and forth on short trips to
their hidden storehouses under the dead palo verde brush.
For half an hour they worked; then they began to explore for
other kinds of food. Before they finished their labors we gave
them opportunity to sample bits of prunes and raisins and
even to get a taste of butter and blackberry jam. The last two
foods posed major problems for them since neither could be
stored in their pockets. The butter they could readily lick up,
but the jam presented a puzzle of a different sort. It was the
blackberry seeds that they wanted above all else and these
were hard to get at, being enclosed in thick sugary syrup. But
the mice were soon equal to the new problem. They picked
out the seeds, then held them in their paws and cleaned them
by licking, until these, too, were ready to go into the pouches.
There was much face and paw washing before they got
through, but they emerged with furry coats perfectly clean.

But tragedy was soon to befall one of them. A small rock
in the embankment behind the fire happened to break loose
from its place and fell down into the fire. The sudden motion

WHITE-FOOTED MOUSE

alarmed the little rodents, and with unbelievable quickness
one of them reacted by leaping right into the bed of glowing
coals, there, of course, to meet his end. A small puff of smoke
from singed hair and a curling up of the body was all we saw.
It was only the death of a small mouse, but it affected us for
the remainder of the evening. Since then I have several times
witnessed this strange reaction of wild mice to fire, which is
an unknown phenomenon to them.

Several times these engaging creatures have taken long
journeys with me in my automobile. One built its nest in the
upholstery of the rear seat while I camped in the desert east
of the Little Colorado River in Arizona. In spite of all efforts
short of trapping, it stayed with me, repeatedly rebuilding
its nest each time I destroyed it, as I journeyed eastward into
Colorado and New Mexico and southwestward into Mexico.
It finally jumped out of the moving auto one early morning

as I traveled along the rough roads of northern Baja California. It surprised me by suddenly appearing and running the length of my arm up to the hand which was high on the steering wheel. From there the mouse made a bold leap out through the window and onto the road.

The deer mice are so plentiful that it is not unusual to find 10 to 15 to the acre in wild areas. They must consume enormous numbers of seeds of wild plants, especially those of the oily-seeded Compositae. Their stores found in shallow holes under rocks and bushes consist of only the soundest, cleanest kinds of seeds. Generally, only one kind of seed is found in any particular food cache. Several times I have found the neat piles between the covers of my bed when for several nights I have not occupied it.

The deer mice are excellent climbers and jumpers. In the juniper country we see places where they have harvested from the high branches the silver-blue juniper berries. They cleverly make vertical cuts into the hard nutlets to get at the oil-rich endosperm within, invariably picking the right spots to make their neat incisions. They do not touch nuts containing sterile seeds.

At night we sometimes hear their high-pitched, almost birdlike singing notes. As one of my correspondents put it, "It sounds as if someone were rubbing a wetted finger tip around the edge of a thin-walled drinking glass." Merritt Cary, conducting his Biological Survey of Colorado, tells of sleeping in an abandoned cabin and hearing their midnight squeaking. "A faint squeal," he says, "in one end of the cabin elicited answers from other parts of the building and the noise was kept up for some time."

The usual nest is a ball of grass lined with soft down of plants, feathers, or wool. The number of young is four to six, and several litters are produced throughout the year. If the mother is disturbed while in the nest with the young, the chances are that she will escape, carrying them with her.

They cling tightly to the nipples as she runs, and if one should lose its grip she may return to grasp it in her teeth, picking it up by the loose skin of the belly.

One very windy night a boy who was camping with me laid his sleeping bag up under a big bladderpod bush, which grew next to a high clay embankment, to secure shelter from the strong gusts. I warned him that he might have rodent visitors during the night. Sure enough, that night he awoke when a white-footed mouse bit him on the nose. I at first doubted his story, but there were clear toothmarks to be seen next morning. This experience had a sequel, an exact repetition just a week afterward when a second boy made his bed under that same wind-protected bush, and was bitten during the night, again on the nose, probably by the very same mouse. Both boys became fully convinced that meat must be part of the diet of this deer mouse, at least.

SPINY POCKET MICE

The silky-haired, bright-eyed spiny pocket mice belong to the genus *Perognathus*. They are given their common name in allusion to the long, spiny hairs on the rump and sides and to the fur-lined cheek pouches, opening like those of the pocket gopher, on either side of the mouth. They are very tiny and have tails which seem in length out of all proportion to the body. This tail ends like an artist's brush in a tassel of long hairs, and we frequently see indications of where it has been dragged in the sand as the animal feeds. Pocket mice are sociable rodents, and we often enjoy their company about our evening out-of-door fires as we camp along the edge of rocky desert mountains. They pay no attention to us but go diligently about gathering into their pouches the crumbs dropped on the ground during the evening meal. If we make a quick motion, they leap out of sight, with the ease of a kangaroo, in jumps two or three feet long. As soon as they get their pockets filled they dash away to their underground storage chambers, only to return quickly for another load. They are timid creatures, and if we find them in their burrows they may quite easily be caught in the hand. Seldom do they make an attempt to bite when held. If held gently for a moment between the thumb and palm they may be quieted sufficiently to be stroked with the finger.

The runways of these rodents are apparent almost everywhere that there is fine, mellow soil to record their numerous and regular journeys to sources of food in patches of seed-laden wild grass, rabbit brush, and atriplex. Their shallow burrows are generally closed during the daytime with a plug of loose earth.

There is a desert-dwelling pocket mouse, called Baird's perognathus (*Perognathus flavus*), which is scarcely more than four inches in total length, and almost half of this is tail. It has the distinction of being rated as the smallest rodent of

GLEN VAR

Spiny Pocket Mouse

the southwestern desert area, perhaps the smallest in America. Its weight is less than half an ounce.

GRASSHOPPER MICE

The small, plump, big-eared, short-tailed grasshopper or scorpion mice feed, as their name indicates, on insects, scorpions, and other small invertebrates. At times they even catch and eat small lizards. They are prone to live in open country but seemingly have no definite places of abode. Their pudgy-footed tracks are frequently seen in the loose soil about the abandoned holes of prairie dogs and ground squirrels, indicating that they often repair to such places to search for insect food. Their burrows are hard to find but usually are located under low bushes, mesquite trees, or weed tangles.

The name "calling mouse" sometimes given them refers, says Dr. Bailey, to their unusual voice.

In camp on a still night one often hears a fine, shrill whistle or prolonged squeak, insectlike in attenuated quality but as smooth and prolonged as the hunting call of the timber wolf, and next morning often finds some of these little hunters in traps near by. In captivity the mice utter their calls from cage to cage, or if taken away from their companions, or if alone when the mating season arrives and warm nights stir their social instincts. Often from their cages in the evening the fine call note rings out, repeated at irregular intervals, and on a few fortunate occasions the writer has watched one throw up its head, and with open mouth and closed eyes send forth its call exactly as he has watched a lone wolf give its prolonged howl from the snow-covered crest of a far ridge. With the difference in size of the animals allowed for, the calls are not so different; it is merely that the voice of the calling mouse is so attenuated that only keen ears can detect it.*

HARVEST MICE

The harvest mice are among the smallest and scarcest of our desert mammals. They live mostly under the cover of

* Vernon Bailey, "Mammals of New Mexico," *N. A. Fauna*, No. 53, p. 136.

grass and thick weed tangles near cultivated fields, on the borders of canals, and in river bottoms. They are mainly seed eaters, but grass stems and fruits are frequently eaten too. Grass tussocks, rubbish heaps, and weed piles are favorite sites for their ball-shaped nests. Their natural enemies—gopher snakes, owls, hawks, coyotes, foxes, and skunks—generally keep their numbers down to a minimum.

12. The Kangaroo Rat

Shortly after my yucca-stalk clock had stopped ticking at Camp Tempus* and the woodpecker family had scattered to take up their abode in new haunts, a new desert neighbor moved in, induced, no doubt, by the abundance of crumbs purposely left about on the ground as an attraction to wild creatures of the vicinity. This new neighbor was the rodent *Dipodomys,* more commonly known as the kangaroo rat. He made his first appearance just before dark and sought for food on the ground in the light of the campfire until we got out our bedrolls and put up for the night. An attractive, compactly built, soft, silky-furred, dainty creature he was, with a head almost equaling the size of his body, and a tail so long that it well exceeded the body length by several inches. On its end there was a tuft of hairs that might have served as a painter's brush. The large, bright eyes shone with great luster. One would not expect bigger ones in an animal

* See p. 229.

twice its size. Most remarkable of all was the face, which because of its peculiar markings seemed to be two faces, one set above the other. The forehead was extremely long, and two deep brown spots below it looked like a second pair of eyes. I could not help thinking of the peculiar helmets the Greek warriors sometimes used to wear, which gave them, too, a seemingly double face.

Kangaroo rats always make the most of any chance to lay up supplies of food, and our new neighbor proved to be an exceedingly busy harvester. No sooner had he crammed his cheek pouches full of crumbs than he was off on leaps to his burrow to empty them and return for more. He seldom approached the campfire twice from exactly the same direction. From out of the surrounding darkness he sometimes came in unsuspectedly from behind, picked up his load, departed, and then soon approached from the side or came in from under the bush which stood in front of us. His usual quiet manner of locomotion when feeding was a kind of scooting forward with body close to the earth and with foot movements so nearly invisible that he appeared for all the world like some mechanical toy moving forward on hidden wheels. Only when surprised or alarmed by some quick motion did he leap about on the elongated hind feet. Then we saw him bounding away in flying leaps like a miniature kangaroo, and always with grace and ease and the speed of a bullet. Like many other small creatures, he seemed to show no fear when we were talking or laughing; even a shout provoked little response. It was quick motions only that moved him to whisk away. Such fear as our motions caused was evidently held in mind for the briefest time. In a moment our visitor would be back at the important work of gathering in food.

Although on a number of occasions careful search was made to find the home burrow where he emptied his bulging cheek pouches, it was never found, principally because he always went to it in the dark beyond the light shed by our fire.

It was difficult to know, when daylight came, which of the numerous holes under bushes was really of his making. Judging from the number of burrow entrances and mounds, we decided that there were other members of his kind very near. Some moonlit night I hope to see him go into his retreat.

Some species of *Dipodomys* excavate their complex dens in soft, sandy soils; others work in heavy soils with considerable coarse gravel intermixed; still others mine in ground almost rocky, provided, of course, that there is some fine soil mixed in. Most burrows are made in the shelter of shrubs or small trees, the more important of these being creosote bush, *Lycium* or thornbush, cat's-claw, ironwood, palo verde, and mesquite trees. Several of the smaller species which build under small bushes make no mounds at all, or only very small ones, indicating that the galleries are neither long nor extensive in their ramifications. The largest of all the species of kangaroo rats, *D. deserti* and *D. spectabilis,* build the largest mounds, and the entrances to the burrows are correspondingly numerous and large. The excavations of these larger rodents often extend over an area of 15 or 20 square yards, and the earth is so honeycombed with galleries crisscrossing one above the other that a person walking across them may suddenly sink almost to his knees or even fall headlong as the labyrinthine tunnels, built in sand, cave in beneath him. Such mounds are particularly common in the southern parts of the Colorado Desert and in the sandy flats of southern Arizona and northern Sonora where *D. deserti* and *D. spectabilis* dwell. Grazing cattle and pack burrows soon become acquainted with the nature of these dens and avoid going over them.

The deepest of the galleries in the large dens may go three or four feet underground. It is in these deep recesses that the animals find effective refuge from the baking heat of midsummer days. There, too, is the nest where the young are born; in the upper-surface tunnels the adults are well above the waters of ordinary floods. In the large dens there are often as many as six to ten entrances. These openings are all of large size, for they must accommodate the animal diving into them in the semierect position that he assumes while on the leap. Some of these openings are occasionally plugged with earth during the daytime, doubtless to keep intruders out.

When a "dipo" is about to emerge from one of the holes, he often announces the fact with a thumping noise made by striking the ground with his hind feet. This thumping sometimes seems to be given as a kind of alarm as well as a signal before approaching the burrow opening and emerging from the den.

Coyotes often try to dig out the kangaroo rats and in doing so make deep holes into the mounds. Foxes depend more on running the animals down or surprising them on the surface while playing or feeding. The fox is often very successful in his quest and secures from *Dipodomys* a large portion of his food. Where kangaroo rats are plentiful, there, too, one finds foxes equally abundant.

Communal living is unknown among these rodents. One occupant to a burrow is the rule except for a short time when the mother and two or three young are together. It is thought that the desire for solitude at home exists because of the concern of the individual for its supplies of stored foods. Occasionally, dipos are forced by plunderers to give up part of their caches, for robbing of the stores is often practiced. If the prowler is caught in the pilfering act, he is quickly pounced upon and, if possible, evicted from the premises. He gets a good thumping, and, in addition, some flesh-gouging scratches inflicted by the powerful, sharp-clawed hind feet. Sometimes when you think the fighters are about to meet in the close combat of battle one leaps high "in air, completely over the other." I have on many occasions seen both of them "do the leap" at the same time, meeting in mid-air. Bloody

MERRIAM'S KANGAROO RAT

wounds and slashed ears and noses are not unknown results
of these conflicts. When no pilfering is going on and everyone is attending to his own business, a sort of good-natured,
silent play often seemingly goes on among them. Sometimes
the play consists of a "waltzing" on the sand; at other times
a kind of leapfrog and tag is indulged in. I have seen two
dipos scoot across the sand, approaching one another until
they touched noses; then suddenly, as if by electrical contact,
they would spring upward, backward, or sideways in a high,
bouncing leap. Another "play trick," rather similar, is seen
when a dipo, nosing about, quite suddenly and for no apparent reason other than pure sport, leaps straight up a foot or
two, as if a spring had been released just beneath him.

Most of the movements, whether they be crawls, runs, or
sudden leaps upward, are almost solely hind-foot perform-

ances, the weak forefeet being ill adapted by size to serve as efficient locomotor aids. The small forelimbs are principally used in rapidly passing food such as seeds into the fur-lined cheek pouches, in digging into the loose soil or sand to help excavate tunnels, or in unearthing buried seeds or some other treasure. Like a true kangaroo, the kangaroo rats sit much, when quiet, on the long soles of the powerful hind feet. When dipos spring forward, the well-developed hindquarter muscles are brought into effective play, sending the rodents on leaps sometimes a yard long. All the while, the tail is brought into cooperative use both as a rudder and as a balancing organ. When leaping, the tail is curved slightly upward. At other times, when the dipo sits upright on its haunches, this long tufted appendage serves as a prop, like the third leg of a tripod.

When I get up in the morning at my desert camps, usually one of the first things I do is to look around the dead campfire to examine the myriads of tracks in the fine dust and see what rodents have been nocturnal visitors. The tracks show plainly that white-footed mice are among the most frequent guests; and more than likely the kangaroo rats have been there, too, helping to finish up the crumbs. Never one crumb, not even a small one, is left. Sometimes I scatter far and wide about the camp whole handfuls of scraps and wild seeds, to see who will come in to get them. It is my firm conviction that every foot, almost every square inch, of earth is hunted over each night by these harvesters.

The kangaroo rat tracks are always easy to distinguish from those of other animals, for the kangaroo rats leave not only the parallel marks of the two long-soled hind feet but also the gently curved shallow furrows made by the long, tufted tail, which is dragged or swished about behind them. In addition, as evidence of their nocturnal activities, they always leave behind them numerous little pits dug by the forefeet to get bits of food beneath the surface of the soil.

Larger cavities or tunnels are excavated by the strong hind feet. These they draw up under the body, close to the jaws, and then send them flying backward, throwing out the sand in a shower behind. At times I see in the fine sand evidences that the animals have been rolling in the dust to remove the excess oil from their coat of fine hairs.

The kangaroo rat's season of breeding is a long one, lasting from early spring to late midsummer. The normal number of young is two or three. They are born blind and practically hairless. I once caught in my hands a baby dipo just old enough to be getting about on his own. It was in the evening just after sunset and I found him as he was nosing about under some shrubs. Curled up in my hand he was no larger than a walnut. When I first held him he bit my finger so severely that I dropped him. He drew no blood, but it was an indication of the strong development of incisor teeth even very early in life. I took the little furry ball home with me and kept him in a three-by-three-foot wire cage. His favorite food was ripe Bing cherries; next came sunflower seeds and hemp. For fully two weeks he was full of pranks and played all day long; then suddenly he became wholly nocturnal. Once he had changed from a creature of the day to one of the night, like his parents, he began throwing the dry earth and sand about in his cage with such diligence and force that much of it went through the screen mesh onto the floor. All night long there were such thumpings and scrapings that I finally had to give him his liberty. No protracted sleep was possible with him around. He had grown so fast that he seemed adult both in size and behavior in a matter of a few weeks.

The food of *Dipodomys* is largely plant stems, seeds, and fleshy fungi. The time of greatest storing of these materials is during the active period of plant growth. In the California deserts this is in the months of spring. In Arizona and Sonora, where there are not only winter rains but also good summer rains, there is a second period of storing in late August and September. A considerable amount of fresh green material is always eaten when available. In lands where competition for grass among grazing animals (cattle, horses, and sheep) and *Dipodomys* exists, the large amounts of such food collected by the kangaroo rats may be a deciding factor in estimating the number of cattle that can live in an area. In drought years this competition may be very serious, and the amount of grass gathered in and consumed by the provident dipos may mean that few domestic animals can survive. In some years the drought in desert areas is so intense that there is not even the little food needed for the kangaroo rats and they, too, perish. In turn, this may mean that the existence of foxes and coyotes is threatened, since they depend much on these rodents for their food. So the endless chain goes on. Any upset in the usual cycle brings changes, and grave maladjustments and serious consequences ensue.

We can add *Dipodomys* to our rather long list of desert animals that live on day after day, year in and year out, with no need for seeking water at streams, pools, or springs. For him it is enough to have some green food occasionally, but even this is not wholly necessary, since his own body is a chemical laboratory wherein water can be synthesized from the elements of starchy food or obtained by the slow oxidation of fats. It is, in fact, in this latter role as self-sufficient chemist that he gets most of the water he needs. This lack of dependence on outward supplies of water makes it possible for him to live over wide areas denied to animals such as ungulates, carnivores, and many birds that must visit the water holes almost daily, or at least once every three or four days, or soon perish.

The kangaroo rats are not rats at all in the true sense, and it is unfortunate that this name is attached to creatures so unratlike in their ways. Rodents they are, even as rats are, but they belong to a family which has affinities with the squirrels and chipmunks rather than with the barn rats and the common house mice. Kangaroo rats are wholly North American in distribution and are mostly confined to the more arid regions, particularly the southwestern United States.

At least 34 species and subspecies of kangaroo rats are known in the state of California alone. Four of these inhabit desert areas—the allied kangaroo rat, the Mohave kangaroo rat, the big desert kangaroo rat, and Merriam's kangaroo rat.

The two most common and widespread in the southern California deserts are the large *D. deserti*, particularly plentiful in sandy areas, and *D. merriami*, a smaller animal making much smaller mounds and found widely dispersed over creosote bush plains. The big desert kangaroo rat (*D. deserti*) is an animal of pale coloration, without vertical tail stripe, and with tail tuft ending in white. Merriam's kangaroo rat is reddish buff-colored, with vertical tail stripe and tail-tuft wholly dusky.

13. Pygmy Mammals

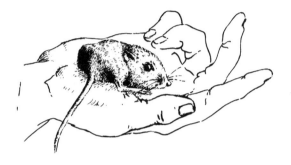

In the desert there are many kinds of mice and mouse-like animals, some of them so small and secretive in habit that they are scarcely known to any but the most careful or lucky observers.

THE DWARF KANGAROO MOUSE

A kangaroo rat in miniature is the little mouse, *Microdipodops*, which was originally called the dwarf kangaroo rat. In 1891 it was first made known to science by Dr. C. Hart Merriam, who at that time pronounced it "one of the most remarkable of the many new and interesting mammals that have been discovered in North America during the past few years." It has the appearance of "a heavy, thickset pocketmouse" with a comparatively large head like that of the kangaroo rat and abnormally large furry hind feet which serve as efficient "sand paddles." As in *Dipodomys*, there are cheek pouches opening near the angles of the mouth and lined with hairy integument. The tail is comparatively short and simple, being without stripes and without the strange little brush of hairs so noticeable in the white-footed mice and kangaroo rats.

Like the kangaroo rat, this yellowish-brown or clay-colored nocturnal mouse makes its burrows in fine, loose, sandy soil where detached bushes offer it protection and also provide the seeds which constitute its principal fare. In bipedal manner it goes about or leaps on its two hind feet, so that the tracks it leaves on the sand are those in small scale of the kangaroo rat, except that they are not parallel, but have the toes turned a little outward.

The most easily accessible region where one may become acquainted with these little dwarfs is a picturesque one and well worth a vacation ramble any time. Upper Fish Lake Valley in Nevada, near the place where the dwarf kangaroo mice were first discovered, is an area surrounded by mountain scenery both austere and grand in the extreme. To the west of it lie the stern and majestic White Mountains and on the east are hills so varied and bizarre in form and in the colors of the rock veins that run in them, that they are often called the Pintos (from the Spanish *pinto*, meaning "painted, mottled"). In the full heat of summer noon their color is a variegated gray-buff and they appear to be veiled in a kind of half-visible white vapor. But when sunset comes the erstwhile pale slopes glow brightly with vivid magentas, greens, yellows, and browns. The old road leading out of Fish Lake Valley to the north takes one through the fine-sand country where the dwarf kangaroo mice and their habitations may be seen. If there has been no wind to disturb the sand, the telltale paired tracks are easily found.

It was on a night in August 1941 that I first chose to camp in this attractive *Microdipodops* country. It was moonlight, and so bright that coarse newsprint could be easily read and every grass stem and every branch of the low, detached, half-dead, puny bushes that dotted the pallid sand hummocks clearly stenciled their forms in black shadows on the silver sand. As my companion and I talked while seated on an observation rock near one of the *Microdipodops* burrows, we several times had a chance to see the big-eyed, soft, silky-furred midgets leaping about like tiny kangaroos or digging with the small forefeet into the almost powdery sands for wind-buried seeds. Once one came so near that I slowly extended my hand, thinking I might actually reach down and touch it, but so alert was it that upon the first-noticed movement it made a getaway leap of fully thirty inches; another similar bound put it well into its burrow. Some idea of the small size of these creatures can be gained by telling you that the burrow opening into which this one popped was scarcely more than an inch in diameter. That this bipedal mouse is an agile jumper is further corroborated by the experience that Drs. Raymond Hall and Jean Linsdale, of the University of California, had with one they had caught at Halleck, Nevada. It "repeatedly jumped out of a can, the sides of which were seventeen inches high. This it did without touching the sides of the can, although it was only ten inches in diameter."

The kangaroo mice are typically Nevada mammals, being confined almost wholly to that state and to small adjacent areas of Oregon, Utah, and California. The two species and thirteen subspecies are known only from the Upper Sonoran Life Zone.

THE DESERT SHREW

By far the smallest and probably least known of all desert mammals is the desert shrew (*Notiosorex crawfordi*). Although it looks very much like a tiny mouse, its primitive dentition and insatiable carnivorous appetite, among other things, tell us that the shrew is in reality a member of that very primitive group of mammals called *Insectivores*. The desert shrew's diminutive, pale, ashy-gray body is scarcely more than two inches long, to which is added about an inch-long, smooth, mouselike tail. Like all shrews, it has a long pointed snout (the Germans call the shrews *Spitzmäuse,* point-mice), but unlike most others, this species has prominent eyes and ears, giving it an even more mouselike appearance. During its waking hours it does little else than hunt for food (insects, larvae, and small rodents) among the grasses and leaves around and under shrubs and trees of its low desert habitat.

George Olin, in his *Animals of the Southwest Deserts,* describes the desert shrew as "an appetite on four legs, guided by a keen nose and aided by small but formidable claws and teeth." A successful hunter this ferocious and active animal must always be, for to be without food for more than six or seven hours means that it must miserably perish. I have seen a desert shrew but once in all my wide travels and then only for a fleeting but most exciting moment. This was some years ago while camping among some ironwood trees in a wash to the east of the Colorado River. It was late in the evening and the shrew darted into a small hole from among a litter of leaves.

So little is known about this tiniest of all the desert's mammals that a few paragraphs are adequate for a full description of all of its known habits. Any observations that you or I may have made or may make in the future will be a valuable contribution to the knowledge of this rare and certainly unique animal.

The desert shrew is a member of the Lower Sonoran fauna of the United States and Mexico and may be looked for from southern Texas westward to Nevada and southern California and southward on the mainland of Mexico to Sinaloa; also on the peninsula of Lower California. It belongs to a subfamily (*Soricinae*) characterized by having the summits of the teeth colored red, in contrast to another group of shrews in which the teeth are completely white.

14. The Pack Rats

Noise-weary city dwellers out for a few days of a primitive sort of vacation sometimes move into old desert shanties, set up simple housekeeping, and prepare for a time of relaxation, a life of simplicity and quiet. But they are not there for long before they begin to complain of queer nocturnal noises, "evidently made by some ambitious ghost or mischievous animal." Objects banged on the floor or wall, shoutings, and cursings are useless. "Whoever the ghost, whatever the animal," they declare, "it must be a big one." They do not realize that the culprits that annoy them and rob them of half their sleep and all of their patience are very gentle but wide-awake, bright-eyed, soft-furred creatures of modest proportion that prefer to work at night. To the long-time desert residents they are known as pack rats or trade rats, but to the serious student of mammals, as *Neotoma*. This last is really a better name, since the animals are not true rats at all, even though to the uninformed they may bear superficial resemblance. Virtually unknown to town dwellers, these animals are abundant everywhere on deserts where there are rocks, shrubs, trees, old camps, and cabins.

Uninitiated persons camping in the open have their troubles, too, especially if their camps are in brushy areas. They will do well to see that their temporary out-of-doors abode is not made near a *Neotoma*'s hut of sticks or piles of stones, for they are almost certain the very first night to have visits from their rodent neighbors and perhaps even have a piece of clothing, a knife, or a spoon carried off in the bargain, too. A lad camping near me once complained of having lost a woolen sock only a few nights before, and, since it was one of the only pair he possessed, he was quite certain that my advice always to keep small objects of clothing out of reach was well worth heeding. Since it was the time of the *Neotoma* breeding season, early March, I daresay some baby pack rats had that year an unusually soft and warm bed. Wool isn't to be had every day for nest lining.

Pack rats are persistent travelers. All during the night they scurry about on the limbs of shrubs or make their way in exploratory excursions over rocks or along radiating trails previously established. Night is their time for picking up insects, seeds, small berries, and wild nuts, none of which come amiss as objects for storage or as food to satisfy immediate hunger. It is also their time for bringing in the numerous sticks, cactus joints, and other objects they use in making or protecting their home. In the vicinity of the *Neotoma*'s domicile, the runways used for foraging are many, and often they lead considerable distances through the brush and grass or along the bottom of sand washes. These are narrow trails that show imprints of numerous pudgy round feet and thus are easily distinguished from the broad trails made by rabbits. The well-beaten appearance of these paths shows that they are often used and that every part of the foraging ground must be visited almost every night. Many times by firelight I have watched pack rats go in and out of their homes. Always I have noticed how remarkably regular they are in using certain definite runways. Some of the well-used routes on rock surfaces appear to have been long established and habitually used, generation after generation, perhaps even for centuries.

Most unusual individual preferences are shown by pack rats in the selection and assemblage of nest materials. Some nests are made of an elaborate assortment of objects—weathered bones, bits of bark, chips and splinters of wood, empty shotgun shells, dung, and stones; others may be built almost wholly or even exclusively of green twigs of juniper. Sometimes the sole material is small rounded rocks, or it may be joints of cholla cactus or only the clusters of cactus needles. Irrespective of the materials, there are almost always lying about the entrances of used nests a few green twigs or fresh green leaves. These are sure signs of occupancy. To some extent, the materials selected are those nearest at hand, but this is not always true. This was illustrated in a nest I saw not long ago. Abundant supplies of sticks and stones were near, but the *Neotoma* had chosen juniper twigs exclusively.

In his ardor for transporting objects, the *Neotoma* will frequently move a whole pile of sticks, bark, and whatnot back and forth over an open space again and again. Later they may wholly abandon these and start moving about new objects that for the moment excite their interest. This is especially noticeable when pack rats inhabit the walls and attics of old houses. An old miner I once met vowed that they do it just as a means of increasing the number and variety of their nuisance noises and to exasperate as much as possible their human neighbors. "A noise repeated a few times I can stand," he said, "but when those pesky trade rats go rumpling sticks around on the attic floor over a period of hours and hours it becomes unbearable." I quite agreed. I've spent my share of sleepless nights, too, because of a trade rat's mania for moving things about.

Stick Nest of Neotoma in a Natural Rock Cave

So ingrained is this habit of object-moving that the pack rats sometimes build their rubbish-heap abodes to unbelievable size. In the juniper thickets of the Mohave Desert along the north borders of the San Gabriel Mountains, I once discovered a nest made up of enough chips and sticks of juniper wood to fill eight or ten barrels. Some of the sticks were almost a yard long and an inch thick. It was an area where, many years past, a lot of wood-cutting had been done by settlers, and that trade rat seemed to have collected every little chip and small juniper stick they had left behind them. This was the typical work of the desert trade rat, *N. desertorum.*

Among the dense cottonwood thickets along the Mohave River near Hesperia and beyond, the brown-footed wood rats (*N. fuscipes*) build wigwam-shaped, ground-level huts that are five and six feet broad at the base and just as high. Up in the cottonwood tree branches, the males construct for themselves high arboreal nests that are as large as barrels, made completely of twigs and larger sticks which they have gathered from far and near.

Many of the huge nest heaps are very old, with new materials added by each successive occupant. In one area I walked among the trees for an hour and estimated that there must be 10 or 12 of these "stick tepees," as I once heard them called, to the acre. Diligent builders those trade rats are. And what a chittering of teeth, what rustling noises one may hear at night as the animals cut the green twigs, nibble at bark, or drag along the ground the materials for their ever-growing conical homes!

When the desert *Neotoma* builds between the large, loosely piled, rounded boulders of disintegration of the granite country, his passion for bringing in wood fragments, spiny cactus joints, and dung finds fullest expression. Night after night such materials are brought in to fill the cracks and block possible entrance of enemies. As time goes on, the

NEST OF WOOD RAT IN COTTONWOOD ALONG THE MOHAVE RIVER

enormous accumulations mat down and become cemented together with solidifying urine and fecal matter. When set on fire, as they are sometimes by curious travelers bent on diversion, they burn for hours, giving off volumes of acrid, foul-smelling smoke and considerable heat. If the rodent occupants are at home at the time, the chances are that they will suffocate rather than try to leave the burning mass.

Animals, like people, have their individuality and, at times, manners strange even to their kind. In the giant yucca forests near Hesperia, I found a place where a *Neotoma* had accumulated a lot of yucca-bark fragments at the base of a fallen yucca trunk and then, in a vent of energy, had carried several dozen pieces of bark chips high up into a near-by standing green yucca tree, tucking them in among the bristling needles. I daresay once it had deposited them, it straightway went off and forgot them. That's an old trade rat for you.

The world is full of unsolved riddles. Although the pack rat has been the nuisance neighbor of almost every desert camp and mine-cabin dweller for more than a hundred years, and in spite of all the speculation and careful study by trained observers of the puzzling nocturnal behavior of the desert wood rat, we know almost as little as we did fifty years ago about these animals and how they walk with such ease over cactus joints. As Vernon Bailey says, "They even climb the spiniest cactus trees and run over the thousands of needle-pointed spines without the slightest hesitation or inconvenience, notwithstanding the fact that the soles of the foot are as naked and as delicate as the palm of one's hand."* How do they manage to carry the spiny sections of cactus stems that so often form the barriers of defense at the entrance of their desert homes? We know that the cactus joints are carried in the mouth, but why don't the needles ever puncture the tender lips, the tongue, or the flesh of their jaws? Particularly does mystery surround the manner of safely transporting the large, spiny, stem segments of Bigelow's cholla, those bristly cylinders of silver-green needles of the desert's most beautiful but most frightful cactus. The fallen joints are full of stabbing spines; they are also exceedingly heavy and given to rolling, so they must always be handled with the utmost dexterity.

The heap of sticks, stones, cactus joints, and rubbish you see piled high against tree stumps or about rocks and bushes is only part of the *Neotoma's* home. This is only the outer structure. Within it there are often tunnels and from one to three chambers lined with shredded bark or fibers. There the animals may curl up and keep warm on cold days, or there

---

* "Mammals of New Mexico," *N. A. Fauna*, No. 53, p. 178.

they may store excess food. The real nest and place of greatest security is generally underground, in one of the numerous deep tunnels excavated in the earth between rocks, or more often among the twisted roots of some desert shrub or tree. This nest is lined with soft bark and grasses, is cup-shaped, and just large enough to accommodate the rat when curled up in sleep. The opening is generally at the top.

Vertical banks of consolidated gravel, full of miniature caves, or cliffs of clay, or the steep, stony banks of deeply cut gullies are especially preferred homesites for the desert *Neotoma* because of the protection they afford from the many enemies, especially digging carnivores such as coyotes. As Dr. Bailey puts it, "every crevice is a temptation to build." Claybanks are often honeycombed with *Neotoma* excavations—at times, so much so that during periods of heavy rains when volumes of water flood the land and rush down the gullies, the weakened claybanks give way and precipitate the animals and their homes into the water below or crush them into the crumbling earth and rubble. When pack rats build in steep-sided banks of clay or conglomerate, the usual large accumulations of rubbish ordinarily needed for protection are not found, and the entrance to the nest may be indicated only by a few sticks and cactus-needle clusters.

The period of gestation of the pack rat is about four weeks, a variation occurring in different species. The two or three young are born blind and remain so about 17 days. At Coolgardie in San Bernardino County, California, I once opened a cactus-covered *Neotoma* home in early March. Under the outer piles of sticks was an upturned rusty washbasin. Under this was the nursery nest, containing a female with three young. The babies were pink, not more than three or four days old. Two were attached to the mother's nipples. Dazed by the sudden light, the mother seemed at first at a loss what to do. She looked up appealingly, sniffed the air, moved her long whiskers rapidly, and shifted her position slightly. The

Joshua Tree Offshoots

JOSHUA TREE NATIONAL MONUMENT, NEAR HIDDEN VALLEY, CALIFORNIA

single, small, unattached youngster quickly reacted to this motion and immediately took hold of a nipple. The mother now, with all her babies firmly secured, bolted over the side of the nest to safety in a rock crevice, her young bobbing and dragging along beneath her as she fled.

The teats of the pack rat are in two pairs and inguinal— that is, between the hind legs, "just like a cow's," as prospector Coffey said. Until the eyes are open, the young remain attached to them most of the time. Their hold is made sure with the aid of the incisor teeth, which in the very young are strongly incurved. Later, when no longer needed in this capacity, these teeth become normal.

Once the eyes are open, the young enter the second period of their development, a time of education through activity and play, and less time is spent in nursing. The paws practice bringing food to the mouth. They wash their faces; they dig into the sand either for exercise or to locate bits of food. The jaws are exercised in nibbling, much of it useless, since many of the things they work on, such as small pebbles, wood fragments, and even fecal pellets, are objects unfit for food. Small scraps of green food, seeds, and tiny sticks are carried about. All these are doubtless purely instinctive behavior patterns which become purposeful activities when adulthood is reached. A lot of time, too, is spent in frisking about the mother and one another, making sudden runs, leaps, and stops, and nosing one another.

By the time the young have reached the age of three months they are weaned. In appearance and actions they now are very much like adults — sleek, soft-furred animals with big, bright, bulging, black eyes, with erect, rounded ears and almost full-sized body. It is time for them to begin the new activities of house-building and finding food. Moreover, they must begin to be alert to the dangers of enemies, ever present on the ground and in the air—snakes and hawks by day, snakes and owls by night.

15. The Pocket Gopher

Neither the mole nor his earthwork tunnels are ever seen on natural deserts. The soil is generally two sandy or too rocky to favor his work of making subterranean runways. Moreover, his food is wholly animal—small grubs, earthworms, and insects, that live plentifully only in soils rich in humus, the soils our deserts most lack. There is thus no sustenance there for the creatures he uses to appease his voracious appetite.

He has left it to his vegetarian cousin, the pocket gopher, *Thomomys*, to excavate the desert soils and throw up the earth in mounds about his dwellings. On deserts, pocket gophers have a wide distribution, from below sea level, as in the Salton Sink, to high elevations in the arid desert mountains, being absent only in the most sandy, salt-encrusted plains or rocky places. In some of the broad *Larrea*-covered plains, these excavators are wholly absent or infrequent, but in many other places, when the winter and early spring rains come, their mounds are seen in numbers, especially in the clayey borders of washes, in the finely comminuted soils of mesas, or in the valleys of the somewhat rocky hills.

Their season of activity is a short one. They work only through three or four winter and spring months, when the topsoil is damp and the annual herbs are flourishing and succulent. The eight months of "arid summer" find them for the most part very quiet, hiding in inactivity in the tunnels where neither glaring light nor much heat can penetrate.

Did you ever try sleeping in a wild flower garden, placing your bedroll right in the midst of the flowers? I did this recently. Just after dawn, I saw a stalk of foot-high, colorful lupine suddenly begin moving violently about. Then a moment later I saw it disappear quickly, pulled underground as if by a mysterious hand. Almost immediately after, another lupine stalk waved about, tottered, and, like its predecessor, went suddenly down beneath the surface of the soil in the same strange manner. After a half-dozen lupine stems had been pulled under, the activity completely stopped.

In a few moments, almost at the very spot, there was a sudden great heaving of earth and out of the middle of the mound appeared the head of a homely, whiskered gopher, with chubby cheeks and beady eyes. This smoky-gray rodent, armed with pairs of great whitish incisor teeth protruding like the tusks of a walrus, popped above ground to take a look around him. It was he who had made the lupine stalks quiver; it was he who had pulled them underground to add to his cache of green foods.

Now for a moment he had stopped eating and was about to extend his underground tunnel. There was a lapse of only a few minutes before there began a great pushing up of soft, damp earth, load after load. As each pile of loosened soil was brought up, pushed forward, and thrown out by the forefeet, our gopher showed his head a moment, only to back down to gather another load of earth. Only once did he come forward far enough to show his body, and then it was with belly dragging close to the ground and with hindquarters still hidden within the burrow. A tender bit of miner's lettuce (*Montia*) was nipped off and transferred to his capacious cheek pouches. That done, he quickly slipped backward, only to go through the act again before finally plugging the opening. Probably not until evening did he again venture forth to feed.

There is a particularly dangerous kind of gold mining engaged in at times by prospectors, which most appropriately may be mentioned in this connection. It is called "gophering," since the men who "gopher" spend all their time alone in narrow subterranean tunnels, which they dig while lying flat on their bellies. In solitude they work, going about—like gophers—along the layers of gold-bearing sand, soil, or gravel. Backing out now and then, while in the same prone position, they bring dirt to the tunnel entrance.

Near Lida, Nevada, there is a small district where such gophering has been going on for years, and the whole area is covered with mounds just like a pocket-gopher-infested field. We found there that one of the old "gophers" was a woman, who had worked her area alone for many years, groveling about in tunnels eight or ten feet underground, sometimes working in under for a distance of forty or fifty feet. Every now and then the cramped underground passages of the "gopherers" cave in behind them, leaving the unlucky miners to dig their way out or perish.

The pocket gopher's main runways are generally made about six inches to a foot underground, depending partly on the character of the soil and partly on the position of the roots or tubers they seek for food. In sandy soil, where cave-ins are possible, they naturally work much deeper than in dense soils. The passage, once made, may be used over a long period, and since new ones are constantly being made whenever the soil is damp, they finally honeycomb the earth in many directions. As the main subterranean galleries are extended, small radiating side tunnels are also made for food gathering, and it is mostly from these that the earth is pushed up and dumped to form the characteristic hillocks. These animals run along their subterranean routes either forward or backward with equal ease. Back-running is probably facilitated by the scantily haired, short tail, which is an organ of high sensitivity and of great aid, as Dr. Merriam suggests, "in warning the animals of an enemy in the rear." Speaking of a pocket gopher he once had under observation, Dr. Merriam noted that "when carrying food to one of his storehouses the animal rarely turned around but usually ran backward to the place of deposit, returning for more and repeating the operation again and again, the to-and-fro movement suggesting a shuttle on its track."

The great digging tools of *Thomomys* (Greek, meaning "heap-mouse") are the two pairs of powerful front incisor teeth, used as a pick for loosening the soil, and the powerfully muscled, long-clawed forefeet. With these they not only dig, but, aided by the hind feet, constantly work the loose earth back under the body. When too much earth has been piled up behind him, the pocket gopher turns about within his narrow run; then with wrists under his chin and palms of his hands held vertically, he pushes the earth along in front of him like a bulldozer, finally discharging it through an opening of one of the short side tunnels made purposely to serve that end. Each load is brought up and then shoved out and up on top of the earth already there. He seldom gets his body length out of the burrow. Ordinarily, the haunches are kept well within the tunnel opening, and these he uses as "sort of an anchor by means of which he can pull himself back into safety at an instant's warning."

Several times each day the pocket gophers go over their runs and extend them to get at new sources of food. Our desert pocket gophers are especially fond of lupines, which are rich in proteins. Almost every thickset stand of spring-blooming lupines shows its gopher workings, with new mounds added daily.

Some people think that the pocket gropher's capacious cheek pouches are used to carry earth from the point of excavation to the soil surface. Nothing could be further from the truth. They are used exclusively for the temporary storage and transport of food. The cheek pouches are sacs of skin lined with soft, short hairs; they extend from the angle of the mouth even as far back as the shoulder. Strong protractor muscles spread out over both inner and outer sides of the pouch. When they contract they draw the back of the pouch forward to empty it. A long bandlike retractor muscle brings the sac, after being emptied, back again to normal position. A strong sphincter or circular muscle closes the entrance to the sac, acting much like a drawstring. As the gopher works forward, extending his tunnel, he nips off succulent roots he comes across, cuts them up, and crams them into the pouches, continuing alternately to excavate and store until the pockets are full. Once the sacs are filled, he backs along the runway to his storeroom.

The pocket gopher is a highly specialized animal. The specialization is seen particularly in the bones and muscles of the forelimb, parts highly developed because of the animal's digging habits. The bones of the fore part of the body are especially thickset and roughened for attachment of the powerful muscles. When digging the tunnels, the efficient forefeet are capable of strokes so strong and so rapid that they produce a continuous buzzing sound which is distinctly audible, especially when the animal is working in hard ground.

In the owl the pocket gopher has a swift, subtle, and sure-striking enemy. Plenty of evidence of this is seen in the numerous bits of skulls and other pocket gopher bones found in the disgorged pellets about every owl nest and owl roost. It is really surprising that so many pocket gophers do fall prey to owls, for the animals are really quite wary and stay above ground or at the entrance to their tunnels only very briefly.

In the spring of the year, when food is most plentiful, the two to six young are born. They are nursed in a dry nest of fine grass made deep in the tunnel. They are tiny creatures, even when big enough to get around by themselves. Few people ever see an adult gopher; still fewer see a baby one.

16. *The White-tailed Ground Squirrel*

The antelope "chipmunk," that lively animal that bounces over the ground, carrying his small, flattened, white-backed tail curled over his back, is the gayest mammal of the desert. Sprightly and restless, he is a favorite of all who know him. You are especially fortunate if this chipper little rodent takes up living quarters in the neighborhood of your desert home, for then you may watch him in all his sportive moods and know his engaging family life at first hand. He is a decent, friendly neighbor of the finest sort. Like most people who live in the desert, you will probably call him a chipmunk because of his superficial resemblance to that mountain animal, but in reality he is only a small striped ground squirrel. Unlike the chipmunk, the stripes on the sides of the body run up only to the shoulder and not to the tip of the pointed nose.

If you who are living in the desert foothills would really get acquainted with this daring yet friendly rodent, put out in your backyard melon rinds, scattered grains of corn and wheat, and scraps from the table. It may be only a matter of days until the "ammos" (from the scientific name *Ammospermophilus*), as I like to call them, are constantly about. You may even be as lucky as I once was when several pairs, drawn by the variety and abundance of my menu, moved right up close and excavated their tunnels beneath nearby rocks and the floor of my hillside desert shanty. Because I was very quiet, they played daily about my doorstep and even at times ventured inside the house. I watched them at their feeding, at the quick nose-bumping and scratching for fleas, even at their love-making. Once I had a chance to observe a male as he sat in a sunny spot just inside the door and gave his long series of sharp, almost birdlike, call notes. For intensity and long continuance they seemed out of all proportion to the small creature that made them. I saw now the vibrating movement of the tongue and jaws, the quick pulsations of the furry, white-striped sides as the strong, rapidly contracting diaphragm forced spurts of compressed air over the strong vocal chords. On hot afternoons I repeatedly watched these rodents quench their thirst by lapping water like a cat from a shallow drinking pan, and then afterward observed them go away to rest in the shade of the mesquite tree nearby. They sometimes contentedly squatted flat on their bellies with the inner face of the "hams" of their hind limbs flat against the sand, a position I have often seen taken by fat little dogs. Among this group of five desert antelope ground squirrels there was a surprising degree of difference in disposition. One of them was very timid; three were very bold in coming to the feeding yard; and then there was the stolid old male bully who thought that everything was put out for him alone and that others should eat only the leftovers, and these only at his sufferance. His capacious cheek pouches seemed always full. In winter they ventured out only when the sun was warm.

In the wild, the desert antelope ground squirrels show particular preference for the rocky foothill borders, but they are not by any means wholly confined there; a fair amount of brush is always essential, since they depend on it a great deal for protection against avian and other enemies. The main entrance to the den is a neat hole in the gravelly earth, probably beneath a boulder, creosote bush, or thorny cat's-claw or cactus. Besides the main opening there may be other openings leading to auxiliary burrows. The openings are by no means easy to find, for there is scarcely even the slightest mound of excavated earth to mark them. At one moment you see the rapidly retreating animal on the run; in the next flash he is gone, seemingly having disappeared into nowhere, dropping suddenly into his vertical hole. Even when you go up to the place where he was seen to vanish, you cannot always find the opening, for it may have been cleverly concealed among the woody basal stems of a thorny shrub. Burrows made in the sides of the vertical claybanks of barrancas are, of course, easier to spot, especially if you should chance to see the animal pop into one.

The burrow generally goes straight or almost straight down half a foot or more, and then meanders among the clutches of strong and tortuous roots for safety against digging enemies. The ground squirrels have numbers of predatory foes, very dangerous ones, in such neighbors as sidewinders and other rattlesnakes, weasels, bobcats, coyotes, road runners who may gobble up the young, and ravens and such birds of prey as the hawks and falcons. But they are usually safe in their underground retreats when darkness comes and the keen-eyed, soft-winged owls are about.

Against daytime foes they are always on the alert. Their big, sharp, black eyes are quick to sense the approach of moving objects. Any sudden motion of an intruder is a cause for immediate alarm. They then may be seen sitting upright on their haunches, looking around and alertly listening in true ground-squirrel fashion. Their hearing is evidently very keen.

When creeping along and feeding, they frequently look up to be sure that all is safe. They seldom walk, less seldom run in the true sense of the word; rather do they scurry quickly from place to place in rapid, bouncing leaps. While foraging, they go considerable distances from their burrows, but they are ready to run home upon the least provocation. When really suspicious, and perhaps anxious, they stop, spasmodically twitch the tail, look excitedly about, and turn the head a bit sideways in listening attitude. They soon bound away a short distance, assume the same alert attitude, and violently vibrate the tail again. As they move toward a place of safety, they go from bush to bush, trying continually to keep behind them a screen of vegetation.

I have no reason to believe that white-tailed ground squirrels ever hibernate even in their places of farthest northern distribution. On sunny days even in midwinter they engage in their usual activities. Cold windy weather makes little difference, provided the sun is shining. In winter the time of greatest activity is midday, whereas in summer it is between sunrise and midmorning.

The ammos are voracious feeders and keep their stomachs full all day. Among the favorite natural foods of these rodents are the seeds of the abundantly fruiting annual herbs and the oil-rich seeds of encelia, many of which they carry away in their cheek pouches to store. In years when the goat nut (*Simmondsia*) yields abundantly, they harvest and store every nut they can get hold of. I must confess being guilty of having several times, when in need of food, robbed the pantries of the antelope ground squirrels for the well-husked, clean nuts. Succulent herbs and the tender new growth of cacti are part of the diet in season. Dr. Joseph Grinnell reports a female taken at Walker Pass on the Mohave Desert which had in its cheek pouches 98 shelled seeds of juniper (*Juniperus californicus*) and another female captured at Keeler which had gathered into her cheek pouches 178 husked seeds of salt grass. Beetles, grasshoppers, crickets, and an occasional fly give choice bits of needed protein food. They may even eat the flesh of members of their own species killed on the highway by passing autos.

Where yuccas are common, the fruits are much sought— not for the bitter hulls, but for the oil-rich, flat seeds which fill the center of the plump, ripening pods. Any summer morning you may see these persistently hungry harvesters perched in the midst of the pannicles of egg-shaped, egg-sized pods, ripping away the covering and exposing the black seeds. The chisel-like teeth are adept at cutting and tearing plant tissue to shreds. Neither cacti nor arborescent yuccas present climbing difficulties for them. They go right up and over the needles or spines, short or long, in quest of food. It seems as easy a job for them to get to the top of a tall tree yucca armed with many sharp-pointed, slender spines as to work their way among the few coarse bayonetlike leaves to the summit of the smaller, short-stemmed Mohave yucca. They descend, head downward, over the spiny "stairway" of the yucca stems as safely as they went up. Even the seemingly inaccessible seedy fruits found at the ends of the prickly cholla stems are not safe if they are really hungry. Somehow the paws are not stuck by the fine needles that protect the cactus fruit.

During the mating season the males are pugnacious and quarrelsome, sometimes killing their rivals. At this season the huge testes descend and are external and the heavily loaded scrotal sac sometimes becomes so long that it trails on the earth and bobs along over the rocks, looking much like a piece of flannel projecting between the legs.

Deep in the burrow the nest is prepared for the young. It serves in winter to keep the animals warm and later is used for the offspring. Feathers or soft plant fibers or the fur from dead animals is used as a lining. Once I left a felt hat on a rock and found it later full of holes, the material having been a prize find for some antelope ground squirrels who were getting ready for a family. J. R. Alcorn tells of finding rabbits killed in traps, with all the fur cleaned off the carcass, presumably to make linings for the nests.

The young, usually numbering seven or eight or even as many as 14, are born from late February to May. They are soon miniature duplicates of their parents, and when old enough to come out they may be seen playing about the home base. I have watched them by the hour. Among a group of young I observed one spring in the mud hills near Mecca by the Salton Sea, a kind of leapfrog was one of the favorite sports. They were as lively as a family of baby bears and were often cuffing one another and playing tag. The mother watched them with little evident solicitude for their safety. The young grow surprisingly fast and soon reach maturity and establish themselves nearby in burrows of their own.

I had a guest a few months ago, just as I was starting lunch. It was an *Ammospermophilus,* who seemed as surprised to be in my presence as I was in hers. She came down out of the rocks and climbed into a desert rue bush, sat upright on a branch, and with her deft handlike paws began to pick the pungent fruits. Some she ate on the spot, others she tucked away in her roomy cheek pouches.

I got out some raisins and one by one threw them down before her. As each landed on the earth, she picked it up. The first one or two she readily ate, then decided the rest should be stored. She was crafty, and every time she left me she went off in a different direction. However, she soon lost interest in raisins, and resumed her harvesting of seeds.

Two weeks later I returned to this same place. Mrs. Ammo spied me and came right over. But this time she was accompanied by five fuzzy-haired babies. They were not much larger than walnuts. I passed out raisins again, but the young were too small to take interest and started to play.

One of my most amusing experiences with this small ground squirrel occurred on a summer day in late June when I was traveling by automobile over a lonely road in the vicinity of Pilot Knob. An animal nosing about in a cactus patch started to cross the sandy roadway. He belatedly became aware of my automobile fast bearing down upon him. Confused, he attempted to reverse himself and run for cover under a roadside bush. But he turned so abruptly that one rear foot slid out from under him, causing him to somersault several times in the sand before he could regain his footing and dash away.

This antelope ground squirrel occupies both Upper and Lower Sonoran zones of a large inverted U-shaped territory stretching from the tip of Baja California north to Oregon and Idaho and southeastward to El Paso and northern Mexico.

Persons crossing the Colorado River from California into Arizona at Yuma will see there an antelope ground squirrel with gray on the underside of the tail instead of white. They have now come into the territory of the Yuma gray-tailed antelope ground squirrel (*Citellus harrisii saxicola*). It is distributed from extreme southwestern Arizona to the eastern borders of Yuma County and well south into Sonora. It has never crossed over into California, the Colorado River serving as a continuous and effective barrier.

Going still farther east over the deserts, the traveler will meet the Harris ground squirrel (*C. harrisii harrisii*). Its pelage in general is darker in color, but the underside of the tail is also gray. It has a much wider distribution than its paler Yuman cousin, being found over the greater part of northwestern, central, and southern Arizona, and south through central Sonora. It is often referred to as the gray-tailed antelope ground squirrel. In general habits, these last two squirrels closely resemble the white-tailed antelope ground squirrel. All are inhabitants of the Lower Sonoran Life Zone. Animals of all three species molt twice a year. Peculiarly enough, the hairs of the tail are shed only once a year, and then in autumn. After the autumn molt there is always a fine underfur to give warmth to the winter pelage.

Dr. Edgar A. Mearns, in *Mammals of the Mexican Boundary of the United States*, wrote of the Harris ground squirrel:

. . . there are few of the Sciuridae (squirrels) that can not climb when tempting food is seen dangling overhead, and the golden bunches of ripe mesquite beans are sufficiently tempting to stimulate the present species to arboreal enterprise; and it may be seen awkwardly hugging the spiny branches or sunning itself on the limbs, with tail dropped, frequently uttering its hollow call-note.

It lays up ample stores of mesquite seeds in its burrow, which doubtless accounts for its somewhat rare appearance above the ground during the coldest weather. It has sufficient intelligence to husk the seeds from their long pods before carrying them under ground. The capacity of its cheek-pouches is considerable. Those of one that I shot contained 44 mesquite beans. . . .

Its mercurial temperament savors of the spiciness of its food. It is much heavier and stouter than the Gila or Rocky mountain chipmunks, and is brimful of playfulness and noisy activity, delighting in the fierce power of the summer sun. As one rides over the mesquite flats, it scurries from underfoot, carrying its tail straight up in the air, uttering explosive chipperings as it hurries to the nearest mesquite bush, under whose shade it is quite certain of finding numerous holes by which to make its escape; but it oftener stops and chirrups saucily, stamping with its forepaws.

Its curiosity is so great that a few sharp chirrups with one's lips will often bring it to the entrance of its burrow, or it may run directly up to within a few feet of one. Then it stops, stamps, and jerks its tail, presently beating an equally precipitate retreat and diving into its burrow with a whistle; and it also utters metallic chirrups and chipperings suggestive of its impulsive nature. It very commonly sits up perfectly erect upon its hind feet, like the prairie-dog.

The antelope squirrels belong to the genus *Citellus* (a Latinized form of a Siberian word) and to the subgenus *Ammospermophilus*, which is a word from the Greek, literally meaning "lover of sand and seeds." The specific name *leucurus* applied to the desert white-tailed "ammo" is a compound of Latin words meaning "white-tail," and has reference to the white underside of the flattened tail. The specific name *harrisii* applied to both the gray-tailed Yuma and Harris ground squirrels honors a collector, Edward Harris, who presented to Audubon the specimen from which the original description was made.

17. The Round-tailed Ground Squirrel

Do you who live on the desert's vast sandy stretches know your quite silent, but no less engaging neighbor, the round-tailed ground squirrel? He is not the vivacious and sprightly creature that the antelope ground squirrel is—in fact, he seems rather dull in comparison; but he has ways worth knowing just the same. A friend of mine who, during the recent war, was stationed in a hospital at one of the desert training centers set up a little zoo as a means of entertaining the convalescent men. Among other captive animals, he had a round-tailed ground squirrel, which proved to be most amiable and one of the greatest favorites among the pets. Contrary to expectations, this creature was found to have quite a number of unusual habits, and the men made frequent visits to its cage.

The round-tailed ground squirrel makes his home in the sands or loose soils of the bleak desert flats, where wind and heat and shimmering light make life quite unbearable for many of the other animals. Befitting his harsh environment, he is a plain-looking fellow with a cinnamon-drab body built on the proportions of a rather slender cylinder, five or six inches long, with an almost earless, round, baldish-appearing head at one end and a rather long round tail at the other—as Dr. Spencer F. Baird once said, "in everything but the long rounded tail he is a miniature of the prairie dog." The hair is soft and silky when fresh, but in summer, when worn, it is rather coarse and stiff. The most attention-compelling thing about him is perhaps his big, almost mischievous-looking black eyes, set in the dull white fur of the sides of the head. The long-clawed feet may seem disproportionately large and stout, the hind feet particularly broad. The soles of the feet are densely covered with long stiff hairs, which help greatly in areas of loose drifting sand. The broad hind feet are the powerful instruments used in kicking back sand or gravel that is loosened by the rapid digging motions of the forefeet when the burrow is being made.

On the whole, the round-tailed ground squirrel is a shy creature, and about all that most people in the desert know of him is that from time to time he scampers, perhaps not too adeptly, across the road in front of the approaching automobile. Or he may be seen feeding on one of his brothers, who has been run over by a passing motorist, although he is primarily an eater of seeds and succulent herbs.

The burrows of this rodent are neither deep nor extensive. Like the underground runways of the kangaroo rats, they often cave in as you walk over them. The tunnels, about two inches in diameter and usually not over five or six feet in length, enter the soil at a slight angle and are simple excavations not over a foot beneath the surface. There is very little heaped earth at the entrance. Most of the tunnels are dug by the squirrels themselves, but they are known also to reside in underground burrows made by other rodents, especially the tortuous ones made by kangaroo rats, animals which inhabit the same type of level-topography, sandy territory. The habit these animals have of running into burrows other than their own increases their safety immeasurably. It means that there is almost always a place of refuge very near when danger threatens. But their curiosity is often so great that they offset this advantage by reappearing at the surface too soon. I have repeatedly watched an animal go underground, only to pop his head from the burrow a minute or two later. If all seemed safe, he would cautiously crawl out and begin to explore and feed again almost immediately. We can imagine the advantage this gives to a patient predator.

In winter these animals remain in their underground burrows much of the time. Spring months are the time of greatest feeding activity, for not only do the young need food, but the succulent food, preferred above all, is most plentiful. At this season these animals eat so much that their bodies often become so distended with green fodder that they can scarcely crawl into their small burrows. The resulting sluggishness makes them easy prey to predators. Even if one is so fortunate as to escape from his enemy and get into one of his underground tunnels, he may not be too long safe there either. Since the burrow is made in sandy or loose, powdery soil, it is quite easy for such animals as badgers and coyotes to dig in after him. Neither is he free from the attacks of snakes, such as gopher snakes, which follow him deep down into his subterranean retreats. Then too, as he crawls about feeding, he must run the risk of being seen by ravens and birds of prey such as hawks and falcons, which are always on the alert at this time of year for small mammals to feed their young. Twice I have seen the little animals carried off in the talons of hawks that had found them feeding on the ground while away from their burrows—one was taken by a red-tailed hawk, the other by a Cooper hawk. It is the habit of this squirrel, when seeking succulent foods, to climb into bushes and low trees such as the desert willow and mesquite; and then of

Young Round-tailed Ground Squirrel

course he further exposes himself to the attacks of these raptorial birds. The inexperienced young are especially susceptible to their many natural enemies.

The young are brought forth in March or April. As is not unusual with animals often preyed upon, these squirrels have great fecundity. The young number four to seven and even up to 12, and there may be a second litter later in the season. The mother has ten mammae, a number none too great with such large families to nurse.

Small colonies of these squirrels are widely scattered over the low-lying sand deserts, but nowhere are the animals plentiful. Ten or 15 to the square mile in suitable locations is probably about the average number.

Really to know their habits requires extreme patience on the part of the observer. I found the best way to get acquainted with them was to choose a warm, sunny day, and then with a canteen of water, some lunch, a notebook, and a pair of field glasses, go out prepared to sit still, for hours if necessary, under a large creosote bush, mesquite tree, or desert willow, and quietly watch. Observing in this way, I once had a squirrel under scrutiny for a period of four full hours—from 12:20 until 4:30 P.M. I saw him first as he emerged from a burrow. He evidently had fleas, for among the first things he did was to give himself a thorough going-over with both teeth and paws, scratching every part of the body that he could reach. Then he tidied himself by licking, particularly on the breast, belly, and forepaws, just as a cat does. Then for a moment he sat straight up on his haunches with tail up behind his back, the forelegs hanging relaxed over the chest and head turned slightly to one side, as the prairie dog does. It really surprised me to see how relatively inconspicuous he was during this time. The gray-buff color of his furry coat harmonized remarkably well with the sandy surroundings, especially when the sun was brilliant. For a minute or more he seemed to listen intently. Then several times he turned his head to look about. After that he resumed his former position on four feet and began to crawl along. For an hour or more he nosed about and fed on the succulent herbage which grew abundantly in scattered patches all about him. Twice during this time he assumed his alert position and gave an explosive, high-pitched, rasping note. When he ate he would sit up semi-erect on his haunches and, while holding the food in his forepaws, repeatedly nibble off small bits, moving his jaws very fast.

Up to 2:30 P.M., when he scratched himself again and went down a nearby burrow, he had moved not more than 60 feet from the place where I first saw him. At 3:12 he came to the surface, but from an accessory tunnel, and began feeding again. Several times he varied his diet by climbing into bushes of desert tea for the small black seeds, first removing the husks or scales while holding the small "cones" in his forepaws.

His only real excitement during the period I had him under observation was when a jack rabbit came loping along. The rabbit seemed unconcerned with the squirrel, but the ground squirrel, much excited, first sat upright on his haunches, then crouched low, and made a quick retreat into a kangaroo rat hole, giving vent to several sharp peeps on the way. He stayed underground this time fully 30 minutes. Several subsequent periods of watching round-tailed ground squirrels made me feel that on this day I had had quite a fair sample of the ordinary activities of these animals.

Four species of round-tailed squirrels inhabit the deserts in the vicinity of the lower reaches of the Colorado River and the upper parts of the Gulf of California. The Colorado River has long served as an effective barrier between the subspecies of Arizona (*Citellus terreticaudus neglectus*) and those of California and Lower California. The distribution of all these is shown on the end-paper map. A quite similar appearing but wholly unrelated *Citellus*, the Mohave ground squirrel (*C. mohavensis*), inhabits a limited area in the northwestern arm of the Mohave Desert and is often thought to be a "round-tail" by uninformed observers. It can be clearly identified when seen at close range by its tail, which has a white underside.

The generic name *Citellus* is applied to a host of ground- and rock-inhabiting squirrels of North America, Europe, and Asia. Those of eastern Siberia show close relationship with the Alaskan species. The specific name *terreticaudus* is a combination of Latin words meaning "round-tailed."

18. *Desert Bats*

The mammalian order *Chiroptera* (hand-winged), which includes the bats of some 2,000 living species, is, next to the rodents, the most numerous order of living mammals; but because bats come out only very early in the morning and at dusk, little is known about their activities by the average person.

Bats are sharply set apart from all other mammals by possessing the power of true flight, and this entails special modification of the forelimbs. In most of the mammals the hind limbs are as large or larger than the forelimbs, but in the bats the opposite is true. One of the bones of the bat's upper arm, corresponding to the human radius, is extraordinarily elongated, and still greater is the lengthening of the bones of the hand, except those of the thumb. A double layer of skin extended between the body and the long digits of the hands, the legs, and often the entire tail comprises the means of flight. The wing membrane connecting the hind limb and the usually long tail is generally supported by a peculiar cartilaginous rod, the calcar, projecting from the inner side of the ankle joints. The breast bone, as in many birds, has a median keel for attachment of the strong muscles of flight. Since the hind limb is connected with the wing membrane, the leg is rotated outward so that the knee joint, like the elbow, bends backward, and not forward in the usual manner. Because of this peculiarity the bat's movement on the ground is at best an ungainly shuffle.

Bats are divided into two major groups: (1) the large fruit-eating flying foxes, some tiny nectar and pollen feeders, and the long- and tube-nosed fruit bats, all of the warmer parts of the Old World; (2) the smaller, mostly insectivorous bats, of the New World as well as a few from the Old World. To this second group belong our desert bats. They usually have short snouts and sharp-cusped cheek teeth to aid them in crushing the hard parts of insects. On the snout and face are glandular pads and skin appendages of complicated and peculiar form, giving the animal a grotesque appearance. Their function is thought to be sensory. On the front lower edge of the ear is sometimes seen a small flat spur called the tragus: it too is supposed to have a sensory function. Its variation in form is often useful in identification.

Although the bat's brain presents a low type of organization, no other mammal possesses such a refined sense of touch. The tactile organs exist in connection not only with the delicate hairs which project from the muzzle, but with the skin of the widely extended wing, the conches of the ears, the peculiar leaflike expanses surrounding the nose openings, and the special rows of curved hairs projecting beyond the ends of the toes. The latter may aid the bat when backing in and about in dark crevices.

The small eyes probably function only for distinguishing light from darkness; but making up for this lack of visual acuity are the highly developed senses of hearing and touch. By means of echo location many of the smaller bats are able to avoid obstacles and locate their prey in darkness. A succession of bursts, each lasting about one-fiftieth of a second and having a frequency averaging about 50,000 per second, is emitted from the small cartilaginous larynx. The echoes reflected from surrounding objects, especially those nearby, give the bat precise information concerning its insect prey and the proximity of things which it must avoid while flying.

The Germans call the bats *Fledermäuse* (fluttering mice), and the English used to speak of them as flitter mice, both designations suggested by their flittering, often erratic flight at twilight and their mouselike color and body form.

When trapping larger insects some bats use a method called pouching. This consists of curving the tail forward so as to create a receptacle of the membrane which the tail supports. Into this receptacle the bat, while flying, scoops the insect. At leisure, the head is bent downward and the food which the pouch retains is chewed up.

Suspended by their long-clawed hind limbs, the desert bats spend the daytime in caves, crevices, unused mine tunnels, and dark corners of old buildings, taking wing a little before or just after sunset to feed. A few of the larger ones may actually feed on crawling insects such as Jerusalem crickets (*Stenopalmatus*) on the ground.

Bats are gregarious animals, often hunting together at night and seeking members of their kind when they roost. This custom probably allows easy passage of parasites, of which there are many, from one animal to another. None of the bat parasites, as far as we know, attack human beings.

A colony of bats occupying a roosting site soon leaves a scent, a decidedly musky odor, and from then on the place will almost always be used again. An abandoned roost is rarely found. "Only the most persistent persecution," says A. Brazier Howell, "will have any effect; even if the entire colony is wiped out, others will soon take possession."

Just at dusk on a recent July evening, I saw a number of

large brown bats flying from an abandoned mine building into a windowless storeroom. Next morning I found a small colony of them hanging on the rafters of the storeroom: all were females. Nearby in some cracks I came upon a colony of Mexican free-tailed bats; again all of them were females, some with young, which, although half-grown, were still nursing. The sexes, it is now known, are often found together only during the mating season.

Recent studies indicate that, while mating may occur in winter, the sperm cells may lie dormant in the uterus of the female two months or more before ovulation takes place. The normal number of young is one or occasionally two. The baby bat clings to the breast of the mother both when she is roosting and when she is flying.

The next day I went inside a nearby mine tunnel and spied two colonies of California leaf-nosed bats gathered in knots of a hundred or more, all clinging to the rough ceiling. Disturbed by my presence, they flew deeper into the dark interior. Further investigation revealed several western canyon bats in rock crevices on the tunnel walls.

The Mexican free-tailed bat (*Tadarida mexicana*), mentioned above, is one of the commonest bats of the desert West. It is called free-tailed because—unlike many of its near relations, the included-tail bats—the long tail extends beyond the interfemoral membrane. It is the smallest of the free-tailed bats in all areas where it is found. This is the bat that for ages has gathered by the millions each autumn to spend the winter in the Carlsbad Caverns of New Mexico. There they hang in great dense masses, suspended by their hooked hind claws from the roof.

When warm evenings of April come, they end their state of voluntary winter torpor and come out of the cave each night in great swarms, scattering over the countryside to feed. At times it takes them two hours to leave the mouth of the huge cavern and they form a veritable black cloud visible at least two miles away. Great numbers of these bats depart to distant places in summer, but many others remain to raise their young.

It is not generally known that in torrid summer or in mild winter some bats can go into a kind of voluntary torpor and, with lowering temperature and respiration, sleep for days or weeks when food is scarce or the weather unfavorable to their feeding activities. Bats wintering far to the north enter into true hibernation or winter sleep. It is quite a different phenomenon, over which they have no control: they then become completely torpid. Resting bats in winter may have a body temperature only slightly higher than the surrounding air of their hide-out. When active during summer nights they may have a body temperature of 104 degrees F. and a breathing rate correspondingly high.

The large pale bat (*Antrozous pallidus*), easily recognized by its pale-buffy fur, light brown wings, and forward-extending, inch-long ears, is another abundant desert dweller, and one of the most attractive. It lives about old ranch buildings, hollow trees, and caves, coming out in early evening, but usually later than the pigmy bat now to be mentioned.

Some evening at sundown or just after, you may notice a small bat swinging above your camp in erratic flight as it comes out of the nearby cliffs or rocky hills to search for insect food. This may well be the western pipistrellid, or canyon bat, sometimes also called the pygmy bat.

Because of its small size, early evening appearance, and extremely quick flight with sudden turns, the canyon bat is rather easy to identify; most other desert bats do not appear until near dark or after, and they are generally much larger in size. Even on evenings of quite cold days this small bat occasionally may be seen.

The late Dr. Joseph Grinnell tells of one occasion when he saw a canyon bat in flight in the glaring noonday sunshine. He noticed it as he was boating down the Colorado River. "The bat," he wrote, "dipped down to the surface of the water where it touched and thence flitted back to a crevice in a near-by cliff." It was probably getting a drink.

The canyon bat is found throughout most of the arid country of the West. To scientists it is known as *Pipistrellus hesperus*. Pipistrellus is a New-Latin word derived from the French word pipistrelle, meaning bat; hesperus is the Latin word for evening, the later part of the day.

At mid-dusk one late April day two of us visited a mineral spring along the north margin of beautiful Panamint Valley. Around the spring were numerous low, squat-crowned mesquite trees, covered with an almost solid blanket of pale yellow flower catkins with a sweet odor. Attracted by the honeylike nectar were many large, dusky-winged geometrid moths flying in clouds above the trees.

Suddenly great swarms of small, pointed-wing bats (which I recognized as canyon bats) fluttered in from one of the nearby slotlike, colorful canyons and began feeding on the moths. Their zigzag flights enabled them to fill their capacious stomachs in a very brief time. They left and others as silently took their places.

Except for man, bats have few enemies. Occasionally a hawk, an owl, a snake, or trout will eat one, but only when other food is scarce. Because of the bat's musky odor, it can hardly be considered a desirable food except when an animal is very hungry.

Studies of captive bats indicate that they eat from one-third to one-half their normal weight in insects every night when food is available. Since their numbers are often great, they are a decided asset to man, especially when injurious flying insects abound: their colonies should be broken up only when their presence is a definite annoyance.

Other bats frequently found on our southwestern deserts are: western mastiff bat, pocketed free-tailed bat, California leaf-nosed bat, pallid cave bat, western yellow bat, long-eared bat, house bat, Hollister bat, Yuma myotis, California myotis, and masked bat.

19. *Skunks*

Sooner or later, if you make your night camps beside brush-covered, rocky hills along the desert edge, you are certain to have a visit from the spotted skunk. Its inquisitiveness is great, and as it makes its nocturnal rounds it will inspect everything connected with nourishment, from camp dishes to food boxes.

Only a short time ago I camped in an area of picturesque granite pinnacles full of shallow caves and crevices. That night I slept in my auto with all its doors wide open. The air was balmy and the moon brilliant. I was disturbed about midnight by a creature crawling over the bedcovers. I merely turned over, and as I did so the intruder slipped down from the sleeping bag and out through the open car door onto the ground. That much I later vaguely remembered.

Next morning I took a cup from my camp table and filled it with water. As I brought the cup to my lips I sensed a strong skunky odor. I now knew who my visitor had been.

It took three washings with soap and hot water to eliminate the odors and get the table and the dishes upon it ready for the morning meal. Everything had a telltale odor.

The spotted skunk is a playful creature, especially when

young, and once it accustoms itself to the company of human beings, engages in all the antics of domestic kittens. A friend of mine had a spotted skunk which he found as a kitten in a plowed field. He and his family and all the neighborhood children lived with it in perfect amity for several years. It slept in a box most of the day, but when night came, it raced about the house, ran up onto the shoulders of its human companions, worried the cat, and even played with the dog. A favorite pastime was to roll and chase a small rubber ball over the floor. It loved to be turned on its back and have its stomach rubbed. As it grew older, it showed anger and impatience in chattering of teeth and an occasional attempt to bite. Although it sometimes quickly arched its back, turned its hindquarters toward its keeper, and menacingly raised its tail, not once did it scent the air or otherwise become a nuisance. It ate, in addition to its regular fare of mice, meat, and eggs, all kinds of cooked vegetables, lettuce, and fruits. If a gray spider got into the house it was quickly chased down and devoured. At the end of four years of exceedingly active life the skunk suddenly died, apparently of old age.

One is always amazed at the actual size of the small, black-eyed creature when examined in a strong light. Its manner of displaying the tail gracefully arched over the back makes it appear, especially at night, to be a larger animal than it really is. The body, exclusive of tail, averages only about seven inches in length, and it is so narrow that the skunk can crawl through very small cracks or knotholes to get into houses or small places. A spotted skunk which visited my Palm Springs shanty used to crawl through a knothole not much greater in diameter than a silver dollar. With much wiggling, it always maneuvered through the hole in a matter of seconds. This animal was very adept in getting around among the sticks as it hunted mice in my wood box and in climbing when it wished to get up the rough wall to a shelf above the cupboard where I kept bits of fat bacon for it.

Its usual gait about the house was a trot, but it could run if it needed to. Ordinarily, because of its ready means of defense, it seldom ran away from anyone. When moving slowly over the wooden floor it waddled or shuffled along. When angry or apprehensive it sometimes struck the floor with its forepaws. Only once did I see it attempt what is called the handstand. That was one evening when a stranger and his little dog suddenly appeared at my door. Quickly the skunk turned and reared its hind parts, assuming the position of a boy trying to stand on his hands. For a moment it appered that the worst was to come, but then it relaxed.

The young of the spotted skunk number three to six. They are usually born in late spring or early summer. Like domestic kittens, they are born blind. They make a variety of strange squeaky noises, especially when the mother is away and they are cold. Until almost full grown they forage with the parent for insects and spiders.

The dens occupied by spotted skunks consist of burrows they dig under stones or buildings, or of small but rather deep caverns under hillside rocks. When the air is dry, there is usually little odor to help us detect the homesite, but when it rains the scent is quite strong. The odor left by the spotted skunk is not long-lasting like that of *Mephitis,* its big striped cousin, and generally after a few days of sunshine it disappears.

In looking over the skeletal remains among the rock debris near the nests and roosting places of raptorial birds, we occasionally find the bones of the spotted skunk. This shows that besides the traps set out by man and the automobiles, this animal must fear the onslaught of owls, hawks, falcons, and eagles.

The name spotted skunk is somewhat a misnomer, for what we see on the sides and back of the animal are not spots, but a number of lengthwise stripes broken up by intervening bands of black.

Striped skunks (*Mephitis mephitis*), quite plentiful in wooded areas of many parts of the United States and Canada, are confined in desert regions almost wholly to the brush and tree-lined borders of the desert's living streams such as the Colorado River or the Rio Grande. The spotted skunks seem able to get along without water, but not these larger fellows. They are pre-eminently insect eaters and hunt in the leaf mold and under decaying logs which are found along stream bottoms.

The female striped skunk is able to nurse up to eight or nine kittens. I remember observing a mother striped skunk on a moonlit night in a mesquite and cottonwood thicket near Needles on the Colorado River, scratching among decaying leaves around a rotting cottonwood log as she searched for beetles and larvae for her five babies.

Occupying the often hot, arid country of southern Arizona and New Mexico and parts of Chihuahua and Durango in Mexico is the long-tailed or hooded skunk. It is a small, slender creature compared with the striped skunk. The tail is bushier and much longer. The long white hairs of the back of the neck and head form the cape or hood, which gives this animal its common name. Sometimes the top of its tail, the entire back, and a narrow stripe along each side are white.

Occasionally I have seen these active creatures shuffling along a trail, leaving behind the marks of their long flat feet. They seem to prefer the late evening and early night hours for hunting along the bottoms of brushy washes and cliff bases of rocky canyons for rodents, small birds, and insects.

In parts of southern Colorado, southern Arizona and Texas, in the large Chihuahuan Desert of Mexico and southward to Chile and Patagonia is found the heavily built but less active white-back, hog-nosed skunk (*Conepatus*). I have seen them only in the warm lowland valleys, where their hair is coarse and the normally black areas are only brownish-black. I am told that hog-nosed skunks living at higher elevations have pelts with much finer and longer hair. This change also occurs among other mammals. A somewhat comparable alteration takes place among certain grasses. The widespread tobosa or galleta grass, which in the hottest desert basins grows stems so coarse and rigid that cattlemen consider it almost worthless as forage, is fine-stemmed and leafy at higher elevations.

This large, slow-moving, shy skunk with a somewhat pig-like head seems especially adapted as a hunter of ground-dwelling insects, especially beetles and their larvae. Its shoulders are stocky, the claws are long and heavy, and its bare flexible snout enables it to locate and root out insects from the loose soil and leaf mold. In prickly pear country the cactus fruits as well as small rodents and birds are eaten.

The skull of *Conepatus* has many special characteristics. The teeth are different both in shape and number from other skunks, and the nostrils open forward and downward instead of on the sides of the muzzle. The ears are extremely small, and the tail is less plumy and shorter than in other skunks. There may be two very dark bands along the sides, or these may be completely united. The tail is generally pure white and hence especially conspicuous in the moonlight.

The peculiar black-and-white combination of the skunks has been regarded by naturalists as a warning coloration. "Such colors," said Dr. E. B. Poulton, long recognized British authority on the coloration of animals, "assist in the education of enemies, enabling them to easily learn and remember the animals to be avoided. Having had one real experience with the nauseous artillery of a skunk neither dog nor man would be other than foolish to menacingly approach or attack one."

Because of their food habits, skunks are among our most valuable mammals and should be protected. If they annoy, they can be caught in box traps which do not injure them and transported far enough away so they will not return.

20. The Badger

At least once a week I go into the remote desert, where my roads are those made by the pioneers and miners and where my companions are the birds and other animals. In such solitary places I can still hear at evening the calls of coyotes and see the steep trails of bighorn, or sight evidence of the badger in numerous large holes scattered over his sprawling hunting grounds.

To me, the badger is a symbol of strength and freedom. I especially like him because he despises ease and shows so little gregariousness; for his midnight meals he is willing to dig hard and deep.

The last badger I saw was ambling over the flat bottom of a sandy wash in western Arizona. Why he was out at midday in bright sunlight I do not know. Perhaps his work of the night before had yielded him no food.

The badger, though well able to fight, is by nature a shy and timid creature. When this one sensed our presence he immediately began moving up the wash in fast waddling gait with his flat body held as high as his short legs would permit.

Eager to see more of him before he got away, the boy who was with me ran after him. For about an eighth of a mile the race was almost an equal one. Then the strong but short-legged badger, unused to such contests, became winded and sought refuge in a thicket of cat's-claw bushes. As I came up I found him wedged beneath a sprawling branch, bravely facing his pursuer. He was hissing and breathing heavily through his nostrils, keeping up an almost continuous savage noise. From time to time he defiantly turned up his nose and curled back his lips, exposing strong white teeth. I prodded the beast several times with a stick, but the only responses I got were a few deep grunts, more snappy snarls and hisses, and an occasional erection of the stubby tail. The air soon became filled with an unpleasant stench as secretions from the anal glands spread over and moistened the long hairs of the tail and hind parts. It is the usual habit of badgers when cornered to attempt to dig their way to safety, but not once did this one make an effort in that direction. It is still a puzzle to me why he had not, while being pursued, bolted into one of the numerous shallow burrows that he had previously dug in the vicinity.

Study of the form and structure of the badger at once reveals a remarkable adaptability to the strange and lonely life it leads. The body is short, flat, and thickset, with short and powerfully muscled legs. The broad cone-shaped head is heavy-boned, the jaws fitted with strong sharp teeth. The neck is short and thick. The long, broad claws of the forefeet are not only sturdy and effective weapons but also powerful shovels, while the strong hind legs throw backwards the soil that has been excavated. The loose, tough hide is underlaid with a very heavy coat of protective fat; the fur is long and dense.

Badgers certainly cannot be included among animals that love the chase, having, as Ernest Thompson Seton says, "bartered speed for strength." Although they are energetic hunters, they seldom are able to run down their prey; they depend on their ability to dig it out.

Having located, with the aid of the keen sense of smell, the presence of a rodent such as a ground squirrel or kangaroo rat, this adept miner quickly enlarges the rodent's burrow so far that it can enter and reach the deepest parts. The victim has little chance to evade him. The badger's appetite is enormous, and he may dig out half a dozen small rodents and as many lizards and insects in a single night. Hunting is done mostly at night, but daytime search for food is not uncommon. During their protracted quest for food they may wander a mile or more, but they make so many deviations from a straight course that they may get only a short distance from the starting point.

When a badger is faced with an enemy such as man or his dogs, as a rule he immediately uses his digging abilities to give him a place of safe retreat. Says Vernon Bailey: "So rapidly do they dig that even while fighting a dog one will often gain a few minutes' time in which to sink a well and bury itself before the very eyes of the hesitating enemy. Once below ground the badger's escape is almost assured, for it digs rapidly and turning around, pushes out loads of the loose earth in front of its breast without emerging from the burrow, and when it is well down, instead of shoving its loads outside, it packs the earth into the entrance and closes the door, and continues to burrow indefinitely with only a narrow chamber between the point of excavation and the closed door behind it."*

J. R. Alcorn of Nevada narrates an incident which well illustrates the rapidity with which badgers can dig. With the assistance of ten associates, all provided with shovels, he tried to reach a badger which had attempted to get away by digging a tunnel in the sandy soil. "We worked," says Mr. Al-

* "Mammals of New Mexico," *N. A. Fauna*, No. 53, p. 344.

BADGER

corn, "as fast as possible for about four hours. At the the end of that time we were at a depth of six feet and had traveled about twenty feet laterally, when exhaustion prevented us from digging farther."*

Some years past, three of us came upon a trapped badger at the north base of the Sheep Mountains of Nevada. The animal was still very much alive but securely held by the jaws of the steel trap, which had closed upon a hind foot. The first thought of this badger had been to dig, and he had excavated and pawed the earth into a great circular heap fully two feet high and more than four feet across, reaching out and down as far as the chain of the anchored trap would allow. As we came up, the animal began to hiss and snarl savagely. We wanted to free the unfortunate creature, but it was so savage that we hesitated to get near.

Close by on the ground lay a five-foot length of pine two-by-four. Armed with this, one of the boys struck the badger on the head, but only hard enough to knock it unconscious. While I held my foot on the head, the jaws of the trap were opened and the badger was freed. It was some minutes before he came to, but when he did he almost instantly put up a show of fierce defense. We soon saw that one result of the head blow had been to paralyze the hind limbs, but use of these gradually returned and the badger started to move away. However, instead of retreating directly, he hobbled along a few yards, then suddenly turned toward us and hissed, then went on again. The performance was repeated six times before he finally shunted off into the brush out of sight.

Badgers are easily caught in traps and will eat poisoned bait without hesitation. They often are killed by government hunters out to rid the range of coyotes "for the assumed benefit of cattle- and sheepmen." Often there are almost as many badgers killed as coyotes. It is a most unfortunate situ-

* E. Raymond Hall, *Mammals of Nevada* (Berkeley: University of California Press, 1946), p. 217.

ation, for badgers keep down the number of rodents, and their burrowing activities do much to aid in soil formation.

Badgers are still to be found in diminished numbers over much of western North America, from the tablelands of northern Mexico to southern Canada "without regard to climatic or physiographic features except as they modify the food supply." They are widespread in deserts where the rodent population is dense and where man's persecution has not led to their extinction.

There is only one species of North American badger (*Taxidea taxus*), but there are several geographic races or subspecies. In the desert regions of southern California, southern Nevada, Arizona, New Mexico, and the plains of northern Sonora and Baja California the badgers are of smaller size and have a narrower skull than those found farther north. They also show a longer white stripe on the back.

The European badger (*Meles taxus*) is a quite different animal from the American species, although resembling it much in appearance and habits. The tooth formula is almost the same, but there are distinct differences in the form of the teeth as well as in the skull and other bones. Both animals are, as might be suspected because of their scent glands, close relatives of the skunks, polecats, fresh-water and sea otters, Asiatic sand badgers, and weasels; they are accordingly placed with these in the large mammal family, Mustellidae. Like most of the mustellids, badgers are valuable fur bearers.

The common name badger is thought to be derived from the word *badge*, in reference to the white mark on the forehead.

21. The Peccaries

In the peccaries or javelinas, as they are sometimes called, we have a small wild pig about three feet long and about 15 inches high at the shoulder, with stocky body and disproportionately large head, which appears to be set imperfectly apart from the body because of the shortness of the neck.

They are quick-moving animals and give the impression of being able to take care of themselves. They betray their relation to the true pigs by the long pointed snout which ends in an oval, flattened, naked disc in which the nostrils are placed. When feeding, they often use this truncated snout to push around in the soil and the cover of brush and leaves. The general body coloration is salt-and-pepper gray, this due to the black and white banding of the harsh stiff bristles, but a lighter-colored collar or stripe, sometimes almost white, encircles the shoulders. A mane of longer bristles runs from the crown of the head to the rump, but it is raised high only when the animal is frightened or provoked to anger. The short, narrowly built legs end in two black-hoofed toes. The tail is so short that it can scarcely be seen.

The peccaries are the New World representatives of the Old World pigs. The peccaries may readily be distinguished by their sharp-edged canine teeth, which point downward, not outward or upward as in the boar; by the presence of only two mammae, whereas the pigs have many, the number of mammary glands corresponding roughly to the number of young. Instead of having a simple stomach, they have a complex one of three parts, more like that of the ruminants or cud-chewing animals. The hind limbs have three instead of four toes, but only two reach the ground.

My acquaintance with this "wild pig" has mostly been in Mexico's arid country, with its thick growth of prickly pear cactus, as we sometimes call the flat-jointed *Opuntia.* While preparing camp one evening in northern Coahuila, a small herd of nine of them wandered out of one cactus clump clearing into another very near us and began biting off the lower, juicy round joints and fruit without regard to the numerous sharp spines and smaller prickles that covered them. Easily audible were the varied small grunts and occasional squeals as they jostled one another. Two of the females had young about a third grown, which kept very close. Their feet had to move very fast to keep up with the quick shifts of the mothers.

Next day I passed through a small Mexican village and saw a grizzle-coated young peccary following two children. They were evidently very fond of it. When the little boy reached down and scratched its short-eared bristly head, short grunts of satisfaction came from its throat.

I am told by those who have kept young javelinas as pets that they are pleasing to have only until almost grown; at that time they sometimes become quite willful and may show their anger by attempting to bite.

One of the drawbacks of having them about the home is

their somewhat musky odor. At times this may be very pronounced and actually quite unpleasant. It is due to the secretion of an oleaginous substance produced in a relatively large gland in the mid-dorsal lumbar region—to be exact, about eight inches anterior to the base of the short, almost invisible tail. This compound gland has a single external opening at the summit of a nipple-like elevation. The secretions are produced by oil and sweat glands, both internal. The capsule surrounding them is attached to a cutaneous muscle under control of the animal, and the odorous secretion can be forcibly ejected as a means of "protection" against enemies. Peccaries have been seen to rub the gland against low bushes, thus perhaps marking a trail for others to follow. This gland was mistaken by early observers for a second navel, and this popular error suggested to the French zoologist, Baron Cuvier, the name of *Dicotyles* (*di-*, two, from the Greek *dis,* double; *kotyledon,* a cup-shaped hollow) as a generic designation for these animals.

Our desert-dwelling javelinas are, on the whole, timid creatures and quite harmless unless cornered. Then they use their canine teeth very effectively. The back edge of these teeth is sharp, so they are able to make nasty wounds. Peccaries are usually found in small roving bands. When set upon by the hunter's dogs, they may give the dogs, especially if untrained, a bad time. Occasionally they kill the dogs. Their behavior, however, is quite unpredictable, and they may all run instead of attacking.

They are usually hunted for their hides or for the meat, which in young animals is considered quite good, provided the scent gland is soon removed from the body. Some are hunted merely for sport. Cowboys sometimes try to rope them, but as Vernon Bailey says, "many good horses are ruined by being ridden over boars, which never fail to cut and gash the horses' legs in dangerous manner."

Although given to seeking food and shelter in the oak and

wild brush country of the low mountains, peccaries also live in mesquite and cactus thickets, on the more level lower areas of dunes and plains. They feed mostly at dawn, at dusk, and at night; then, during the middle of the day, particularly if it is hot, they lie under cover of thick brush or in shallow caves or excavations along the banks of deep ravines. They drink water when near, but if fleshy cactus joints are available these may supply all the water needed by these highly adaptable animals.

The peccary's only real enemy other than man is the large, heavy, powerfully built jaguar, which, being a skillful and sly hunter, finds the javelina rather easy prey. Smaller predators, such as coyotes and bobcats, sometimes prey upon old or sick peccaries, and occasionally the young, but, unless caught alone, the "desert pigs" are quite able to defend themselves. As a generally harmless member of our native fauna the desert peccary deserves the full protection of our wildlife laws.

There are two species of peccaries. The collared peccary (*Pecari tajacu*), with at least ten subspecies recognized, is to be found from Texas west to southern Arizona and south through Central America. The white-lipped peccary (*Tayassu pecari*) or warree haunts the dense forests of southern Mexico and ranges southward to Paraguay. The latter is a somewhat larger animal (about 40 inches in length), of blackish color. It is distinguished by a large white patch on the lower jaw, and the white lips. It generally runs in large herds of 50 to 100 or more, is quite pugnacious and at times ferocious, and in inhabited districts may do much damage to field crops.

22. The Ring-tailed Cat and Near Relatives

One April afternoon many years ago, I hiked up the long shady brush-bordered wash from my camp among the junipers in Tavern Gulch to see if my old gold-miner friend, Joe Glavo, had returned from his winter stay in Lone Pine.

I knocked on the door. No one answered, but from within the cabin came a sort of shuffling noise.

I opened the rough-board door to investigate, and in the half-light I saw among the cans and boxes stacked on an end-shelf a lithe animal of catlike form and size intently watching me. It was a pointed-nosed, big-eyed, big-eared black and gray-brown creature with a long, fluffy, banded tail. Its fox-like face was alert and gentle.

This was my first sight of a cacomixtle, or ring-tailed cat. Instead of fleeing, the timid creature merely retreated behind a box and, raising his head, continued to peer at me. Gently I withdrew and closed the door.

Shortly Joe arrived. He told me that when "Caco" first moved in, the place was swarming with mischievous deer mice, which scampered around and gnawed half the night. Two nights after Caco arrived, he had caught them all.

Back in the cabin we saw no trace of the cat. "He's probably under the house or prowling around outside," Joe explained. "He'll be coming in soon through that hole behind the stove for his canned fish and honey supper."

Joe went on to tell me that two years previously a family of ring-tailed cats had lived with him. Caco, Joe thought, had been one of the three kittens, which he had tamed with regular feedings of canned tuna and sugar.

"I used to give those kits a little wooden ball to play with," Joe recalled. "Indoors or out, they were always battering it about or cuffing one another. But surprisingly soon they began acting like adult cats—didn't play with their tails any more, or frisk about as much."

As predicted, Caco showed up for his supper. He came in cautiously, but soon began eating. His long-clawed paws were very dexterous. Supper over, old Joe picked Caco up, put him on his shoulder, and stroked him.

The ring-tailed cat or cacomixtle (ka-ko-*mish*-tlay), as the Mexicans call it, was long ago classified with the raccoons and the coatimundi in the mammalian family *Procyonidae*. All of these agile, intelligent animals have banded tails. The ring-tails (there are two species) now are considered sufficiently unique to warrant a separate family classification, the *Bassariscidae*. They belong to the genus *Bassariscus*, a name derived from the Thracian word *bassaris*, meaning fox, and the Greek diminutive ending *iskos*. It is a name doubtlessly coined with reference to the animal's foxlike face.

Cacomixtle is an Aztec word which, like many others, was carried by the Spaniards over Mexico and eventually to the United States. Cacomixtle appears in the Aztec and Toltec codices—books of pictographs and phonetic signs painted on paper of maguey fiber or deerskin parchment.

The ring-tail differs from its raccoon cousin in its more slender elegant form, sharper nose, and longer tail (as long as the head and trunk), longer toes, and smaller teeth.

This attractive animal is found in rocky terrain of arid brush and tree areas of the far western United States, from southern Oregon southward to the tip of Baja California; and eastward and southeastward through the mesquite and cactus thickets of Texas and Mexico proper. Guatemala is the southern limit of distribution.

On the Mexican Plateau, where it is most common, it is often locally numerous in the arid brush and wooded districts and in the smaller towns, where it makes its den among the stones of the many walls separating the fields. The belief is that it will not live where water is not easily accessible. Since ring-tails are almost wholly animals of the night, few people have seen them in the wilds.

They are omnivorous animals, feeding upon juniper and mistletoe berries, cactus fruits, grapes, and grasshoppers. One observer saw them eating dates in the date gardens of Baja California. Studies made on the Edwards Plateau in Texas indicated that in autumn insects made up the largest item of the ring-tail's food, with plant material second. Small mammals were the principal food in winter. In summer, insects were first, plants second, spiders third. The conclusion drawn was that the "beneficial food habits of the animal more than make up for any damages done."

Cacomixtles are very active creatures. Their gait, when moving rapidly, has been described as a "loping, humping along, with tail straight out behind, drooping toward the end." They are good climbers and will go high into trees and brush in search of food or to escape enemies. When kept indoors as pets, they enjoy climbing the door and window screens. Dr. Walter P. Taylor tells of a pet ring-tail that played with a pointer dog. Tame cacomixtles are usually gentle, affectionate, and seldom given to biting.

Of this animal in captivity, Victor H. Cahalane wrote: "When seriously disturbed or when approached by strangers, anger or fear [is] expressed by a succession of growling clucks, or a series of low hoarse barks on a background of deep growls. Wild, trapped ring-tails, when first approached, [may] utter a succession of piercing screams."

Usually the number of young is three or four, born in late April, May, or early June. The stubby-nosed short-tailed toothless sucklings are blind and their ear canals are closed for the first month of life. The only noise they utter is a metallic squeak, but later this develops into an explosive, coughing, foxlike bark, or at times a muffled whimpering sound. Weaning takes place near the end of the third month. By this time the animals have a distinct, sweetish, musky odor due to the secretion of a clear amber fluid from the anal glands. The fluid appears when the animal is frightened, or when it shows strong resentment or anger while being handled.

The coati, coatimundi, or cholugo (*Nasua narica*), also a near relative of the raccoon, walks on the soles of all four feet and usually carries erect its long banded tail. This brownish-gray, long-snouted animal at first sight appears to be a queer combination of baboon, bear, raccoon, and pig.

Although not an attractive animal, it makes, when taken young, a fine pet full of clownish habits. Like baboons or javelinas, coatis travel in small, often noisy groups of five to 10 or even up to 20 animals, made up of sociable females and their young. They hunt for food in the open, arid brushland, using their long flexible piglike snouts and strong webbed and clawed front paws to root up small rodents, insects, larvae, snakes, centipedes, and scorpions. Dry berries of juniper and manzanita, and occasionally small birds, also are eaten.

RING-TAILED CAT

In many parts of its range the coati is almost wholly arboreal, but in parts of southern Arizona, southeastern New Mexico, and northern Mexico it inhabits true desert areas, and at night and sometimes during the day climbs through the palo verde and mesquite thickets. In climbing, it uses the tail for both balance and support. One of these animals, which Lloyd Ingles had as a pet, used to climb as high as a hundred feet into pine trees.

Because of its upturned nose the Germans call coatimundis *Rüsselbaren* (snouted bears). The New Latin generic name *Nasua* applied to this animal refers to the snout. The specific name *narica* is a variant of the same Latin noun, with the intensive suffix *ica* added to emphasize the length of the nose.

Coatimundis (there are two species) are found from mid-Arizona and southern Texas southward into the tropical forests of South America.

The intelligent, stream-frequenting raccoon often comes down into the margins of deserts where streams of the bordering mountains emerge onto the desert flats. It also is common on the mud flats of such streams as the Colorado River and the Rio Grande, which traverse the desert lowlands in their course to the sea.

Habitat of the Colorado Desert raccoon (*Procyon lotor pallidus*), characterized by its light coloration, is from southern Utah and southern Nevada to northern Baja California and eastward along the Gila River into mid-Arizona. I have seen its tracks in mud along the lower streams of Baja California's Sierra San Pedro Mártir, where it evidently subsists largely on the small granite-colored tree frog (*Hyla californica*), which inhabits the streams, and on insects such as grasshoppers of the marginal rocky banks. Seeds of mesquite and screwbean trees, and cactus fruits are probably eaten too.

23. *Some Desert Sparrows*

Among the many small sounds of the desert—the chirp of cicadas, the song of small birds, the drone of the different wild bees and flies—you are sure to hear the simple, melodious song of *Amphispiza*, the desert sparrow. It is a song often described as a *cheeet, cheeet, cheeeeeee,* with a throaty near-trill at the end. The singer has a general color of gray, brown, or ash, a very noticeable black bib patch, and two clear white stripes along the side of the face, one below, one above the eye. When singing, he generally perches on top of a creosote bush or other tall shrub. If you approach too close, he will retire to a distance and again begin singing. At intervals he changes his position on his perch or drops to the ground, where he looks for the many small seeds of annuals which are always present in the sand. If it is the breeding season, the pair are at their best, both in song and in plumage.

The desert sparrow is, except in the northern parts of its range, no mere summer visitor, but for the most part resident throughout the year. In winter, desert sparrows often flock in small groups. They begin actively singing about the middle of February, but the rest of the year they are never wholly quiet. On many a near-breezeless summer morning they are often among the few singers one hears, and certainly among the cheeriest.

Robert Ridgeway, of the United States National Museum, gives the desert sparrow's range as: "Arid plains from western Texas (west of 103° W. longitude) to the coast of southern California (San Diego County, etc.) north to northern Nevada and Utah, south into Chihuahua and Sonora, Lower California."

The nest is a small cup of fine, soft plant fibers and grasses such as are obtained from filago, the annual eriogonums, and wool grass (*Eriochloa*).

SAGE SPARROW

GAMBEL'S SPARROW

A favored site for the bird nest is within the thorny branches of one of the cholla cacti, although it is also found near to the ground in other twiggy shrubs. Three or four small bluish-white eggs comprise the normal set. Two broods are often raised each season, the first about mid-April or early May, the second some six weeks later.

One morning long ago, when we traveled about the desert from one water-hole to another on burros, I was making my way over stony ground where there were large branching specimens of deerhorn cholla when I heard the agitated distress song of a sparrow; soon, from my position in the saddle I looked down into the sturdy, cup-shaped nest of the desert sparrow, set well in the protecting spiny branches of the cactus bush. There I saw a red racer devouring the nestlings, his long, slender form draped over the spiny branches. The distressed birds were anxiously flitting about, uttering strange notes of alarm and, at intervals, a kind of hurried song. I threw the stick I was carrying to prod the burro, and the racer was driven off; but already three of the nestlings had been disposed of. I dismounted and chased the racer a considerable distance before ending his career. It was indeed a surprise to me to learn that a snake such as the racer could climb up among the branches of the spiny cholla.

There is another pleasing, though we can hardly say conspicuous, sparrow we desert people should know. That is the Salton Sink song sparrow. It is now more or less common in the Colorado Desert lowlands where water-loving plants are present along irrigation canals of the Imperial Valley south of the Salton Sea and along the bottoms of the Colorado River. It is worthy of special mention here not only because of its simple and melodious song but also because of its extraordinary, pale coloration, it being recorded as lightest in color of all known song sparrows of the genus *Melodia*. The customary blacks, browns, and grays we expect to see forming the sparrow color pattern have been so much bleached out, as it were, that they are here reduced to amber-brown, and smoky- and silver-grays; even the underparts are more brightly white and extended than is usual. It is another of those many instances of desert races of birds showing decidedly lighter coloration than closely related species of the higher mountain or near-sea areas.

This sparrow is much in evidence in spring. Where the areas immediately contiguous to the Colorado River have long been subject to yearly inundation, the Salton Sink song sparrow has shown a remarkable adaptation, not only in its nesting habits but also in the timing of its nesting season. Dr. Joseph Grinnell long ago pointed out that the birds were given to unusual avian wisdom, deferring their nesting time until after the usual high-water period, that is, until late May and early June; also, he noted how they build their nests much higher above ground than is usual elsewhere so they may be above the mud left by the flood waters on the arrowweed and willows in which they nest. In the Salton Sea vicinity the usual nesting time is mid-March or early April.

Since the building of Hoover Dam in the Boulder Canyon Gorge, the periodic floods of the Colorado River have been largely controlled, if not wholly eliminated. It will be interesting to observe the total reaction of the birds to this new situation. Will they continue to build nests high and late in accordance with the ancestral custom, or will they nest close to the ground and early as do their neighbors in the Imperial Valley?

Several other sparrows are more or less common in the desert area; one of these is the sage sparrow. This bird is a resident of the broad sagebrush-covered basins and valleys of the high deserts of the Great Basin, but is not unknown on the warm lower deserts in winter and early spring. Along the brush-covered Colorado River this sparrow has, as Dr. Grinnell observed, "the habit of skulking along the ground among the close-set bushes," thus avoiding easy observation. The Gambel white-crowned sparrow is also a winter visitant of the southern deserts of California and Sonora.

Other sparrows known to winter, at least in part, on the southern deserts of California are the Western vesper sparrow, the savanna sparrow, the Western chipping sparrow, the Rocky Mountain song sparrow, and the Lincoln sparrow, the last two largely confined to the stream-side brush thickets along the Colorado River.

24. The Rock Wren

Soon after the War of 1812, the United States War Department, looking forward to the erection of new frontier forts and revisions of the laws for Indian trade, decided to send an expedition under Major Stephen H. Long to explore, geographically and scientifically, the western portions of the newly acquired Missouri Territory. Major Long was especially directed to ascertain the position of the headwaters of the Platte River. This work of exploration was undertaken in the summer of 1820, and Thomas Say, sagacious student of insects, was chosen to go with the party in the capacity of naturalist. He in turn was accompanied by an able and enthusiastic ornithologist named Titian Peale, just turned 19. Say prepared the report on the birds. Among the most interesting species he saw and described was the now well-known rock wren, to which he gave the scientific name *Troglodytes obsoletus*. The type specimen on which he based his description was taken on the South Fork of the Platte, probably by young Peale. In 1847 the generic name, *Troglodytes*, assigned to the new bird by Say, was changed by the German ornithologist Jean Louis Cabanis to *Salpinctes*. Both names were well adapted to the bird and its habits, *Troglodytes* being Greek for cave dweller and *Salpinctes*, the Greek name for trumpeter. The first name alluded to the bird's nesting site, the second, to its clear vibrant song.

The rock wren is now known to be widely distributed throughout the West. From British Columbia south to Lower California and the northern Mexican mainland, and from western Nebraska to the Pacific, it is everywhere at home where rocky ledges, piles of boulders, or shale slabs offer it places favorable to its nesting habits. Although most common on deserts, *Salpinctes* is by no means confined there. It nests in the high, forested mountains, too, and even above timber line; also in the near-sea-level cliffs of the Pacific Coast, and in the Farallon, Santa Barbara, and San Nicolas islands. As Leon Dawson observes, "We have here the most remarkable breeding range of any bird in the world."*

Rock wrens which breed at high altitudes drop to lower levels when autumn approaches. Those of the far northern habitats go south to warmer regions, but in the low southern deserts they take no heed of time or seasons. They remain both in torrid summer and in the cool of winter in their often desolate arid home.

In size, the rock wren approaches the desert song sparrow. It is larger than the canyon wren and may be readily distinguished from it in haunts they share by its generally pale, earthy-brown coloration,† absence of clear white throat and breast patch, and longer, broad-feathered tail. This tail on alighting is spread fanlike and shows a distinct edging of light

---

* William Leon Dawson, *The Birds of California* (San Diego, Los Angeles, San Francisco: South Moulton Company, 1923).

† John Cassin and George N. Lawrence said: "The name, obsoletus [L. *obsoletus*, indistinct, faded], applies well to this species, the feathers all having a faded appearance very difficult to define." *Reports of Explorations and Surveys*, Vol. IX, 1858.

buff and a subterminal band of black. The plumage is soft and lax, the bill slightly curved and about as long as the head. The notes of this bird, too, are distinctive.

Perhaps the most amazing trait of the rock wren is its extraordinary nest building. In good "rock wren country" where the birds are plentiful, it is possible to find half a dozen of the nests in a day's search. Some will be old nests, some trial nests or abandoned incomplete ones, but all will show ingenious planning. Hundreds of hours of searching and miles of climbing have rewarded me with the discovery of many a rock wren home. No two nest locations, no two nest structures are exactly alike. The imagination and adaptability of this artisan are great, both in locating suitable sites and in preparing and shaping the nest within its cranny.

Sandstone escarpments, steep granite rocks, lava cliffs, or walls of earthen gullies offer the ideal nest sites, since they generally are pitted with the many cavelets, crypts, and crevices in which the nest may be safely hidden. Some of these builders select high crevices, even to heights of 40 or 50 feet on vertical surfaces; others choose rock covers at ground level, where they are much more subject to the menace of snakes and egg-molesting rodents.

The birds have a queer habit of placing near the entrance to the nest either a sort of paved pathway made of little stones or an approach of small heaps of thin rock chips or flattened pebbles. There may be a half-pint measureful of these stones, or even a quart or more. When one is hunting for nests, these little collections of potterylike rock fragments usually offer the best guide to the nest's location. As a rule, the nest, if it is in a vertical rock surface, will be located above this rock pavement a foot or two; if the nest is under a shelving rock, it will be near and just behind the pavement. Were it not for these telltale pebbles or rock-fragment heaps, the location of many a nest site would never even be anticipated. Occasionally this guide to the nest labyrinth is missing, and then one must depend on luck or upon actually seeing the birds entering the crypt or crevice. The small rock chips are carried to the nest sites in the bird's beak. Their primary use seems to be to serve as material for building up at the entrance to the chosen crypt a wall behind or above which the nest can be built. When the nest is finished, there is above it an opening only large enough for the birds to pass in and out. The fragments are sometimes brought in from considerable distances, and since they are often an inch to an inch and a half long, their transportation must considerably tax the carrying ability of these wall-building masons. It is my belief that the small pile of stones just below or near the entrance is made up, at least in part, of fragments which have been found unsuitable for building the wall and which have therefore been rejected and allowed to fall and collect in a heap below. There are, however, altogether too many rocks in the usual collection to account for the phenomenon wholly on this basis. One of the finest nests I have seen had only about a dozen stones in the wall, but there were over a hundred flat pieces of rock below it. These were scattered over an area of more than two square yards with no suggestion of heaping. In this case the masonry material consisted of flakes of lime or *caliche,* all about the same size, and brought in from a distance of more than a hundred feet. Mrs. Vernon Bailey suggests that the assemblage of small stones must help the birds in marking the particular crevice of the nesting site, especially in sandstone walls full of innumerable crevices.

The nest itself is not a bulky affair, but is rather small, as we might expect of a wren, and with a foundation of random-size twigs, fine grass, and rootlets. The shallow cuplike hollow of the nest is lined with bits of shredded bark, fine grass, and hair.

The rock wren female incubates four or five or even as many as seven or eight eggs—white ones with a few fine distinct spottings of chestnut brown around the larger end. Two such clutches a season are not infrequent. The second egg set is being incubated while the birds of the first brood are still in the vicinity of the nest. The incubation period is about 14 days.

The increase in rock wren population is very noticeable by the end of the summer, but the number is often greatly reduced by the following spring. Snakes, wood rats, falcons, owls, shrikes, and even antelope ground squirrels no doubt take their toll.

Once the nest is occupied with eggs or young, the parent birds are constantly about. They approach their hidden rock retreat with caution even when no one is near and increase their fidgetings and roundabout approaches very much if an observer comes close. One midmorning J spent a full half-hour by a nest built under a flat rock along the edge of a dry stream bed in the piñon-covered mountains. It was early June, when most of the vegetation was very dry, yet the birds seemed to experience little trouble in quickly locating all the food they needed to feed the babies. Insect larvae, moths, and spiders were brought in at the amazing rate of one every three or four minutes. I later watched this family again when the young had left the nest, and I could not detect that the parents' feeding duties had at all decreased. From dawn to darkness the five fluffy-feathered young constantly crept about on the rocks begging open-billed for food, often flying forward to another rock to meet the parent approaching with food-laden beak. The young birds often stay with the parents until quite full grown. As late as the last of November I once saw five rock wrens, two adults and their young, flying to-gether in a canyon of the desolate Indio Mud Hills. It was evidently the last of a late-hatched brood not yet separated. Later I saw two of the wrens hunting insects in *Bebbia* bushes, showing that it is not rock crevices alone that get at-tention from these rock-dwelling birds.

In dry Cushenbury Canyon, in the San Bernardino Mountains, I saw three young wrens bobbing about on the rocks begging for food and parental attention. Finally they and the parent birds flew across the canyon and started up the steep rock-strewn slope. The parents left the young down below while they flew some 40 feet above into a thicket to hunt food. The young kept up their begging notes (*de-de-de-de-de,* the notes following each other in rapid succession). Suddenly, I heard a single clear excited call — *turee* — from above. The three young birds immediately scuttled off the rocks for cover under some bushes; there, like baby quail, they remained in absolute silence. The next instant a falcon swept silently over, not more than a hundred feet above. That admonishing note had not been given a moment too soon. The alert mother bird had sensed what I was totally unaware of.

No bird of the wren family is a more true troglodyte than this "wren of the rocks" or *roitelet des rochers,* as the French Canadians say. Not only does it build its nest in crannies of the rocks, but almost the whole of its time is spent flying, running about, or singing on the rocks; and most of its food is gathered from among them. The whole body of the bird shows unique adaptation to its habits in its rocky domicile. Drs. Grinnell and Storer, in their book *Animal Life in the Yosemite,* speak of this adaptation thus:

In shape of body and head it is notably flattened, a feature which enables it to creep far into horizontal fissures and into crevices between boulders; the bill is very long and slender, enabling the bird to reach still further into remote niches, in its search for an insect or spider; the legs are short, but sharp-clawed toes are very long and have a wide span to permit the bird to cling firmly to vertical or even overhanging rock walls; the coloration, *in toto,* is that of the average barren rock; when the bird is examined at close range the indistinct fine pattern·of white and dusky dots is seen to resemble, to a suggestive degree, the minute patterning of the rocks.*

* Joseph Grinnell and Tracy Storer, *Animal Life in the Yosemite* (Berkeley: University of California Press, 1924), p. 531.

The rock wren puts in a long day. It is about the earliest bird out in the morning and the last to go to its retreat at night. Unsuspicious and seemingly indifferent to all sounds which are not associated with danger, it creeps about on the rocks, occasionally flying to new places to bob and dip and utter its series of rapid, screeing notes. Again we see it delving into crevices and dark tunnels to rout out spiders and pick up insects and their larvae. Almost no sooner does it disappear than it mysteriously bobs up at some unexpected point a few feet to a few yards away, there to give again its bell-like tinkling note or an admonitive *turee, turee, turee.* With this wren, as with the small cony of the high mountain solitudes, lone rock spits and pinnacles are favorite perches. There you will see to best advantage those quick bobbings so characteristic of the bird. This strange action is also engaged in by the water ouzel of our mountain streams. When excited or surprised, the bird may turn completely around in its bobbings, at the same time giving frequent short bursts of song.

In the mating season you may see the queer antics of the *liebespiel,* the animated maneuvers of courting. The female, crouching low to the rock surface, crawls about almost like a mouse, spreading wide her dusky feet and tail and uttering faint squeaky notes. The male spreads his tail and flies about, now in front, now behind her. After a moment the two fly to another location, there to repeat the curious performance.

Water is no great problem for the rock wren, since spiders and hiding moths, insects, and insect larvae are always juicy bits supplying the liquid needed. Like most desert dwellers, the birds drink water at springs or from rock pools after rains, but they are not strictly dependent upon such sources of water. This no doubt accounts for the rock wrens' occurrence, even in hottest summer, in dry, desolate places remote from water.

25. Scott's Oriole

No bird is more intimately associated with the desert's tree yucca forests than Scott's oriole.* The flash of jet-black and yellow as it flies, and the voluble song of meadow-lark quality after it comes to rest on the topmost branch of a tall yucca, usually serve as the means of immediate identification of this handsome oriole of the high deserts. If the near-robin-sized bird is a male and in close view, it can be seen that the whole head, throat, breast, and upper back are black, while the belly and lower back and basal portion of the tail are a brilliant, deep lemon-yellow. The wings, except for some spots, bars, and edgings of ivory white, are

* Twenty other desert birds are known to nest in the tree yucca. As observed by Wilson C. Hanna, ornithologist of Colton, California, they are: Bullock's oriole, white-rumped shrike, costa hummingbird, desert sparrow hawk, Western red-tailed hawk, American raven, Pacific horned owl, long-eared owl, Pasadena screech owl, Western gnatcatcher, California house finch, Brewer's blackbird, Arkansas kingbird, San Diego titmouse, Western lark sparrow, cactus woodpecker, red-shafted flicker, Western bluebird, Northern cactus wren, Baird's wren.

for the most part bright black, as is also the lower two-thirds of the top of the tail.

Perhaps the principal reason this oriole is so closely connected with the tree yucca is that there it finds a sure anchorage for its half-hanging, cup-shaped nest, and also some or most of the fibers useful in its construction.

Sometimes the nests are made wholly from yucca fibers. Several nests I have seen, taken from tree yuccas of the broad alluvial slopes on the north side of the San Bernardino Mountains, were made almost wholly of grass fibers with only a small representation of yucca fibers. One had sagebrush (*Artemisia tridentata*) leaves scattered through the walls. Wilson C. Hanna, of Colton, California, showed me a similar nest in his collection. In no case were the fibers of yucca leaves sewn into the nest to hold it. The nests were rigidly anchored by grass leaves which passed from the nest up and around the yucca needles. Each had a soft lining of fine grass or hair. Four of the nests were built over old ones, a not unusual practice.

The nest is generally suspended three to ten feet above ground at the junction of a yucca branch and the main trunk. It is placed in such a position on the underside of the branch that it is hidden from an intruder's view. Usually it is concealed not only by the leaves to which it is fastened but also by other dead yucca leaves which hang down from the trunk. I have spent many an hour of fruitless search for old nests in winter when there were no birds around to give me a clue. During nesting season, especially when food is being carried to the young, it is, of course, much easier.

The birds do not always build their nests in tree yuccas, although that is by far the favorite site. Where tree yuccas are lacking, other yuccas, such as the widespread Mohave yucca (*Yucca schidigera*) or the big-fruited Spanish bayonet (*Y. baccata*), are chosen as nesting places. When building in these smaller yuccas, the birds may pick away the pulp of several of the somewhat green leaves, thus exposing the strong inner fibers. These are frayed out along the edges, and as the nest is built they are woven into it in such a way as to support it firmly. Along the western edge of the Colorado Desert in California these orioles are occasionally found building in Washingtonia palms. In the Arizona deserts, and also to some extent in California, they sometimes build in the pannicled flower stems of the agave, or even in paloverde trees.

Few people have ever watched the actual building of the nest. Since the work of sewing and weaving and laying of the grass and yucca fibers is so much concealed by the protecting yucca needles, what really goes on can be judged only by noting the construction of the finished product.

The nest is built in late March or April. Three or four bluish-white eggs, spotted with dispersed markings of chocolate and light black-brown, form the set. By mid-May the young birds have generally left the nests. A second brood for the season is not uncommon, especially if the first clutch of eggs has been disturbed or destroyed.

These birds are ever active and restless, flying frequently from one yucca-top "singing post" to another. At times you may see them descending to the ground, where they hunt caterpillars and insects, or going into low bushes to eat wild fruits. The high, clear notes so frequently given as they perch have not only a melancholy but also a ventriloquistic quality which makes it difficult to locate the birds until one sees them fly. A pair of eight-power field glasses is helpful in observing these orioles, for it is not easy to get close to them.

W. E. D. Scott says:

Few birds sing more incessantly. The males are of course the chief performers, but now and again near a nest, while watching the birds, I would detect a female singing the same glad song, only more softly. At the earliest daybreak and all day long, even when the sun is at its highest and during the great part of the afternoon, its very musical whistle is one of the few bird songs that are ever present. ... during the height of the breeding season often many were singing within hearing at the same time.*

Speaking of the young birds, Scott writes:

Young taken from the nest when about ready to leave become very tame and familiar, and one I took in this way began to sing before a year old, and was so tame as to be allowed the run of the house. It was very intelligent and inquisitive, and would frequently alight on my chin or head and strive to open my lips with its bill; or in the same way my eyes if I closed them.†

The general range of this oriole includes the desert areas of southern California, southern Nevada, southwestern Utah, southern Arizona, central New Mexico, western Texas, and parts of Lower California and mainland Mexico, even south to Vera Cruz. In late August or September our American birds go south to Mexico and return in late March and April. Occasionally, one sees the Scott's oriole in the warm southern deserts in midwinter. Migrant and vagabond birds sometimes wander even into areas coastward from the deserts. I have myself seen the birds outside the tree yucca forests or piñon-juniper country. There they are often observed.

The Scott's oriole was first described and named *Icterus scottii* in 1854 by Lieutenant D. N. Couch from birds he observed and collected in Coahuila, Mexico. "I have named this handsome bird," he says, "as a slight token of my high regard for Major General Winfield Scott, Commander in Chief of the U.S. Army."‡ Like so many others with whom I have corresponded and talked, I had always thought that the name, Scott's oriole, was given in honor of W. E. D. Scott, the gifted

* William Earle Dodge Scott, "On the Breeding Habits of Some Arizona Birds," *The Auk*, II, No. 1 (January 1885), 1.

† "On the Avi-fauna of Pinal County, with Remarks on Some Birds of Pima and Gila Counties, Arizona," *The Auk*, IV, No. 1, 22.

‡ *Proceedings of the Academy of Natural Sciences, Philadelphia*, VII (April 1854), 66.

ornithologist, who was the first to write ably of the habits of this bird. As far as I can learn, the earliest use of the common English name, Scott's oriole, was in Cooper's *Ornithology of California*, published in 1870.

The current scientific name now in use, and also the oldest, is *I. parisorum*. *Icterus* is the generic name for all the American orioles. They bear no close relationship to the European orioles. *Icterus* is from the Greek *ikteros,* "a yellowish bird." The specific name *parisorum* was given "in honor of the Brothers Paris" by Charles Lucian Bonaparte, in his *American Ornithology, or History of Birds Inhabiting the United States Not Given by Wilson.* Who the Paris brothers were nobody seems to know. Bonaparte left no word on the subject, and no one has since offered an explanation to clear up the mystery. The common name, "oriole," comes from the Old French *oriol,* in turn derived from the Latin *aureolus,* "golden."

26. The Prairie Falcon

Of all the birds of prey, the bold, swift prairie falcon seems to me most typical of the desert. No other bird appears at once so daring, so resourceful, so defiant when faced with danger.

I first sighted the nest of a pair of these clay-colored cousins of the duck hawk in a pothole some 300 feet aloft on a high limestone cliff of Potosi Mountain of southern Nevada. It was in the latter part of June. Long before I approached the base of the perpendicular escarpment the birds had seen me coming through the piñons and announced their concern with agitated flight, high-pitched cries, and harsh, screeching notes. As I came under the nest site the birds began a wild, high-pitched cackling, which they kept up continually. Often after approaching in a wide arc they flew directly above me, then zoomed with folded wings menacingly to within ten feet of my head. I could hear the swish and whirr of the air past their descending bodies. Then off they shot, soaring upward and outward in graceful sweeps. Often they turned completely over. At times, when for some moments the parent birds had flown far away from the nest site, I could hear, high above, the faint cries of the young. Occasionally one of the falcons would come to rest on a crag, watching to see what I was going to do next. Only once did one of them go to the nest. That gave me my one opportunity to see the falconets; they crowded up to the edge of the nest, doubtless expecting food. When after a half-hour or more the parents saw that I was not disturbing their family, they quieted down and I neither heard nor saw any more of them. I do not doubt that they were watching me, though.

Late in March one year, another pair of falcons was observed in the Pickaninny Buttes of the Mohave Desert. These buttes are great granite formations shaped by chemical disintegration and exfoliation—the last remains, doubtless, of old, old mountains of considerable height. Here and there on the huge, bizarre rocks are great vertical fissures, niches, and potholes. In one of these potholes at the upper head of a deep fissure, at an inaccessible height, there was a falcon nest. It faced broad, open country, with visibility for miles around. I discovered the site after noting the white, limey fecal and urine stains on rocks just below it. The birds spotted me the moment I approached. A strong southwest gale was blowing. At times, one or both of them would swing almost directly above me and without a single wingbeat remain almost motionless, in defiance of the wind, for moments at a time. Suddenly, with rapid strokes of its long-pointed wings, one would dart forward, come to a dead stop, poise there a moment, and then let the wind smoothly carry it backward in a broad, graceful sweep.

Because I remained quiet and did not approach too closely, several times I was able to see the female enter the nest hole. She approached it from below. When quite near she suddenly folded her wings and smoothly shot upward into the nest opening. Just as she alighted, she opened and closed her wings as a brake. Then she sat motionless on the edge of the nest, watching me silently for a long time.

On several occasions after she had sat there for some minutes, I made a wild, cackling call in rapid repetition, and this evidently annoyed her, for she would suddenly bolt from the cavity uttering sharp, piercing cries as she flew above me.

The male, the smaller of the two birds, had a watching post high on the cliff. From there he could see the pothole where his mate was, as well as the surrounding country. Here he sat motionless over long periods of the day. From time to time, he flew in high, wide circles over the buttes. A sort of auxiliary sentinel post was a small ledge quite near the nest. Great white urine and fecal stains were on the rocks below it; also there were the remains of mammals and birds—bones, fur, and feathers. This was probably where the prey was brought, torn apart, and eaten when there were no young in the nest or when the parent birds fed alone during the incubation period.

Falcons and ravens often nest close together, possibly serving as sentries for each other. The ravens generally build large stick nests on open but sheltered ledges with a good outlook of the open country. In the vicinity of this falcon nest there were two raven's nests and two nests of red-tailed hawks. It was very evident that both the falcons and the ravens disliked the presence of the hawks. Several times I watched a pair of ravens annoying the hawks by flying above, behind, and alongside them or making swift passes at them. The red-tails generally paid little attention. With the falcons it was quite different. When the paths of the falcons and red-tails crossed, the falcons swooped down shrieking, and the hawks would change their course or turn partly over as if to dodge.

Most of the falcon's hunting is done quite early in the day and again in late afternoon. Twice I witnessed the sudden taking of a horned lark, once the capture of an antelope ground squirrel. In neither case was there any warning of the attack. The falcon shot down from a height of perhaps a thousand feet, striking with great force and accuracy. The talons dug into the victim, and the assailant was off almost before I had time to realize what was happening.

John G. Tyler of Fresno, California, speaking of the behavior of the falcon, says:

A moody creature at all times, peevish and whimsical, the Prairie Falcon is a bird of extremes. One never knows just what to expect from this handsome falcon and the expected seldom happens. He may fairly dazzle us with a burst of speed as he comes in to his cliff nest over the sage-covered ridges; but our admiration fades as we behold him sitting stoop-shouldered and motionless, for an hour at a time on some low mound in a pasture, a picture of listless dejection.

A pair of ravens in a nest not fifty feet from the falcon's own pot hole may be tolerated for days at a time with no act to indicate that the falcons are even aware of the presence of their neighbors. Then a sudden outburst of anger, totally unprovoked so far as human eye can detect, may mark the beginning of merciless and unceasing persecution. Indeed, they may even dispossess the ravens entirely and use the wool-lined nest while the falcon's own favorite pot hole or ledge goes untenanted.

Sometimes the canyons echo with their noisy cackling as the female falcon strikes again and again at the observer who approaches her nest cliff and yet, when upon a return visit we expect the same thrilling demonstration, she often flaps silently away with all the cramped awkwardness of a sparrow hawk just aroused from the duties of incubation.

With a roar of wings the male sweeps along a canyon wall, dashes into a feeding flock of quail, snatches a victim and beats away like some giant swift: but when we hope to see this marvelous exhibition of flight repeated we find him moping around sparrow-like on the ground in some summer fallow field scrutinizing the bunches of stubble for a chance hidden meadowlark or Savannah sparrow.

A wounded falcon, or one who has changed her nesting site only to have the new location discovered, can give an exhibition of unmistakable anger which defies all attempt at description; but an overfed mid-October bird as it sits dreamily on a roadside fence post is usually too utterly lacking in spirit to attempt anything that requires more energy than a lazy flight to some more secluded perch.*

During the nesting season falcons take larger game such as rock squirrels and rabbits. I have never observed the procedure, but Leon Dawson says: "In the case of larger game the quarry is knocked headlong by a crashing blow after which the assailant turns to try conclusions as to weight." Then picking up the victim in its talons the falcon flies to its nest. The bird's eye is not only large but also capable of remarkable accommodation. "It is almost," says Dr. T. D. A. Cockerell, "as though the soaring falcon possessed a telescope which could immediately be converted into a microscope as it swooped upon its prey."

As I wandered over the rocks of the Pickaninny Buttes, I found mammal and bird bones scattered in crevices, on ledges, and on the tops of domes. It is a well-known fact that falcons thus dispose of food refuse from the nest. On rocks beneath the nest were pellets of fur and broken-up bones which had been disgorged by the young birds. Says F. H. Fowler of Palo Alto, California:

The process of casting up a pellet is a serious and sea-sick business. When the symptoms of casting first attack a falcon it draws its feathers down flat, stands up full height, sticks its head and neck outward and upward, and for a few moments looks bereft of its senses. It then starts to duck its head in a series of quick jerks, at the same time contorting its neck violently from side to side. This muscular action appears to force the relatively large pellet from the bird's interior upward into the crop. The sidewise contortions then cease and the pellet is cast up by a series of up and down pumpings of the head and neck.†

* "Observations on the Habits of the Prairie Falcon," *Condor*, XXV (May 1923), 90.
† "Studies of Food and Growth of the Prairie Falcon," *Condor*, XXXIII (September 1931), 196.

The amount of food consumed by a falcon family is enormous. The young birds grow very fast, and the hunting powers of the parents are taxed to the limit. In his studies of falcon young, Mr. Fowler found evidence that between May 6 and June 6, 1928, the parental pair at one nest had brought in the following food: two mourning doves, eight burrowing owls, three horned larks, nine California jays, 15 meadow larks, three Brewer's blackbirds, two shrikes, one rock wren, one chicken, one pocket gopher, and eight ground squirrels and Nelson spermophiles.

The number of young in a brood is three to six, hatched from creamy-white eggs with many spots and blotches of reddish-brown. The ill-formed, helpless falconets at first are covered with fine white down. At about four weeks the contour feathers are well started. At the end of five weeks the young leave the nest and soon after fend for themselves.

If you wish to see the falcon at its best—in flight, in variety of responses, in the number of strange calls and cries—you must choose the period of courting, nest-locating, and rearing of the young. It is quite a different bird that greets you at other seasons. The flight then is less spirited, the call notes few. When in August I visited the hangout of the Pickaninny falcons it was hours before I saw sign of the birds; later, when they did come in, there was no excitement over my approach.

27. The Shrike

As you went on your midmorning walk, did you chance to see, on top of a barren shrub, a tall tree yucca, or settler's fence, the handsome butcherbird or loggerhead shrike? You will see him on one of his several lookout posts, at or near the outer boundary of his feeding or breeding territory, guarding against trespassers. The shrike marks out boundaries and establishes himself as sole proprietor of a certain area of several acres, within which no other shrike may dwell or even forage. This pattern of establishing a definite territory and driving out other birds of the same species is not limited to the shrikes; it has been observed in many birds, but in most cases, especially migratory species, the territories are, for the most part, defended against usurpation or trespass only during the breeding and nesting season. But with the shrikes there is never a time throughout the year when they lose their sense of proprietorship.

In the breeding season the most important drive behind this behavior of the shrike is, of course, the desire to protect the nest, the young, and the mate. In other seasons it is to obtain an adequate supply of food. Dr. Alden Miller thinks that in our deserts the territory defended by a pair of shrikes during the breeding season may extend over an area of 13 to 40 acres; at other times, when food is the chief concern for the single bird, it is probably slightly less in extent.

During most of the year the shrike is solitary. Once it establishes itself in a certain area it seldom leaves it. And in order to defend the territory, it maintains watching posts where it can easily detect the presence of a trespasser. In the tree yucca country such posts are generally atop the old flower stalks at the ends of the highest branches of the yucca tree. Trees, tall shrubs like the ocotillo, telephone poles, or fence posts are also utilized. On such high points it will sit for unbelievably long periods, ever watchful, from time to time singing strange defiant notes of warning. If another shrike appears near the watching post the singer immediately becomes excited and belligerent, and drives the intruder away, at least as far as the border of the territory, uttering sharp, angry notes, *bzeek bzeek*, over and over. Once the offender is driven off, the shrike returns to its post.

Male and female birds, except during the breeding season, have their own feeding territories, which they defend against all encroachers. But during the mating time and also during the season of rearing the young, a territory is shared and defended with especial vigor.

Dr. Miller wrote of this defense phenomenon of shrikes as he observed it in the northern San Joaquin Valley. Of a particular pair he says:

Members of the resident pair were sitting on fence posts about ten yards apart, one bird, probably the male, singing occasionally. A succeession of sharp notes (*bzeek*) was heard from a third shrike which had appeared at the edge of the territory about sixty yards distant. This was immediately answered by similar notes from the defending "male." This invader sang a few trills, then came closer, approaching the "male" of the resident pair, and sat on the adjacent fence post. The "female" of the pair was on the

HIGH DESERT, WITH JUNIPER AND PIÑON

opposite side of the defending "male." The two "males" remained rigidly on guard, neither moving in the slightest. One of them, I could not be sure which, gave a few song trills. After about five minutes both birds suddenly jumped into the air, the defending "male" came within striking range, and a series of sharp clicks of the bill and a few screeches, low buzzing notes, and staccato vocal notes were heard. The flight of the two continued for a few yards, when the defender returned to the "female" who had remained quiet and seemingly undisturbed throughout the performance. The repulsed invader towered in a most erratic manner and flew high over the hills at the edge of the valley half a mile away, apparently most intent on departing with rapidity.*

On our deserts the only bird with which the trim-appearing loggerhead shrike may be confused is the mockingbird.

* Alden H. Miller, *Systematic Revision and Natural History of the American Shrikes (Lanius),* University of California Publications in Zoology, Vol. 38, pp. 157, 158.

The shrike's flattish, heavy head, the conspicuous black bar running through the eye to the base of the heavy, hooked, and notched beak, and the contrasts of light slatey grays and black and white are field marks no mockingbird can ever show.

Lanius ludovicianus, the loggerhead shrike, is widespread over North America. There are quite a number of different races;* these are divided into two groups, those with light-colored rumps and those without. Our desert shrikes, like all those common to the Great Basin Biotic Province, belong to the white-rumped group. The adjective "loggerhead" applies to the large, blockish, thickset, flat-topped head, "logger" being a dialectal name for a log or block of wood.

This bird is a good hunter. From his position on the foraging post, he seems to see everything that goes on around him. The motions of a lizard or an insect stirring on the ground or in a shrub will at once alert him, and, if he is hungry, he will drop from his commanding lookout to pick it up. A blow or two with his heavy, notched beak brings it to a quick end. He then carries it to a near, exposed perch and eats it. If any parts remain, they are either dropped or hung on a thorn or other sharp spit. Insects, especially the larger flying ones, he may snap up on the wing, flying directly behind them until he overtakes them. The shrike impales his larger prey upon a thorn or wedges it in a small crotch in order to flay it. The feet, unlike those of the birds of prey, are weak and unable to grasp and hold large struggling prey so it can be torn to pieces. At times, the victims are placed on the impaling thorn to dry for future need. One recent morning I came upon a shrike tearing apart and noisily crunching a dried desert brown-shouldered lizard he had long ago spitted on a mesquite thorn. The number of impaled insects varies from season to season and with the individual bird. It is a

* Birds of the subspecies *nevadensis* occupy most of the middle and southern Great Basin; birds of the subspecies *sonoriensis* are dwellers of the Colorado Desert and southern Arizona.

fairly common practice for the shrike to hang its prey on certain thorns to which it has become accustomed. The impaled creatures may be eaten within a few hours or a day after being killed.

There is a belief that at times the shrike kills for the mere love of it. We are probably safer in saying that locating, capturing, and killing of prey are instinctive acts, controlled in part by hunger and in part by the need to store food for the future.

When one is out camping in the spring and early summer it is always well to spend several days in a particular vicinity. One is likely to see the activities of a half a dozen nesting birds in a small area and find it to advantage to make a consecutive series of observations in order to get the complete picture of the birds' habits over a period of many days. With camera and notebook one should watch intently, first about one nest, then about another, visiting each several times a day. During a recent spring season I spent such a time of observation in the Joshua Tree National Monument, and among the birds I watched with greatest interest was a pair of white-rumped shrikes. I first noticed them while they were occupied with courting and hunting a nest site. The female, watched and closely followed by her mate, flew about among juniper shrubs, lycium bushes, and thickly branched Joshua trees. I knew their final decision on a nest site when I saw the female leave a small three-branched yucca, fly to the ground, and pick up a twig. The birds were very shy and it took much patient hiding to see the nest built. The bulky foundation laid among bristling needles in the crotch of the tree was made mostly from twigs of the desert wild almond. The deep cup was lined with fibers from yucca, a few stray feathers, several horsehairs, fine leaves, grasses, and bits of woolly filago. On the second day, after the nest was complete, from behind my rock-pile blind I saw the female lay her first egg. At that rare moment I was hidden only about three yards from the nest and I saw her every motion.

Eventually, five palish-green eggs were laid and incubation began. Only the female shrike attended the eggs; the male aided by defending and feeding her. At the end of 16 days all the eggs had hatched and feeding of the young began. At first, they were given only small portions of insects, but later whole beetles and moths. As the birdlings grew larger, I noticed the first spewing forth of pellets of undigested food particles, such as tough wing-covers of beetles. With the grown birds this practice of ejecting pellets of undigestible matter may often be witnessed.

The young birds, when first out of the nest, were a noisy lot and very greedy. The old birds were there constantly, both feeding and defending against intruders. Once, approaching behind a screen of bushes, I surprised the young birds sitting huddled together on the limb of a shrub waiting to be fed. At once, added to the anxious screechings and raucous notes of the parents, came a perfect hubbub of grotesque cries—not of fear, but of ferocious belligerence—from the fledglings. In order not to frighten them I remained for only a few moments.

Two weeks later I returned to the spot and found that the family of young butcherbirds had dispersed, but not beyond the territorial limits established by the parents at the beginning of the nesting season. Most of their time was still spent near the nest site, and I occasionally came upon them as they begged with open mouths and vibrating wings for food. A month later they were gone, no doubt staking out new territory for themselves.

The desert loggerhead shrike is no fine singer, but not exactly a poor one, either. He has a surprising number of notes. Some are decidedly unmusical, harsh, and discordant; these are the ordinary call notes, alarm notes, or notes of defiance and warning. Some notes are plaintive. Others, especially when given as part of a series, are decidedly clear and pleasing, and even of musical quality. Listen during the period of early spring and again in late summer when the song is made of trills, repetitions of liquid-clear notes, and intervening burrs, all given in numbers more than usual. During the nesting season, perhaps as a matter of precaution, few songs are heard. I have noticed even more reticence in song during late autumn and winter. It is often asserted that the shrike is a mimicker of other birds, but no evidence of this is found by those who have studied the song carefully.

The flight of the shrike is strong, often undulating, and generally rather close to earth. The short, rounded wings move in rapid, steady beats. As the bird flies across a field and gets ready to alight, the wings are spread and there is a short upward glide to the perch. Sometimes, especially when foraging, it makes a direct down-drop from its perch, leveling off with a direct, even flight and a final upward landing as it approaches the new perch. The shrike spends much of its time on its foraging post in comparative quiet, looking about or preening. This is especially true during midday hours; only in the early morning and late afternoon when actively feeding does it fly about much. Dr. Miller has estimated that the daily distance covered in flight during summer months may be between 20 and 40 miles.

Watch the shrike for a few hours, especially during the period when the young are being fed, and see the number of Jerusalem crickets, grasshoppers, and moths he picks up for himself and his family. Although at times he is truly *Lanius*, the butcher, he is on the whole a very beneficial bird. Careful studies show that at least 80 per cent or more of his food consists of noxious and harmful insects.

28. The Cactus Wren

The cactus wrens, along with their near relations the canyon wrens and rock wrens, belong to a very specialized group of wrens inhabiting the warmer parts of both the Americas. They are unique among their kind in their large size and the possession of fan-shaped tails, the individual feathers of which widen toward the end. In the cactus wren the tail spreads wide when flying. When the bird is sitting on a branch, the tail is carried in a depressed or hanging position; this is especially true when the bird is singing. Never is it cocked high and forward over the back as so frequently may be observed in the small, short-tailed house wrens, so familiar to residents of the temperate regions of the world.

The cactus wren is the largest of all the wrens, with body length up to eight inches. It is not a handsome bird. The upper part of the head and neck is a rich brown, with a contrasting stripe of white reaching from the beak over and beyond the eye. The back is grayish-brown, marked with sharp black and white stripes; the lighter, loose-plumaged underparts are boldly punctuated with large to small black spots, those of the throat and forebreast being conspicuously large. Both the brown wings and the tail are barred with white. When the birds are seen at close range, a striking feature is the clear, blood-red to orange iris of the eye.

This large desert-dwelling wren is wary, with the habit of running or flying close to the ground while screened by bushes. This makes it difficult to get a good close-range view of him. The best opportunity to view the birds is when they sing, for then it is usual for them, especially the males, to perch on the top or near-top branch of a cactus or thorny bush.

One morning just after sunrise I left my piñon-country camp on a walk of several miles, the object being to visit a number of scenic points and at the same time make a census of the season's birds and their nests. Inasmuch as it was then mid-April, there had been for several weeks an unusual buzz of activity in the avian world. Since my tour of the week before, half a dozen new nests of cactus wrens had been completed in needle-crowded cactus bushes, and several of the previous year's nests had been made over to serve as spare or roosting nests for the male birds.

It was no particular trick to find the new retort-shaped wren nests, for they were large and in plain view. Moreover, the big, brown male birds were noisy, their loud clattery or chutty notes carrying far enough to advertise to all visitors the area they had marked out for their domain.

The new, straw-colored nests were ellipsoid-globular in shape and fully the size of a man's head. They were set deep in the spines of cholla cactus and were made of small twigs, fine-stemmed grasses, colored flower pedicels, dainty red-stemmed buckwheats and gilias, all rather loosely but intricately put together. Each nest had, running outward at a slight angle to the horizontal, a tubular passageway for entrance into the dark, cavernous, feather-lined interior. Some of these tunnels were short (three or four inches), while

CACTUS WREN

others were two to three times as long, but all had the bristling, spiny protection of cactus needles at the entrance.

One of the old made-over nests interested me most of all. Instead of being the usual three or four feet above the ground in a cactus bush, the site was 16 feet high, in the forking, needle-studded branches of a tall tree yucca, above the reach of snakes and beyond the paws of most egg-eating rodents. This was the highest-placed nest of a cactus wren I had ever seen, but I remember one of my fellow ornithologists telling me of one he had found in an athel tree in the Imperial Valley, 33 feet above the ground.

This nest had been built the preceding year as an incubating nest, and the old materials were now somewhat gray from weathering. Since then it had been dressed up a bit by another bird, with new plant stems and the addition of a new "front porch." Old feathers lining the interior had been pulled out, a new batch of flicker feathers put in, and six inches of entrance tunnel, the "front porch," added to an already long one. The nest was a real feather bed inside. It was now serving, perhaps all winter had served, as a warm, wind-tight roosting nest. It is well known that the cock birds are given to this practice of using refurbished nests. Just below my cabin at Palm Springs I had a male bird occupying such a roosting nest all winter, and every evening just after sundown, quite regularly, he would pop into it. The similar-appearing females, too, use these roosting nests in winter.

Another old nest which I found seemed to have been so hastily and flimsily put together that the roof had caved in, and even part of the bottom had fallen out. The usual cactus wren's nest is not at all of this sort; on the contrary, it is so compactly constructed that it may last unbroken for years after desertion. This one may have been a spare or "busy-work" nest, such as the males are reputed sometimes to make without any thought of occupancy. Or it may once have been a hot-weather brooding nest made late in the season, it was of such light construction that it was possible to see the incubating birds and later the active young through the thin side walls. I have found several nests of this kind in my travels in the hot southern deserts.

The wrens as a whole have a reputation for big families. The cactus wren very often has a second brood. The usual number of eggs is four to six, but clutches of seven have been known. The eggs have either a white or a salmon-pink ground color, with a thick peppering of small cinnamon spots; hence they often appear an almost uniform "flat-salmon" or a wine-cinnamon color. They are the handsomest of all wren eggs.

The commonly used name, cactus wren, is suggestive of the bird's most usual habitat. Most of the nests are in the spiny cactus thickets, and it is in the vicinity of these plants that the birds find their chief forage grounds. However, in Sonora and southern New Mexico these large wrens also build their nests amidst the clustered stems of the red-flowered desert mistletoe, and in many cases the nests are almost completely concealed by them. The protective cover afforded by the thorns of the cat's-claw also occasionally affords attractive sites for nests. There is a tendency among cactus wrens toward a sort of communal association, so we often find a number of nests built in a restricted area.

I once found one new and four old cactus wren nests in a large branching staghorn cactus—evidently a very advantageous building site. Another shrubby cactus contained one new and one old cactus wren nest as well as a recently abandoned La Conte thrasher nest.

The cactus wrens are industrious hunters of spiders, insects, and insect larvae, often of the harmful kind, and the number taken, especially when the young are to be fed, is prodigious. It is said that fully 75 per cent of the food is of animal nature. They hunt on the ground, for the most part, working radially about the nest site.

In January one year two companions and I found near our camp, just after sundown, the winter roosting place of a cactus wren. It was in a deerhorn cactus growing in a broad, sandy wash on the north slope of the Chuckawalla Mountains. A weathered cactus wren nest several seasons old had been made habitable by the addition of a rather large, tubular front hallway of long, dried plant stems. As we went by the nest a second time, about half an hour later, the bird, now gone to roost, became frightened by the noise of our approach and bolted from the nest, finally coming to rest in an ironwood tree. Next morning I saw a pair of cactus wrens in an ironwood tree right at the camp, then later heard them singing. One of them was probably the bird we had frightened from its nest the night before. A few minutes later, one of the wrens descended to the floor of the sandy wash, and there, not more than 60 feet from us, started to overturn small stones with its beak, searching for insects. Some of the stones weighed more than the bird itself. One weighed fully six ounces; another, slightly smaller, was greater in girth than my thumb and three and a half inches long. The wren sometimes merely pushed some of the rocks forward to expose the insects.

The song is one of the most striking things about this bird. To the stranger coming for the first time into the cactus wren's desert habitat, the song seems most unwrenlike and a bit coarse and monotonous, but when heard over and over again in early spring before sunrise, when the air still smells of evening primroses, encelia, and creosote bush, it comes to have a fascination. One of the most common songs is a harsh trill reminding one, as J. D. Cooper, author of *Birds of the Pacific States*, said, "of the marsh wren but much louder and more ringing." When disturbed, the bird sounds more like the common wrens in its scolding notes. This is a well-spaced, throaty *chut-chut-chut* which may change to a somewhat higher-pitched, excited *chair-chair-chair,* as Ralph Hoffman has rendered it. The males do most of the singing, and in the prenesting and nesting season they keep it up hour after hour, even through the heat of the day, although it then may be less frequent. Even in winter they occasionally sing, but the day must be sunny.

The males are especially quarrelsome at mating time. They then chase one another and engage in berating duets of song and wild calls. Peace among rivals is seldom known.

Among the cactus wrens' enemies are the smaller owls, some of which are known to tear into the nests. Many of the nests are also sooner or later destroyed or damaged by wood rats, wild mice, and ground squirrels, which eat the eggs and probably also the young. I once saw a white-tailed antelope ground squirrel ripping up a large nest. When he reached the inside, the feathers really flew around. One would think that the cactus needles he had to climb over, to say nothing of those protecting the nest itself, would have deterred him.

No sooner are the cavernous brood nests abandoned in late spring by the parent birds than other creatures move in. I have found lizards, especially the small utas, crickets, white-footed mice, and even small snakes in them.

The cactus wren is a permanent resident of the warmer desert regions of the southern parts of California, Nevada, Utah, Arizona, New Mexico, and Texas, and of northern Mexico. Their distribution is spotted, for they will not go where there are only vast stands of creosote bush, nonspiny atriplex, and other low, thornless vegetation.

The scientific name of the cactus wren is *Heleodytes brunneicapillus couesi.* The generic name *Heleodytes* comes from the Greek *heleos,* a marsh, meadow, or lowland, and *dytes,* a dweller, an inhabitant, some of the South American near relations, known as marsh wrens, being inhabitants of rush-grown swamps and grassy marshes. *Brunneicapillus* is compounded from Latin words meaning "brown-haired," reference probably being made to the brown head. In the subspecific name *couesi* we have commemorated the name of one of America's most noted writers on birds, Dr. Elliott Coues, author of *Key to North American Birds, Birds of the Colorado Valley,* and *Birds of the Northwest,* books every desert bird student should own. Said T. S. Palmer: "He imparted to his bird biographies a charm and vividness few writers can hope to attain."

29. *California Road Runner*

Of all the feathered dwellers in the desert there is none that has such an amazing stock of peculiarities as the California road runner. He is the desert's bird wag, as full of comical manners and as mischievous as the jay or the nutcracker; yet, unlike these birds, he is never obtrusive in his familiarity. Every morning he goes down on the trail below my shanty and saunters along, waiting for me to come with my pail for water, well knowing that I will chase him and give him the fun of beating me to the corner. Just as I am almost upon him, he leaps into the brush out of sight and is not seen for an hour or two. This born gamester has been found time and again pursuing the ends of surveyors' chains as they were dragged along by the lineman, or, on golf grounds, running down stray balls with the eagerness of a playful dog.

You will never mistake the road runner. The bristle-tipped topknot which he raises and lowers at will, the reptile-like face with its deep-slit mouth, and the long tail which so unmistakably registers his emotions, make him a bird of most singular appearance.

This strange cousin of the cuckoo has earned his name

from his habit of sprinting along roadways, especially when pursued by horsemen or moderately slow-going vehicles. In the old days of California, when tourists were frequently driven over country roads in tallyho coaches, it was no uncommon sight to see this bird running a half-mile or so in front of the fast-trotting horses. Another common name, "chaparral cock," is given in allusion to his living in the chaparral or scrub forest of the semideserts; and he is called "ground cuckoo" because of his inability to leave the ground in long-sustained flight.

Formerly the range of the road runner included the grassy plains, chaparral-covered hills, and arid mesas from Kansas to the Pacific Ocean and from central California to Mexico. With the settlement of the land and the increase in the number of gunmen, this unique bird is rapidly becoming rare, and the familiar Maltese-cross footprints which he leaves along dusty roads are now all too seldom seen except in the wildest portions of his former range.

The road runner makes no regular migrations and is seldom seen except when alone. He prefers the protection of thorny, low-growing mesquite and saltbush thickets, and once he chooses a clump of mesquites, he seldom leaves the vicinity and may be found there year after year.

Like a policeman, the road runner apparently has his beats, and anyone who watches him day after day will note how punctual he is in passing certain points at definite times. An invalid on the Colorado Desert recently called my attention to the fact that a road runner passed her porch regularly at 12:25 P.M. every day for over a week, never varying by more than a minute or two. A gentleman who some months ago put up a new board fence tells me that a road runner almost daily jumps on the upper rail and runs at top speed the full length of one side of the fence. He invariably does this at the same time of day—just about noon.

I became acquainted with a young road runner as a pet

in the home of O. H. Wickard, at Antelope, California. The bird stayed in the house at night but went out early in the day.

First on its program was generally a sun bath. Mounting one of the granite boulders about the house, he would puff out his feathers until his body looked round as a ball, spread his wings, and lower his tail. In this position, he would sit quietly for some 30 minutes. Sun bath over, he would go into a cactus patch. In a succession of dizzy leaps and jumps and hurried flights and runs, he would go round and round a cactus clump, perhaps as many as 20 times. He always seemed to make an effort to assume as many different clownish attitudes as possible. This over, the road runner might then go to the house and annoy the cat a while. Dogs he had no use for. Even a very small Pekingese would send the bird fleeing in what appeared to be terror.

Cat-teasing consisted of rushing toward the animal with spread wings, extended neck and head, and wide-open mouth, followed by a snapping of the beak and a strange sound of rattling in the throat. The cat often countered this noisy, showy charge with a quick bat of its paw. Then the bird would deftly retreat and rush at the cat again. Both seemed to enjoy the sport. It generally ended after the cat ran away, with the road runner giving chase for a yard or two.

This road runner was unusually fond of fuzzy objects such as loose wads of cotton and milkweed seeds. He would run round and round the room, holding the object in his beak. Crayons he found in a box on a shelf were picked up one by one and thrown to the floor; flowers in a vase fared likewise.

From time to time his amusements were varied by running from the open door, picking up a leaf in the garden, and then dashing inside with it. Once he picked up a sizable piece of glass, brought it to show to his mistress, and to her amazement, swallowed it without ill effects. As she sprinkled the family wash he hugely enjoyed having her sprinkle water on him. When the neighbor's barefooted children came in, he would rush at them, make a rattling noise in his throat, and then peck at their toes, often frightening them from the house. If they had shoes on he pulled at the buttons or the ends of the shoestrings.

At night the bird slept inside the house on a branch of a tree nailed above the door, or on top of the iron-cased wall clock, his tail pushed flat up against the wall. The striking of the clock he wholly ignored, and he went to sleep even with the lights on; to evening conversations he gave no heed.

One evening a stranger came in and sat down in a chair near the clock. Old Roady jumped from his sleeping perch onto the visitor's head, and from there to his lap, where he made repeated stabs with his beak at the visitor's fingers.

One summer morning one of the boys found the pet caught in a spring trap set out for the rabbits that had been eating the garden vegetables. One foot was so nearly severed from the leg that amputation was necessary. With only a stump left, it was no longer able to leap or run, either in sport or while hunting for food.

But Old Roady was resourceful. For several days he spent most of the time lying in the shade; before the week had ended, however, he was hobbling around, even attempting to run on his stump. On the third day after the accident I saw him with the aid of his wings jump upward and snatch cicadas from the branches of shrubs. He was soon back at most of his old tricks. The end of his leg sometimes got a bit sore from overuse, but the callus was soon thick enough to stand much abuse, and before a month went by he was again visiting at the homes of the farm neighbors. Often he stayed away all morning and traveled several miles. Once he frightened a housewife by bringing her a live snake, he apparently enjoyed her excited screams. He usually stayed out in the brush all morning, seldom coming into the house until noontime. If the boys tried to find him he was very clever at eluding them by crouching low under the bushes.

This road runner was very fond of watermelon, but he ignored all other fruits. Scraps of meat, crickets and grasshoppers, fence lizards, and small horned toads were his favorite foods. Several times he was caught eating baby pack rats.

The Mexicans consider the road runner, or *paisano,* a purveyor of good luck and a desirable neighbor, and he is not unwelcome when he comes, as he often does after getting better acquainted, into the yard to share a bit of grain with the barn fowls.

The *paisano's* appetite is as queer as his looks. He eats many things you would not expect a bird to eat. He swallows horned toads, grasshoppers, mice, centipedes, millepedes, cutworms, spiders, bumblebees, and occasionally even snakes, baby wood rats, and newborn rabbits. Cactus fruits and the berries of the sumac are among his vegetable foods. His flesh-eating habits sometimes get the better of him—for instance, when he finds bait in traps. Too often the trapper, making his rounds in the morning, finds the feathers of a road runner which was caught by the steel jaws and in turn eaten by a coyote or fox.

The road runner has extraordinary ability as an insect catcher. In the stomach of a road runner taken near San Diego, 36 cicadas were found—insects which the entomologist finds very difficult to take on the wing. Again and again I have seen the road runner leap into the air and snap up a large grasshopper. Then he will stand and seem to gaze into the distance for a moment, moving his long tail delicately up and down.

The road runner, like some other desert birds, notably the cactus wren, sometimes secures its food in a manner quite similar to that of the seashore-dwelling turnstone, which has the peculiar habit of turning over small stones and other objects with its short, stout beak in order to find food.

While on a rather recent trip through the Indio-Mecca section of the Salton Sink in the Colorado Desert of California, I came upon a large flat of dried mud, the result of an overflow of highly sedimented irrigation waters from a cultivated field. While lying exposed to the sunshine and drying, the fine sediment had formed an upper crust which had broken up into large irregular-shaped lamina or blocks, slightly upturned about the edges. Shrinkage had caused fissures between the concave plates three-quarters of an inch wide and fully as deep. This peculiar dried-mud surface was located in an open space in the midst of a thicket of honey mesquite and quail brush. The surrounding brush afforded excellent shelter for birds. Among those that I observed was a California road runner, which came out of the brush. Although I was plainly in view at the edge of the mesquite tangle the bird paid no attention to me, and after running halfway across the 60-foot space it stopped suddenly and began tilting and then overturning with its rather long, strong beak the large concave plates of caked dry mud. He seemed quite successful in his quest for food, often obtaining several insects under a single mudcake. This procedure was repeated until some 30 of the cakes had been lifted on edge and thrown over. Some of these plates were seven or eight inches across and almost two-thirds of an inch thick, and very heavy. After about ten minutes of this, he ran off into the brush.

Curious to see what insects he had been getting, I turned over several of the undisturbed mud plates to find rather small, gray-black crickets, just under the upturned margin of nearly every block.

Lizards are the road runner's chief fare; these he picks off the rocks, and one blow of his bill is enough to kill them. One of the common names of this bird is "lizard eater." Especially during the nesting season many reptiles are taken. The baby birds are almost raised on them. Dr. Harold Bryant ranks the road runner as one of the worst natural enemies of lizards and snakes.

Early in May one year I saw a funny sight, when, with a

whirr of wings, a road runner sprang on a lizard and pinned him to the sand with his bill. As is common practice with the lizard, he detached his tail. The road runner picked up the lizard's body and then tried to get the squirming tail into his mouth. He tried again and again to pick it up without letting go the rest of the lizard. Finally, after the lizard's bones were well cracked and his jaws were pressed together to get the ends of the mandibles close together, he picked up the tail. Holding his head high, the bird then ran off with his wriggling prize into the brush.

It is not often that you come across the nest of this bird, but a few days later I was led to the nest and found the mother sitting on a pile of sticks, the ill-made home placed some seven feet above ground in a juniper shrub. With her mottled and speckled plumage she was so inconspicuous that I should never have seen her had she not jumped off the nest as I approached within a few feet of it.

What interested me as the days went by was not so much the rude home, lined with almost everything from a snake skin to bits of manure, or the yellowish egg within it, but the patient mother, who sat almost seven weeks on the nest, first with the eggs and then with the young. The period of incubation was not so unusually long nor were the young birds so slow in growing. It was merely her method of hatching the eggs, which were laid at considerable intervals; incubation began as soon as the first egg was laid. Thus the first of the brood was ready to leave the nest when the last ungainly birds were breaking from the shell.

If a female road runner is approached when on the nest, she generally remains quiet until the intruder is right upon her; then she slips over the back of the nest and flies a short distance away, where she can still see the unwelcome caller. At times she has been known to permit herself to be caught rather than forsake her young.

A member of the Cooper Ornithological Club, J. R. Pemberton, gives a most interesting report concerning the actions of a female road runner whose nest he found some ten feet above ground in a sycamore tree. As the observer began climbing up to the nest, the bird hopped to the ground. Mr. Pemberton says:

Immediately it began to squirm, scramble, and drag itself away across an open space and in full view. The bird was simulating a broken leg instead of a broken wing! The bird held its wings closed throughout the demonstration, though frequently falling over on its side in its enthusiasm. The whole performance was kept entirely in my view, the bird gradually working away from the tree until it was some 35 feet distant, when it immediately ran back to the base of the tree and repeated the whole show. I had been so interested up to now that I had failed to examine the nest, which, when looked into, contained five young probably a week old. When I got to the ground the bird continued its "stunt" rather more frantically than before, and in order to encourage the bird I followed, and was pleased to see it remain highly consistent until I was decoyed to a point well outside the grove. Here the bird suddenly ran away at full speed and in a direction still away from the nest.*

There are many versions of the imaginative tale of the chaparral cock as a killer of rattlesnakes. The rattlesnake is caught asleep and surrounded by a circlet of cholla cactus joints by a clever road runner. The rattlesnake awakens and, realizing that he cannot escape, bites himself and dies. There are many frills and variations to this story.

In winter as soon as the morning sun is out, the road runner may be seen. Mounting a large boulder, then turning his back toward the sun, he opens up and ruffles his feathers. He now looks more like a mammal than a bird, with his tail hanging down and the full exposure of the numerous soft, downlike barbs at the bases of the feathers, which in their fluffiness look like thick fur. This is a good time to see the road runner at close range. Purposely now he seems to ignore your pres-

* "Variation of the Broken-wing Stunt by a Roadrunner," *Condor*, XVIII (September 1916), 203.

ence and will permit you to approach until you can see the white ring of his eye. Several times I have quietly crept up on one and watched him for ten minutes at a time preening, running his bill through his feathers, and gaping and stretching his long black jaws.

The road runner relies mostly on his legs for escape. Like the ostrich, he uses his wings mostly as auxiliaries in running or jumping. It would be a mistake, though, to say that the road runner never flies in the true sense of the term. Several times I have seen one, when hard-pressed, fly almost an eighth of a mile. He looked very awkward. If surprised when on rough ground, the fleeing road runner generally spreads his wings and volplanes across the gullies. If disturbed when on the mountainside, he may glide downward a quarter of a mile to the valley below. It is a beautiful sight.

The road runner has scarcely a vestige of song, his only emotional utterances being a strange whistling note, *oo-t*, ending in a loud clatter, chipper, or crackling noise made by rapidly bringing his mandibles together; and a loud *coo* given most often during the nesting season. The whistle sounds as though the breath were being drawn in when it is produced. But the *coo* seems to be an explosive utterance. Many times in the spring I have been awakened in the morning by this last peculiar song.

30. The Le Conte Thrasher

"If you want to see a bird that can *run* you must watch for the little brownish bird that's got a long sickle bill," said Charlie, my cowboy friend, with whom I had been talking about the fleet-footedness of the comical road runner. "They're the greatest dodgers and runners and hiders you ever saw. There's only one way you can catch them, and that's by chasing them down on horseback. But it's risky business trying to get one that way. Suppose your horse tumbles in a badger hole when you're chasing the bird at full speed and you land in a bunch of cholla. I knew a cowman once, over on the Whitewater, who had that happen to him. He started out full gallop and chased the bird from one bush into another. But the bird was a good runner and quick. Just when the cowman thought he had his bird, his horse stepped into a badger's hole and threw him into a cholla. He was all stuck up with dozens of prickly cholla joints; from head to foot his clothes were pinned to his skin."

After hearing this recital of the bird's running abilities from Charlie, I was anxious to get a sight of one. I shall never forget that day when I first saw my Le Conte thrasher. Almost quicker than my eye could follow him he dashed into a bush, and by the time I reached the spot I saw him speeding a hundred yards away. Like the road runner, he preferred running to flying and took wing only when hard-pressed. Since his color was so near that of the gray sands and vegetation of his range, he slipped out of sight easily. Nowhere is the Le Conte thrasher plentiful, and I watched carefully through many seasons before I felt I really knew this wary bird.

Collectors tell me that, with his powers of running and dodging, he is one of the most difficult of all birds to shoot and that the only way for the gunner to get him is on the run.

Though rather rare birds, the Le Conte thrashers are always about in greater numbers than you are aware of. Almost the only way to make a census is to count the nests of the season. I have traveled for days and have seen but one or two of these thrashers about when I well knew by signs that there were many more in the vicinity.

They generally keep pretty well to the brush-tangled washes where some protection is offered. A field of cholla cactus is sure to be sought out as the most suitable place for the nest. They will occasionally build in paloverde trees, but the cacti are always their first choice.

The nests are generally inconspicuously placed in the center of the thickly spined, branching tops of the cacti and consist of rather coarse thorny twigs. They are easily distinguished from the nests of the cactus wrens by their open tops. The inside is usually lined with vegetable wool gathered from a small woolly plant known as filago.

The female, like most of the thrashers and like the wren tit of the foothills, is a close sitter and seldom leaves the nest until the intruder is right upon her. Then she slips silently over the far side of the nest and is gone, with never a cry of alarm.

French Gilman, of Banning, California, because of his long residence on the desert, is perhaps better acquainted with the habits and mannerisms of the Le Conte thrasher than are most Western birdmen. With his permission, I am here giving in effect his words concerning the call notes and singing habits in general of this hermit bird:

My introduction to this interesting bird, *Toxostoma lecontei*, was during the summer of 1882 when with his whistling note he confirmed my earlier belief in ghosts. In a mesquite and creosote bush thicket at Whitewater Ranch on the Colorado Desert was buried a Mexican horse thief who had died with his boots on. Near this thicket I frequently wandered, though it was said to be haunted. On several occasions a whistle sent me to the ranch house to see what was wanted, but when I got there it was always to find that no one had whistled. This puzzled me until I found the noise came from the thicket, and of course it must be the Mexican ghost. This I believed until, a few days later, accident revealed to me the real whistler, a Le Conte thrasher. The note of the thrasher can be mistaken for that of no other bird. It resembles closely the whistle a man employs in calling a dog—short with rising inflection at the end. So striking is the resemblance that it is nearly impossible to distinguish one from the other. The calls are uttered at intervals of about a minute, when the bird is in the mood, and are easily imitated. If the imitation is accurate, the bird will continue answering for a long time, but care must be taken not to repeat the whistle too rapidly or he sees through the deception. In addition to the call note he has a very attractive song which resembles that of an uneducated mockingbird, though fuller and richer and pitched in a higher key.

The only drawback to the song is its infrequency, even when the birds are most abundant. You may be in their midst all day and see several pairs, but if one song rewards you it may be counted as a red-letter day. At least this has been my experience of nine years in particular. For some time I doubted the statement made by some writers that the Le Conte thrasher was a fine singer, but I was finally shown by the bird himself. While standing one evening on a highdrifted hill of white sand about two miles west of the rim of the ancient Salton Sea, I heard the sweet strains of a new bird song and began to look for the singer. I expected to find a mockingbird whose individuality had been developed by the desert solitudes and who had learned a new song. On an adjoining sandhill, perched on the exposed tip of a sand-buried mesquite, I saw the singer—a Le Conte thrasher. Perhaps environment enhanced the music, for the spot was a most lonesome, forsaken one, near an ancient Indian encampment and burial-ground, but I have heard no sweeter bird song and the memory still lingers. Since then I have heard the song a few times, but not oftener than once or twice a year, though I have frequently been among the birds. Not only do they seldom sing, but the whistling call note is not often heard. They appear to be silent, unsociable creatures, never more than a pair being found together, unless a brood of young birds and parents, and then only until the former can shift for themselves. *

Other thrashers known to the Southwestern desert area are the sage, the Bendire, the Palmer, and the crissal. The most widespread is the crissal thrasher, for it ranges over almost the whole of Arizona and New Mexico. The Bendire thrasher is a bird of southern Arizona and extreme southwestern New Mexico and adjacent Sonora. The sage thrasher is a common winter visitor to desert areas of southeastern California and southern and western Arizona. All of these birds except the sage and the Bendire thrasher have long curved beaks which are used as picks to unearth ground-dwelling insects. Although each bird has its characteristic behavior pattern, there are many habits which they share in common. All are ground feeders and have large, strong feet. Most of them are singers of rare ability; some are imitators of the songs of other birds common to the region. Dr. Elliott Coues long ago made the following observation: "There is a curious correlation of color with shape of bill, the short-billed species being the most richly colored and heavily spotted, while the bow-billed ones are very plain with no spots whatsoever on the under parts."

* M. French Gilman, "The Le Conte Thrasher," *Condor*, VI (July 1904), 95–98.

31. Gnatcatchers and Verdins

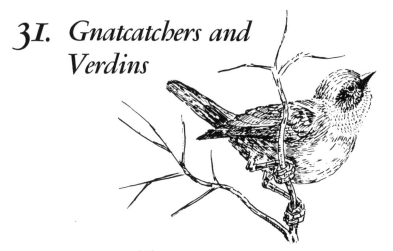

The plumbeous (lead-colored) gnat-catchers, though not the smallest of the desert birds, are surely its noisiest scolders. Their raspish song, anything but musical, is uttered with such frequency and in such a defiant tone that it always sounds as if they were berating and throwing challenges to everybody in the neighborhood.

Never still, they go from bush to bush, turning this way and that, their tails constantly wagging. They hunt in pairs; one, generally the male, takes the lead, and the other follows close by. As they move rapidly about, scolding and chattering and scanning the bushes for insect eggs, small caterpillars, and beetles, they remind us of the talkative chickadees, except that they are not quite so adept at turning themselves upside down on the branches. I have known them to utter four different notes in half as many minutes, each with its peculiar variations.

One afternoon, while walking under a large paloverde tree, I found a gnatcatcher cleaning mites from his feathers. He spread his wings outward and backward and brushed

NEST OF VERDIN
THORNY SHRUB, MOHAVE DESERT

them over the top of his tail, and then bill-scratched his breast and underparts. Hardly had he begun this before he was scratching his neck and head with his feet. This billing and scratching and brushing went on for about 15 minutes. He barely noticed my presence.

The plumbeous gnatcatchers have a sharply defined geographical range. They are found more or less all the year throughout the deserts of southeastern California and Arizona. They jealously guard their territory against the Western and black-tailed species. Occasionally one will see a pair of black-tails on plumbeous territory, but the trespassers are few, for they receive rough handling. This is especially true at nesting time. Both species of gnatcatchers are noisy scrappers. The plumbeous is generally the aggressor, and he drives out his rival at any cost of feathers.

Another tiny bird, the verdin (shown on p. 201), lives in the same region and is of the same nervous temperament and restlessness. The novice may confuse the two birds unless he learns the exact field marks that distinguish them. Both are birds with grayish or lead-colored backs and fluffy, lighter underparts. The male verdins, with their bright olive-green crowns and yellow heads, need never be mistaken for the dull-colored gnatcatcher; but the female verdin is not so easily distinguished. The yellow and green of her coat are restricted to two small patches, one on the head and one on the neck just beneath the bill, and the colors are almost always of so dull a hue as hardly to be seen when the bird is in motion.

A good time to become familiar with the verdins is during the breeding season, for you will then learn to associate them with the large retort-shaped nests which they place in the wild lavender, mesquite, and other thorny bushes, and you will see both male and female together, making it possible to compare their markings. Without appearing much disturbed, the birds will let you sit for hours under the nest while they come and go.

The nests are easy to locate, for they are large and conspicuous. Those that I have found on the Colorado Desert were almost always located in the upper crotches of the paloverde and the desert lavender bushes, which grow so plentifully along the gravelly washes and in the canyon bottoms. On the Mohave Desert, where the *Hyptis* (the correct name for the so-called wild lavender) does not grow so plentifully, the nests, like the gnatcatchers', are placed in the mesquite and cat's-claw bushes. There are generally two nests built close together, sometimes in the same bush. This pairing of nests is easy to account for when we learn that the verdins, like the canyon wrens, build roosting nests as well as breeding nests. The larger nest is the one built and occupied by the female for nesting purposes, while the smaller is built by the male and is for his sole use as sleeping quarters. After the young have been reared, the female uses her nest for the same purpose.

The verdins wherever possible utilize the material of old nests in the construction of new ones. Last winter I took down an unoccupied nest of the season and placed it under the eaves of my house, where it served as a decorative feature. When spring came, the verdins (evidently the same pair that had built it in the spring the year before) spied it and proceeded to tear it to pieces, bit by bit, and make it into a new nest. They took every twig of it back to the lavender bush and made the nest in the same branch from which I had taken it. When this nest was done, it was almost as large as my head. So many feathers and leaves were put inside and protruded from the small opening at the end that the fat nest looked as if it were going to burst.

When I returned to the desert in the autumn I found these same birds still in possession of this nest and the roosting nest that was built beside it soon after. They were getting ready for winter and were relining their old domicile. Frequent trips were made to a gully several hundred yards away, and there—probably from an old nest—great numbers of feathers and sticks were secured. The remade nests looked as good as new ones.

Generally only one bird was working at a time. When bringing in material the female verdin always paused a moment beneath the nest before going inside. Then, after fastening in place the stick or feather she had brought, she flew to a twig near by and chippered briefly.

32. Vultures

Every autumn and every spring there takes place on the Mohave Desert one of the most remarkable phenomena of bird life—the spectacular gathering of thousands of turkey vultures.* These two assemblages have probably taken place for centuries with no cessation or variance.

The autumn gathering of the birds usually takes place in early October, the spring assemblage in middle and late March. The larger of the two gatherings occurs in autumn. Then, from hundreds of miles around, the birds come in, and soon we see their great communal roosts in the cottonwood trees, especially dead ones, along the Mohave River bottoms from near Hesperia, California, to the site of old Camp Cady. In the morning before sunup the vultures are so crowded on the dead branches of the trees that their black-feathered bodies are plainly visible from a distance of half a mile. There may be hundreds of them in a single roost. Sometimes one

* *Cathartes aura septentrionalis,* from the Greek *kathartēs,* purifier; New Latin, *aura,* South American name of the bird; *septentrionalis,* northern.

large tree may hold as many as 30 or 40 birds—six to eight lined up close together on a single horizontal limb. As the sun comes up, they turn about, fluffing their feathers and stretching their wings, one at a time. It reminds one of the similar action of the California road runner. This goes on for an hour or so. After that the birds exchange positions on the trees. Then, one after another, they sluggishly take off, joining others in that slow, cyclic flight that continues without interruption all through the day.

By nine o'clock every bird is in the air in that eternal gliding that carries them around and around like autumn leaves in a slow-moving whirlwind. We see them move in ever changing circles up to heights almost beyond human sight and gradually down again. Sometimes 20 or 30 of these formations, each composed of about 60 to 100 birds, are to be seen at one time along the Mohave River's course and over the hills or low plains to the east, even as far as the Ord Mountains and the vicinity of Twentynine Palms. In any one formation, some of the birds circle clockwise, others move counterclockwise, the whole group slowly drifting now in one direction, now in another.

From all I can observe, little or no food is taken during this period. There is little enough carrion for the few that are permanent summer residents of the area in normal seasons.

Then one day, driven perhaps by hunger, the turkey vultures begin their migration flight. Lee Smith, who lives at the site of old Camp Cady on the Mohave River east of Daggett, tells of seeing in late October of 1945 such a flight of 417 turkey vultures, "all flying at low altitude dead east along the river's course as if toward the Colorado River." I myself have witnessed such migrations, but with fewer birds, headed directly south over and along the crest of the Little San Bernardino Mountains. In a few days the whole sky is cleared of birds, and except for a few stragglers not another vulture is seen until the return flight the following spring. Middle and southern Mexico apparently is their wintering place.

The turkey vulture we have on our southwestern deserts
is the same bird that is common over much of the Western
United States, but, bird of silence that it is, it seems to fit unusually well in the vast, still desert.

The name "buzzard" sometimes applied to this bird is a
rather unfortunate one, since in England this term refers to
a kind of hawk. Turkey vulture indeed seems more appro-
priate.

The first description of the turkey vulture in ornithological literature was made by the same picturesque German
traveler who described the piñon jay, Alexander Maximilian,
Prince of Wied. Of birds he saw at New Harmony, Indiana,
the type locality, he wrote:

> The turkey buzzards were seen hovering in the air, and, after
> wet weather, were often observed sitting in the sunshine, with
> outspread wings, on the highest tree. If we shot a bird, and did
> not immediately pick it up, it was sure to be devoured by these
> ravenous creatures. If the buzzards were driven away, the cun-
> ning crows supplied their place. The whole air was soon filled
> with these buzzards, hovering round and round while numbers
> of others sat together in the high trees. If we shot at them when
> flying they immediately vomited.*

Most of the turkey vultures' daytime hours are spent in
flight as they scan the land below them for carrion. The birds
are often seen singly, in pairs, or in small companies of three
or four, swinging in wide circles. Set with wings to the wind,
they soar high above the earth, hour after hour. Their manner
of flight, with expanded wings tilted slightly above horizontal
and wing tips showing an upward curve, makes the birds
easily recognizable even when flying at immense heights.

When turkey vultures are drifting or gliding, you see these
birds at their best. If you would see them at their worst, seek
them out on a shimmering, hot mid-August noon as they sit

---

* Alexander Maximilian, *Early Western Travel*, ed. R. G. Thwaites
(Glendale, Calif.: A. H. Clark & Company), XXII, 190.

C. S. PA

VULTURES

in silence on a fence post, or on the ground, before a putrid carcass, their wings partly open to help ventilate their bodies, their small red heads held somewhat drooping. They have then an appearance that is hot, stuffy, and drowsy. It is a picture of dejection that fills the observer with the fullest sense of the day's still, stifling heat; the rank, foul-smelling air that rises from the carcass augments the feeling of repugnance.

Birds with black feathers must necessarily absorb much heat as they sit in the hot sun. They have no sweat glands to aid in keeping down the body temperature. By holding their beak open and breathing hard and often, as well as by holding their wings out and puffing their feathers, the body heat is somewhat reduced.

It is surprising how soon turkey vultures appear over a spot where an animal has died. Once the carcass has been found, a crowd soon gathers; nor do they leave, if undisturbed, until they have reduced it to a skeleton. The manner in which these birds detect the presence of carrion has been a subject of frequent speculation. It is probable that the senses of both smell and sight are involved, sight being much the greater aid. Where highly putrid flesh is hidden from sight, the bird's eyes may detect a clue to its presence in the sarcophagid flies which hover about. The manner in which communication is effected between the birds which first find the carcass and others which soon gather to partake of the gruesome feast is perhaps explained by Canon Tristam's observations on the high-soaring griffon, an Old World vulture.

The griffon who first descries his quarry descends from his elevation at once. Another sweeping the horizon at a still greater distance observes his neighbor's movements and follows his course. A third, still farther removed, follows the flight of the second; he is traced by another; and so a perpetual succession is kept up so long as a morsel of flesh remains over which to consort. I can conceive no other mode of accounting for the number of Vultures which in the course of a few hours will gather over a carcass, when previously the horizon might have been scanned in vain for more than one, or at most two in sight.*

When disturbed at feeding, the turkey vultures always leave before the intruder gets too close. Several hops and several strong wing beats get them off the ground. Generally they rise and circle, watching for an opportune moment to

* *Ibis*, 1859, p. 280.

return. Vultures accustomed to eating carcasses of rabbits killed on the highways seem to lose some of their wariness and, although not running undue risks, are slower to leave and return much sooner.

In western United States the turkey vulture frequently nests in the rocky canyons of rough hill or mountain country. The one, or usually two, eggs composing the set are laid in a secluded niche upon the bare rock or earth, with sometimes a few sticks about, perhaps as an aid in keeping the eggs in position. The nest, like that of the raven, soon becomes "a place of unbearable stench" because of the befouled carrion brought in to feed the young. Once the eggs are hatched, there is always added the litter of old bones, decaying flesh, and body ejecta.

The smooth-shelled, creamy-white eggs are beautifully decorated with variformed splashes and spots of bright brown, the number of such markings varying from egg to egg. Western buzzards' eggs show on an average more brown than those of Eastern birds.

The young nestlings have a fuzzy coat of white down, and it is some time before they sprout feathers. They are fed, like young pigeons, wholly by regurgitation. The food given them is the decomposed animal matter first eaten and partially digested by the parent. While the adult bird stands upright, the nestling inserts its beak between the opened mandibles of the parent to take the regurgitated food. The feeding is a lively affair, much resembling "a tussle, both birds swaying their heads up and down and from side to side and balancing themselves by raising their wings."[*] The young birds grow rapidly. At first they are unable to swallow, and this is the reason the parent birds ram their beaks far down their gullets.

[*] A. G. Lawrence, quoted in A. C. Bent, *Life Histories of N. A. Birds of Prey,* Bull. 167, U.S. National Museum, p. 16.

Thomas H. Jackson, writing in *Bird-Lore* about the young birds, says:

Young Turkey Vultures at a very early age display more intelligence than the young of any other raptores with which I am familiar. Their eyes are open from the first, and in less than a week they move about their home, hiss vigorously, and show considerable alertness, but do not seem to have any fear at that age. At two weeks they show a great increase in size and weight but otherwise have changed little in appearance. They soon resent being disturbed and snap at the intruder, and as they get older become quite pugnacious, rushing at one with extended wings, uttering continually their loud hissing sound, which comes the nearest to any vocal performance I have ever heard from these birds. Their beaks are quite sharp and capable of injuring an unprotected hand.

On being approached they retire to the farthest corner of their den and there disgorge the contents of the stomach or crop.*

The turkey vulture has no song or cry, since it has no syringeal muscles. When cornered, as at the nest site in a cave, the bird sometimes utters strange hissing, wheezy noises. J. R. Pemberton, a trusted observer of birds, recorded another sound. He writes:

On August 9, 1924, while resting on the summit of a ridge of the Elk Hills, Kern County, California, an adult Turkey Vulture circled close to me a number of times. It distinctly gave voice to a low-pitched nasal whine, slowly repeated at intervals of about three seconds and greatly resembling the whine of a small puppy. The beak was not opened during the emission of the sound. The bird was close enough to me that I am positive the note came from it; in addition the extreme barrenness of the ground at the spot precluded the possibility of the sound coming from another animal. I am unable to find any reference to any sound emitted by this bird, in any literature at hand other than the well-known hiss usually given as the only sound known to be made by it.†

* *Bird-Lore*, V, 184–87.
   † "Voice of the Turkey Vulture," *Condor*, XXVII (January 1925), 38.

There are seemingly no places too remote for these birds. I see them circling in the cool winds above San Gorgonio and San Jacinto peaks, or sailing in majestic sweep in the high, heated air currents that emanate in summer from furnacelike Death Valley. Wherever there is death, there, too, is the turkey vulture, waiting for the carcass. These birds never attack the living. Both their claws and beak are structurally too weak; moreover, they possess none of the daring of the hawks and falcons.

I have never seen turkey vultures persecuted or disturbed by other birds. They are "peaceable, harmless," never offering violence to any living animal, and for the most part they are respected in return. The raven, carrion feeder too, would probably fare as well if it did not meddle with other birds' eggs and nestlings. Of all creatures the buzzard must fear only man. This is unfortunate, for here we have a bird of distinct value doing what few other creatures do—clearing the countryside of the dead. Few other birds exhibit such gliding and graceful maneuvering.

The turkey vulture, like all scavengers, should be encouraged about the habitations of man. Nothing rotten, no carrion escapes his attention. The generic name *Cathartes* means "the purifier," and wherever he is, he becomes the most valuable sanitary officer of the area.

I have seen the smaller, black-headed vultures (*Coragyps atratus*) only occasionally in southern Arizona and far northern Sonora, but southward in more humid, cactus- and acacia-covered Sonora and Sinaloa they are common about every village and ranch. The denser human population means a greater number of carcasses of goats, cats, dogs, and burros. Unlike the red-headed turkey vultures, which range much farther to the north (even to southwestern Canada), the black vultures are seldom migratory. At times flocks move about, but the periods are not regular nor is the direction of movement necessarily north-south. Such territorial changes as occur are probably dependent almost wholly on the necessity for finding new sources of food.

In their funereal, dusty-black feathers, black vultures are only attractive in flight. The feather-bare neck and small head are gloomy black, the skin often wrinkled. Compared with the turkey vulture's tail, the black vulture's is quite short and broad, barely extending beyond the closed wings. The wings, too, are shorter, but little less capable organs of flight. Wingspread of the black vulture is about four and a half feet, compared with the near-six-foot wingspread of the turkey vulture. On the underside of the black vulture's wings, and seen in flight, is a white to silver-gray area, which serves as a good mark of identification.

As with other vultures, these birds are scavengers. Their hooked beaks are well adapted for rending holes in carcasses. The eyes and mouth of the dead animal are first attacked; the flesh is then extracted through openings in the skin. The birds next insert their whole head and neck and, if the carcass is that of a horse, burro, or large ruminant, eventually the entire body inside the large abdominal cavity. At times of easy feeding, they may eat until they are so heavy that they can scarcely leave the ground in flight.

No animal is long dead before the vultures congregate. Often the village dogs feed alongside the birds. If the dogs are large, the birds usually wait until the dogs have finished. If the vultures crowd in too soon, the dogs often growl or snap at them. The birds then spring up for a moment, only to gather near again and patiently wait.

Although they are, on the whole, peaceful toward other birds, among themselves black vultures are not wholly amiable at feeding time. They push and frequently attack one another, "fighting with their claws or heels, striking like a cock with open wings," all the while making sniffing or hissing sounds while the mouth is held wide open. These sounds are like those made when a red-hot poker is thrust into cold water.

The birds are incapable of making true vocal noises because they do not possess the voice box or syrinx of singing birds.

Black vultures drink a great deal if water is available, and are even fond of bathing. I once saw a morning gathering of about 500 birds on the flat sandy banks of the Mayo River near Navajoa, Mexico. At any given time about one-third of the flock was in the shallow water, the birds drenching their feathers and then walking in the sun to spread wide their wings and preen. They paid little attention to me and I was able to approach very near.

The one or two eggs of the black vulture, pale green or cream-colored with spots of brown, are laid upon the ground under bushes or in a cavity of rock or tree. As with the turkey vultures, the parents feed the fuzzy-feathered young by regurgitation. Almost two months pass before they leave the nest; not before three months are they able to fly well.

33. The Piñon Jay

In the year 1833 there appeared in the upper reaches of the Missouri River a unique bachelor traveler. He was a German, dressed in "white slouch hat, a black velvet coat, rather rusty from long service, and probably the greasiest pair of trousers that ever encased princely legs." This was Maximilian, Prince of Wied, a man of broad culture, well versed in the natural sciences and appreciative of good art. Several years before, he had left his ancestral home in Germany, with a desire to see the distant wilds of North America and especially their Indian inhabitants. He had embarked on an ambitious journey that took him down the Ohio and up the Missouri River to its junction with the Yellowstone in Montana. As he traveled, he kept accurate notes, and he had with him an artist of extraordinary ability to record the Indian costumes and the beauties of the country he visited. The account he wrote of his journey, together with a marvelous atlas of colored plates, appeared under the title *Reise in das Inners Nord Amerika.* It passed through several editions in French and German and at last there appeared an English translation by H. E. Lloyd, edited with notes and an introduction by R. G. Thwaites.

It was Maximilian who first described in ornithological
literature the turkey buzzard. He also discovered and named
that unique bird, the piñon jay.

"Opposite the mouth of the Maria River," he says, "we
saw a herd of eight antelopes and several others at other
places; likewise Virginia deer, and many birds, especially jays
and sparrow hawks. On Maria River, in particular, were various kinds of birds in high trees. Here Mr. Mitchel had shot
a blue-headed jay which was hopping on the ground."* In a
footnote he adds: "This bird, which is nearly allied to the jay,
or the roller, has not yet been mentioned by either Townsend
or Audubon. In the form of the bill, its figure, and mode of
living, it much resembles the nutcracker; only the nostrils are
not covered with bristles, like those of the jay and crow, but
lie quite free on the fore part of the skin of the nose. The
angulus mentalis comes out further than in *nucifraga*.† As
this bird seems to form a new genus, I call it, from the above-
mentioned peculiarity, *Gymnorhinus cyanocephalus*."‡

The bird to this day is sometimes called Maximilian's jay,
but much more often it is referred to as the piñon jay or blue
crow. As its first vernacular name implies, it is a constant
resident of the desert's dwarf pine forests, being widely distributed in arid parts of Utah and Nevada, west to eastern
California; east and south through Arizona, New Mexico, and
Baja California. It extends its habitat beyond the range of
the piñon tree to wild and arid parts of Idaho, central Montana, and northwestern Nebraska. It is sometimes errone-

---

* R. G. Thwaites (ed.), *Maximilian's Travels*, p. 169.

† *Nucifraga*, the Clark's crow or nutcracker.

‡ *Gymnorhinus*, Greek for "naked nose" because of the hairless nostrils; *cyanocephalus*, Greek for "blue head." The general body color is
dull blue, pale on the abdomen but deeper blue on head and neck and
darkest on the crown.

ously called a crow because of its crowlike manner of walking and its behavior.

The piñon jay is a social bird; almost without exception it is found in flocks, small to large. These birds nest in scattered or even close proximity to one another. Feeding, too, is done in companies, either in trees or on the ground, the members of the flock keeping up a continual hubbub of scolding and cawing notes. These jays roam widely over the country, the birds in the rear of the flock rising, anxiously calling, and flying partly in gliding manner beyond those in the front ranks. This leapfrog flying goes on for hours at a time. Especially is this noticeable if the flock is a large one, say of several thousand birds. I recently witnessed such a restless company on the move. There were many stragglers coming up from the rear, cawing loudly and making an awful fuss as if they had been neglectfully and shamefully left behind. This large flock took three-quarters of an hour to pass the site of my camp. Returning to the place of this spectacular flight a month later, I saw not a single bird.

In the midst of a leisurely moving bird flock, it is especially interesting to hear their many kinds of call notes. There is the note of anxiety, and every now and then one without the tone of urgency. And last, there is the gossipy chatter and jabber. A song in the true sense they never have.

At nesting time, these birds scatter and settle down for a short time. They are then often seen in pairs or companies of three or four in the piñon and Joshua tree forests, and the few guttural notes take on a new quality. They sometimes nest again and again in the same locality or even in the same trees; if they change the site there is always much preliminary exploring, hours and hours being spent at it. The nest, when complete, is a bulky one, generally saddled on a horizontal branch some distance out from the body of the tree, and placed three to eight or even ten feet from the ground. As a rule, it is not particularly well concealed. It is made of twigs and dry grass and lined with hair and feathers, and, in the sheep country, often with wool. Sometimes as many as a hundred nests may be located in close proximity. J. C. Braley, writing in *Condor,* sums up his experience with nesting piñon jays as follows:

Some of the Piñon Jay females, on being flushed from their sets of eggs, got clear out of the country and they did not come back under twenty minutes to half an hour. Two females were lifted off their eggs by me and these eggs were only slightly incubated. Still others came back into the nest tree and stayed close around, calling continually. At no time did the male bird come in when the female called. The males usually fed in a large flock one-fourth to three-fourths of a mile distant, sometimes in one direction and again in another, from the nests. On coming in with food, a male usually perched on the top of a tree forty to fifty feet distant from the nest and called the female off to be fed. While being fed, she made a screeching series of calls similar to those of a young bird and continually fluttered her wings, and if the male flew to another tree, she followed him, begging for more food. Having finished feeding, the male flew back to the feeding ground and the female flew directly to the nest, making it very easy to find. The feeding was closely observed and was solely by regurgitation, an unusual procedure for any of the crow or jay family. The female has a call when near her nest that closely resembles *krook, krook.* The male has a peculiar whistle-like note when one is near a completed nest and a very jaylike note when the female is disturbed from her nest.

. . . The Piñon Jay colonizes during the nesting season: sometimes three occupied nests were found in one tree.[*]

The food varies much with the season. When the piñon nuts begin to ripen and fall from the cones in mid-September, the birds feed heavily upon these rich morsels for several weeks. Other wild nuts as well as fruits and seeds are eaten as they appear. Insects are sought for on the ground and even in the air. Several times I have seen these sharp-beaked jays dexterously snapping up flying grasshoppers in mid-air.

[*] "Nesting of the Piñon Jay in Oregon," *Condor,* XXXIII (January 1931), 29.

However, they were not as adept at this as the desert mockingbird is. They generally first flew upward from their observation point on a yucca, then, after hovering a moment, descended rapidly to snap up the grasshopper. Search for other foods sometimes draws flocks of birds far out on the sagebrush plains and grasslands and even into coniferous forests other than those of piñon-occupied mountains.

Water holes are visited daily if possible. Even if the flock is a large one, only a few birds will drink at one time. The rest, as sentries, will warily move about in the nearby trees or bushes, jabbering to one another. Under these circumstances, it may take a flock of several hundred birds an hour or more to drink.

C. E. Aiken reported the following curious flight behavior of the piñon jay at Fort Garland in October 1874:

I saw probably a hundred of these birds in a dense rounded mass, performing evolutions high in the air, which I had never before known them to do; sweeping in wide circles, shooting straight ahead, and wildly diving and whirling about, in precisely the same manner that our common wild pigeons do when pursued by a hawk. This singular performance, with intervals of rest in the piñons behind the fort, was kept up for about two hours, apparently for no other purpose than exercise.*

Does not this remind one of the play-flight of ravens?

One of the best places to observe the piñon jay is in the Joshua tree forests. They often alight and sit for moments at a time on the pinnacles of the stiff-needled branches. Unless one is very quiet, the birds are almost certain to keep at a distance. They show great wariness in spite of their inquisitive nature. I have seldom seen them come right into camp as does the Clark's nutcracker or the Canada jay.

Few people have taken the trouble to get acquainted with

---

* In Henry W. Henshaw, *Report upon Ornithological Collections Made in Portions of Nevada, Utah, California, Colorado, New Mexico and Arizona During the Years 1872, 1873, and 1874 (Wheeler Survey)*, p. 333.

this interesting bird. To many people its piñon country home holds few attractions; water is scarce, the country is generally rocky and sparsely settled, and even game is scarce. To me no wilderness land is more charming. Its genial sunny climate, its bright skies, its quiet and friendly loneliness are most appealing. Summer days are warm but not too warm in this high desert hinterland; nor are autumn, spring, and winter days without supreme attraction.

34. The Raven

I once met a grizzled old prospector out in the Amboy country, traveling along a one-track stony road in "a glorified buckboard and three-burro outfit." He was headed southwest, he said, "to look for diamonds." "If you can find a volcanic cinder cone," he said, "go to its exact center and then head due southwest for exactly 20 miles, no more, no less, and you're sure to find *real* diamonds—providing there are none of those ravens sitting 'round when you get there. I almost had diamonds twice but for them awful, evil birds. They're against your luck every time—they're the devil's own children. Every time I see one crossing over my head, I say to it, 'Curses be on ye.'"

A strange notion, you say, but not more so than many foolish conceptions that have been held through the ages concerning the raven. Alexander Wilson in his classic nine-volume work, *American Ornithology*, devotes several pages to equally queer superstitions. Indian lore, too, is full of references to the evil role of the raven. He is designated as a bird of prophetic evil to be despised or feared. It is an inheritance of ill will he cannot seem to live down.

The raven is always a sleek-looking bird, for its body is a lustrous black with bluish-green or purplish reflections.* On the nape of the neck there is a grayish-white patch, but it is concealed. This hind neck patch is whiter and more extended in desert ravens than in ravens west of the desert divide. In both sexes the plumage is otherwise identical.

In comparison with all his near relations the raven is remarkably large; in fact, he is the largest of all passerine (sparrowlike) birds. Sometimes he is mistaken when in flight for a turkey vulture, although his head and neck are not bare, nor does he hold his wings definitely upward and teeter or rock from side to side when soaring, like the vulture. He should not be mistaken for a crow either. Crows are smaller birds and are generally seen flying in sizable flocks. Ravens are, as a general rule, seen singly or more often in pairs or small groups. Perhaps the most conspicuous difference is in the manner of flight. The crow flaps its wings almost continually and seldom sails with outstretched motionless pinions. The raven often "soars in the buoyant and well-sustained manner of certain Raptores," although a flapping flight is not uncommon. The raven's call note is a coarse *cor-ac, cor-ac;* the note of the crow is much more vehement, a distinct *caw* often repeated, especially in flight.

On the California deserts there are no crows, with possibly a few vagrants in Death Valley, Imperial Valley, and adjacent Borrego Valley. Crows keep close to the more moist interior and coastal areas and do not even venture into the cottonwood bottoms and cultivated fields along the Colorado and the Mohave rivers.

---

* The brilliant young Bavarian zoologist, Dr. Johann George Wagler (*System Avium*, 1827), first described and gave to this raven its scientific name, *Corvus corax sinuatus.* The subspecific name *sinuatus* refers to the notch on the tommia or cutting edge of the bill.

The Western raven is widespread, but locally distributed over our most arid deserts and throughout the rainy coastal belt of the high mountains of western United States and over almost the whole of Mexico. Ravens are unusually abundant on the coastal islands of southern California.

The raven is an unusually conspicuous bird of our deserts, particularly the Mohave Desert. There it finds the least persecution from man, that great archenemy of wildlife, and wide areas of open terrain for extensive foraging; moreover, there are rocks among which it can locate its large stick nest.

Along the highways, on railroad right-of-ways, around corrals and water holes and springs where cattle come to drink, in open creosote plains and Joshua tree forests, you will see this bird. Dr. Joseph Grinnell once spoke of the raven as the tramp of the desert railways, because so many of these birds fly or walk up and down the tracks to feed on the scraps of food and other refuse thrown from the trains, as well as on the animals, from snakes to mammals, killed by the trains.

Ravens, it is said, mate for life and are hence often seen in pairs. In late spring, summer, and early autumn, one sometimes sees small groups of four or five or even six, but these as a rule are family groups not yet broken up. About the time of the mating season assemblages of many birds may be observed in pastures, along streams, about cattle pens or feeding troughs. French Gilman, custodian of the Death Valley National Monument in 1933–34, tells of seeing as many as 40 ravens gathered about the feeding station he maintained to attract wild animals near the overflow ponds a half-mile below Furnace Creek Ranch. On the road between Victorville and Lucerne Dry Lake, I once saw 17 of the birds sitting in close formation on the ground beside the highway. As I slowly approached, they flew up, but then reassembled not far away. This was an unusual number to see in the open desert at one time. It was in October, long after the mating season. There was no common source of food.

Ravens are rare birds in the Salton Sea Basin. The few one sees probably have nests in the steep faces of the box canyons that twist and branch through the conglomerates and clays that make up those charming but unfortunately named formations called the Indio Mud Hills.

The Shoshone Indians called the raven *hih*, the Paiutes, *ad-dah*. Most of the European peoples knew one form or other of the raven and their names were all onomatopoeic, that is, imitations of the raven's call note. Thus the old Anglo-Saxons called the bird *hraefn*, the old High Germans, *hraben*, the Greeks, *korax*. The Latin *corvus* is from the root *kar*, "to sound," and is at least akin to the Greek *korax*.

The common note of the raven heard to best advantage as it flies low overhead is, as noted before, a coarse, guttural, but sonorous *cor-ac*. Another note is sometimes given about the nest. Before storms there is still another, apparently fearful note.

Roland Case Ross, writing in *Condor*, tells of the peculiar notes he heard during the mating season:

While on the north end of Catalina Island April 6 to 9, 1925, I was enabled to observe at leisure some of the breeding antics of the Western Raven (*Corvus corax sinuatus*). A large flock that was gathered there gave daily aerial and vocal exhibitions. The most striking effect was produced by the vocal abilities of these usually croaking, growling dignitaries. When a flock of some numbers would be playing in the air in a general sort of melee, a high-pitched clamorous cawing, very crow-like, was the usual thing. Lower voices were heard, in the quality and burring utterance of the nutcracker. Single pairs gave rapid runs (on an upward scale) that had a ringing quality of wooden nature, like castanets, and were musical enough to remind one of a xylophone.

Another peculiar sound was made in a number of instances by a bird when completing the "roll." Upon reaching upright position such birds made a sharp "pugh" very like a cork drawn from a bottle. My first impression was that it was the result of a certain wing-flash in gaining position; but later, birds in ordinary flight gave the same note, so I concluded it was vocal. Another puzzle was the "whiff whiff" of steady flying birds. It was so strong and distinct a sound that a single bird flying down the valley awakened me on two different mornings by this sound when at a considerable distance. Mr. M. W. deLaubenfels expressed himself at the time as thinking this was a volitional effort, as numbers of times a pair of birds would go overhead and only one would be giving the sound. Could it be a sexual characteristic?*

In early spring during the mating season the raven is an amazing flier, a performer of all sorts of acrobatic tricks. To see these usually dour birds turn clown is a spectacle never to be forgotten. One stunt that is always exciting to watch is the tumble or "roll." The bird descends rapidly with legs down-stretched, then suddenly and with great ease turns halfway over, only a moment later to roll himself back into an upright position. This performance is repeated again and again. There are also games of tag and mock jousts. All this curious behavior is accompanied by an astonishing variety of animated and noisy croaks, chuckles, gruesome sounds, and even half-attempts at singing.

"Several years ago," says Wilson C. Hanna, "about the month of March, I saw a party of ravens on the side of a steep hill south of Victorville. The hill was not high and there were probably fifty or more ravens gathered there, most of them being perched near the top as if to witness the fancy flights of their companions. One, two, or even half a dozen of the birds would fly from their perch and go through fancy flying stunts before their friends, circling, swooping, flying upside down, flying fast, and flying slow—each seeming to do its best to outdo the others. The flyers would be returning to the perch all the time, and others would take off as if to say to the others that their flying was nothing, *"Just watch me,"* and they would go through their best work. I wish that you could have seen the performance and I hope that I may again have such a pleasure."

When after much searching the right spot for the aerie is located, the pair start building the nest. A bulky, deep-cupped affair it is, eight or ten to 20 inches high and 16 to 18 inches broad. On the Mohave Desert gray sticks of creosote bush

* "Field Notes on the Raven," *Condor*, XXVII (1925), 172.

and *Lycium* are used. Once I found a nest with the leg bones of jack rabbits laid in among the creosote sticks. The nest lining is often bits of hairy cowhide taken from carcasses, sheep or rabbit wool, shredded cottonwood bark, and occasionally grass.

The nest is generally placed high upon an almost inaccessible shaded ledge, but sometimes it is built on rock shelves not more than 12 feet from the ground. For many years I have camped from time to time below such a low-placed nest. Each year it is occupied anew and fresh material is added. The birds always drop a great clutter of sticks just below on the ground. Sometimes there are so many of these sticks that I have used them to build my small campfire. Ravens are not averse to appropriating and making over to their needs the last year's nest of a red-tailed hawk, or of taking over the site of a falcon's choice. Once settled, the ravens meet no opposition or persecution from the original builders. The occupied nest is generally smelly and often alive with fleas. If the unoccupied nest is disturbed or, sometimes, if the birds are aware that it has been found, they may temporarily abandon it, but it is quite certain they will return later to deposit their eggs. In the San Bernardino Valley they are known to nest among the rocks of the noisy quarry on Slover Mountain. The blasting and the noise of workmen and nearby trains seem to disturb them little, if at all.

A full set of eggs numbers three to seven. The base color of the eggs is pale green, olive, or even gray with peppery markings, streaks, brushlike markings, blotches, and figures of brown or purplish-brown. The egg size is about that of a young pullet. After the set is complete, the parent birds incubate it in turns for about three weeks. If a female is on the nest, the male frequently perches nearby on a rock, watching for intruders. If one comes, he flies about and past the aerie, uttering a low note of alarm, and the alerted female slips off the nest.

The young, awkward and hungry, are in the nest about a month. During this period the old birds are almost continually hunting. Soon after daylight you see them flying low and with great deliberation, their heads moving from side to side as they search for wild mice, young rabbits, nests with eggs, or carrion.

A great source of food for the raven are the rabbits found in the early morning after being run over by automobiles during the night. In his search for food the raven does not hesitate to rob the nests of other birds. No eggs are too small, not even hummingbird eggs. Often in spring we see the raven harried by pairs, more often by flocks, of small birds flying about him, scolding and furiously venting their anger. He pays no attention to such pygmy annoyers, but flies deliberately on his way.

Attacked by the larger birds, he moves with much more caution. Recently we saw a raven worried by a pair of sparrow hawks whose nest on a cliff ledge he may have just robbed. The small falcons were making sharp dashes at him. Often, after rapidly descending, they almost rode on his back. Then the raven would turn a half-flop, attempting to ward off the attack, and adroitly right himself when the hawks came menacingly near. Several times in an effort to thwart them he turned completely over. The sparrow hawks kept right after him until they had driven him out of their domain.

Wilson C. Hanna sent me the following observation on the relation between ravens and the golden eagle:

Early one spring I noticed that the Golden Eagles were on hand at Slover Mountain and about ready to lay the eggs of the year. I also noticed that a pair of Ravens were showing much interest in the rocky point of the mountain near the eagles' nest and that they resented having the eagles in the vicinity. The ravens would swoop at the eagles while they were perched on the rocks and make life so unpleasant that they would fly away. The ravens took after the eagles as they flew away in much the same way that small birds attack the ravens or large hawks. Both the ravens and eagles were noticed on several different days, and always with the ravens resenting the presence of the eagles. The outcome was the eagles did not use their nest that season, and I believe the ravens also failed to nest on the mountain that year.

The white-necked or desert raven (*Corvus cryptoleucus*) is so small for a raven that it may be mistaken for a large crow. Its voice is a deep, hoarse-voiced *crannk, crannk* or *quark, quark*. It was given the specific name *cryptoleucus* (Greek, hidden-white) because of the basal white portion of the neck feathers. These are noticed only when they are raised or ruffled by strong gusts of wind. The beak is comparatively heavier and shorter than that of the common American raven seen on deserts farther north.

These birds are at times abundant in the low warm deserts of southeastern Arizona, and in arid parts of Arizona, New Mexico, western Texas, and north-central Mexico. In pre-railroad buffalo days they were also found in Colorado, western Kansas, and western Nebraska. They are usually found in flocks, sometimes in congregations of almost unbelievable numbers, especially at roosting time.

35. *Woodpeckers*

For many years it has been my custom to name my numerous temporary desert camps in honor of the first bird I have seen after arrival. Generally I have chosen to use the generic name of the bird rather than the vernacular one; thus there is Camp Asio, where I came upon a pair of long-eared owls, and Camp Salpinctes, where I saw a pair of rock wrens busy nest building. Occasionally I name a camp in reference to some unique feature. Thus it was that I named a camp site Camp Precipice and more recently identified a place as Camp Tempus; and here are the details.

The site I had chosen for the night was a most picturesque one on the borders of a wild, dry arroyo, overlooking the broad Mohave. Besides some low scrub junipers and an attractive scattering of other desert shrubs, there was a great host of the desert variety of Whipple's yucca, some in bloom and some in fruit. The sun had just gone down; deep carmine stains were lingering on the pale sky. A steady soft breeze from the high San Gabriel Mountains was sweeping down. The campfire had been started; its woodsy odors were in the air and the meal was in preparation when there sounded the howls and barks of coyotes hunting. The animals seemed so near that my companion and I rushed out into an open space thinking that we might actually see the serenading dogs. We weren't that lucky, but we enjoyed the concert just the same, and while we stood there listening, I heard, so I thought, the regular ticking of a clock. Neither of us had a watch, but the ticking went on and on, holding our attention so that we momentarily forgot about the coyotes. Could it be some insect stridulating, some wood-boring beetle larva or rodent working its jaws? We listened, but no solution to the mystery presented itself.

We were standing beside a clump of yuccas from which four fruit-laden flower stalks pointed some ten feet upward. "There's your clock," my companion suddenly exclaimed, and reaching over, he pointed to a long, semidetached, paper-thin, dried chaffy scale or bract beating in the wind against the stalk from which it was partly torn. Every time it whirled around it clicked in perfect tempo. Although we listened and watched for a full five minutes there was never a break, never a variation. Several times in the night I woke up to hear our natural clock beating off the half-seconds. A second camp was made there a week later and the queer timepiece measured the moments as before; and so we christened the place Camp Tempus, from the Latin *tempus*, time.

There were, however, other things besides the coyote cries and the "vegetable clock" that captured our attention at Camp Tempus. The following morning I saw a noisy family of cactus woodpeckers, and found also in a nearby yucca stem the excavation in pith that had been their home.

The cactus woodpecker is truly a desert bird. Nowhere is this bird found beyond the desert's borders. For the most part we may say, too, that it is the only breeding species of woodpecker in the area it inhabits. Even in the desert, however, it is not found everywhere; its range is restricted to areas of scanty trees, and brush, "where diggable woody stems and trunks" are of sufficient diameter to allow for nesting excavations. I have never found it in the monotonous creosote bush basins of the Mohave or in the sand dune areas near Yuma, such places being wholly unsuited to its nesting habits. Where small trees such as smoke trees, desert willow, and cat's-claw grow along the broad sandy washes that lead rushing torrents of cloudburst waters from the rock-choked mouths of mountain canyons, where tree yuccas, agaves, and junipers dot the detrital slopes of barrancas and mesas, this bird is most at home. A good neighbor he is, often shaming his human neighbors by his diligence.

If on the desert you see a small woodpecker with upper parts broadly and distinctly barred with black and white, it is certain to be one of the ladderback woodpeckers, as the desert folks often call him. The male has a distinctive red head-cap.

At least 15 forms of this species are known. Of these, two occur in southwestern United States and Lower California, the remainder in the mainland of Mexico and areas south to Honduras. *Dryobates scalaris symplectus,* the form called the Texas woodpecker, is found in southeastern Colorado, west and central Texas, and nearby Mexico. The form *D. scalaris cactophilus,* called the cactus ladderback woodpecker, is the one specifically treated in this chapter. Their behavior is quite similar. According to the American Ornithologists' Union's 1931 *Check-List of North American Birds,* the cactus ladderback ranges from "central western Texas through New Mexico and Arizona to extreme northeastern Lower California and southeastern California, north to extreme southern Nevada and southwestern Utah and south to northern Durango."

Usually one is first apprised of the presence of the ladderback by its single high-pitched note, *"ts chik,"* most earnestly given. Next you see him inching his way along a tree limb or flying with the strong wing up to a yucca stalk or dead juniper "snag." Once in a while you catch him, in search of insects, scratching on the ground at the base of a tall cactus plant.

The hearing is very acute, as it is in all the woodpeckers. Absolute quiet, as well as slow movement on the part of the observer, is essential if he wishes to make close observations. Except during the nesting season and a short time thereafter, the birds are solitary, shy, and retiring, and were it not for the sharp, squeaky notes occasionally given as the birds fly or alight, one might miss them. For a short period during spring they drum rapidly on dry wood with their chisel-like beaks. Some ornithologists think this is an attempt to test the suitability of the wood for nest excavation.

The bill work of this small woodpecker is seen on many cactus stems, tall agaves, and tree yucca limbs. He occasionally works in the dense wood of mesquite and screw bean or the softer wood of cottonwood or willow. Many of the excavations, wherever found, are shallow, abortive ones yielding neither food nor nesting cavities. Like his cousin, the Texas ladderback, he sometimes gouges cavities in fence posts or telegraph poles. Go along the line of the Southern Pacific Railroad in the Colorado Desert area east of the San Gorgonio Pass, and you can see where many of the poles have been drilled into. In some of these poles there are as many as three or four cavities. It is a situation that presents a real maintenance problem to the railroad.

The nest cavity I found at Camp Tempus in a yucca flower stalk was about five feet from the ground. A neat circular aperture an inch and a half in diameter led into a flasklike cavity fully 12 inches deep. Few ladder-back nest cavities are as deep as this. There was no nest lining; the soft pith was no doubt sufficient in itself.

Another nest, this one with three young in it, I found in an agave stalk near Rockhouse Canyon on the Colorado Desert in mid-May. It was 28 inches above the ground. I had come along the trail with my pack donkey, and had sat down upon a rock. A clump of agaves was not more than ten feet away, and from somewhere in the vicinity I heard faint squeaks and hissing noises. Suddenly a ladderback wood-pecker slipped up, perched a moment on one of the agave stalks, sidled around it, and disappeared. "Oh, a nest with young in it," I said, and, sure enough, on the opposite side of the stalk I found the opening. As I looked into the hole, the parent bird hastily popped out, disturbed by the noise. I had a small metal mirror with me, and, using this to direct light into the cavity, I could just see the upstretched heads of four two-thirds-grown birds. The cavity could not have been more than seven or eight inches deep. I soon retired to a distance and for half an hour watched the parent birds bring-ing food.

Sometimes they came just to check. Once a red-tailed hawk appeared. The parent woodpeckers seemed agitated for the moment, then soon went on with the feeding.

When I last visited my old friend Cabot Xerxa at Two Bunch Palms, he called my attention to a birdhouse he had made of sawed pieces of the leaf stem of the Washingtonia palm. He made it to attract other birds, but a little ladder-back moved in first and occupied it at night. The bird did not like the conventional man-made door opening, so he con-structed another to his own liking with his chisel-like beak. The birdhouse seemed more fitted to family life with only one door hole, so Mr. Xerxa closed the larger man-made opening; whereupon the male ladderback went out and found himself a mate. A family was reared to maturity.

The cactus woodpecker lays from two to six eggs; the usual clutch is four or five. They are pure white, more or less shiny, and somewhat oval in form. The young are probably hatched naked, in true woodpecker manner, but the young birds when leaving the nest are well feathered. Those I saw at Camp Tempus I judged to be several weeks out of the nest.

The feather markings were much like those of the adult birds. The scarlet crown patch of the male birds was clearly evident against the black of other parts of the head and nape.

The food of the cactus woodpecker is not essentially different from that of its near cousins, the Nuttall's and Texas woodpeckers. Wood-boring beetle larvae, which it procures from dead and dying trees, especially from mesquite and ironwood which grow along the sand washes, and from willow and cottonwood trees about springs, are the principal fare. Quite a lot of foraging is done in low cactus bushes and on the ground, where it picks up ants, caterpillars, and occasionally a few seeds.

I have seen three other species of woodpecker in desert situations. One of the fairly common species of the upper yellow-pine belt of the San Jacinto Mountains is the southern white-headed woodpecker (*Xenopicus albolarvatus gravirostris*). In the winter of 1915 when I taught the little 12-pupil school at Palm Springs, California, a bird of this species spent the winter there. The children often watched him as he flew up and propped himself with tail and feet on the telegraph pole that stood in front of the school. Near the top of the square pole there was a hole into which the bird often poked his head. At times he went entirely inside. After that season I never saw the bird again.

The ground-feeding, red-shafted flicker we occasionally saw at Palm Springs, too. Although not typically a desert species, it frequents wooded desert washes and rocky piñon and juniper country and sometimes builds nests in tree yuccas of the desert uplands.

During spring migration small flocks of the Lewis woodpecker (*Asyndesmus lewisii*) make short stays among the scattered small trees of the piñon and Joshua tree forests of the high desert mountains. I remember one small band which spent a full week in late March in the Little San Benardino Mountains. The black-backed, gray-bibbed, and rose-bellied birds were expert at catching insects in flight. Like small crows they flew, making direct sallies from their watching posts on the dead piñons to snap up the insects, much as the flycatchers do. They were a noisy lot and whiled away much time in playful flights from one treetop to another. They remained in a very restricted area the whole time. Once a California woodpecker came near and he was promptly herded out of the territory they had temporarily chosen as their own.

There are two other woodpeckers every desert visitor should know—the gilded flicker and the Gila woodpecker. Both are birds of the giant cactus country and in the trunks of the succulent trees they excavate their burrows and often construct their nests. The gilded flicker (*Colaptes chrysoides*) gets its name from the yellow of the underside of the wings and tail. There is no scarlet crescent on the nape of the male, as in the northern flicker, which it somewhat resembles. On the breast are large round spots of black. Its habits are in general those of the red-shafted flicker.

The Gila woodpecker (*Centurus uropygialis*) during the breeding season is usually seen in the giant cactus areas but at other times it may inhabit the willow and cottonwood thickets of river bottoms such as are found along the Gila River of Arizona and the Colorado River. It is resident in extreme southern Nevada southward and along the west coast of Mexico to Jalisco. It has a crown patch of bright red and a yellow belly. The head, neck, and under parts are a "dirty gray," and the back, wings, and rump are finely but conspicuously barred with black. The characteristic phainopepla-like note, a clear *hu-it, hu-it,* often calls attention to the bird's presence before it is seen.

36. Desert Hummingbirds

Some years ago in a desert town, I became acquainted with a likable boy whose father had the multiple distinction of being the town's druggist, undertaker, coroner, and owner of the village graveyard.

"If he'd been a doctor he could have taken care of us folks completely from the cradle to the grave," said one of his townsmen.

That summer I invited the young man to join me on a botanical collecting trip on the desert side of the San Jacinto Mountains, and he promised to join me on a July Sunday morning at the railway station in Riverside.

On the day of our departure I learned from the morning paper that the village where the boy lived had been practically wiped out by fire, his father's drugstore and undertaking business included.

"Surely," I thought, "I'll never see that boy today." However, I met the train, and there he was with knapsack and blankets.

"What else was there to do but come?" he said. "The town's burned down; we lost about everything we had. Dad said, 'This is a good time for the whole family to go on a vacation.' So he left this morning on a fishing trip; Ma's gone to see her friends in the city, and I'm here to go with you and stay as long as I please."

The brilliance of the boy's red blankets intrigued me the moment I saw them. Their unusual quality was so evident that I was curious to know their origin. When we camped under the desert pines that evening, I asked him about them.

"You see," said Bob, "my father is the coroner. One time several trainloads of Chinese were being taken east to Kansas City to work on the rail lines. Two of the men died en route and Dad had to take care of the bodies, which were carried out of the train in blankets. Since no Chinese would think of ever touching the blankets again, they were left with Dad."

We slept that night on a bed of piñon needles. It was cold, so we put the blankets on top of our out-of-doors bed to keep us warm. The fact that one of the red blankets was thus exposed brought us a rare bit of luck. Since this bedcover was a brilliant, almost cinnabar red, it could probably be seen by almost any keen-eyed creature as far away as a mile. Hummingbirds are always attracted by red, and they found the blanket the very first day. From that time on for the next two weeks we had them about us almost continually.

It gave us a look into hummingbird life we had never had before. The red blankets fascinated them through most of the day. Six, eight, ten of them might be poised over the blankets at one time. They would hover a while, then dart sideways, only to be back a moment later. They would never actually alight on the blanket; seldom did they get nearer than 18 inches. Almost at dawn they would come and hover right over our faces.

As hummingbirds go, they were a fairly well-behaved lot. There were the usual menacing thrusts and chasing flights but little of the belligerent behavior we so often see in some of the hummingbird species such as the Allen's and calliope

YOUNG MALE RUFOUS HUMMINGBIRD

"hummers." What most impressed us as they poised in mid-air above our scarlet blanket was their dexterity.

Although some of these birds were Anna's hummingbirds, the majority were probably rufous hummingbirds. There may have been among them some Allen's hummingbirds, since it is almost impossible to distinguish these in flight from the rufous hummingbirds. The Anna's "hummers" nest in the mountains, but these rufous hummingbirds did not breed in the region where we were; they were only transients, attracted by the abundance of wild currant, gooseberry, and wild flowers at a time when the desert valleys below were dry and barren.

At another time I made my camp near a patch of red-flowered penstemons and horse thistles. The air above these gaudy flowers was alive with hummingbirds—this time Allen's hummingbirds, with bodies of iridescent green and brown and red.

The pugnacious males were guarding small patches of the flowers, each such feeding preserve being about 25 feet in diameter. The limits of the prescribed territories were so definite that a trespassing bird might at one moment be outside limits and after moving two feet be attacked vigorously. Both males and females were harassed when intruding. Not only were the beaks used to stab offenders, but at times the birds seemed actually to be grappling with one another. The males sometimes attacked in mid-air; at other times they drove the trespassers into a low bush and fatally stabbed them.

A casual winter desert visitant is the black-chinned hummingbird (p. 236) with shimmering band of violet across the throat just below the black chin.

The common hummingbird on the shrub-covered deserts is the costa. The male is bronze-green with an exquisite bright-hued gorget or ruff of violet. Not long ago I watched a female costa constructing a nest along the edge of a rocky gorge. She was building it on the end of a long creosote limb

Costa Hummingbird

where the breeze was swaying it gently back and forth most of the time. Trip after trip she made to bring in plant down and fibers. With her long, slender beak she put the materials in place and then pressed her breast against them to give proper shape to the inside of the cuplike structure. It was tiny, but it took most of a day to complete.

Three days later a strong wind began to blow. It kicked up the sand and filled the air with clouds of dust. I went to check on the nest and found the bird calmly sitting on the nest, as it and the bush lashed up and down and back and forth, often through an arc of 60 to 70 degrees.

Later, after the two tiny eggs hatched, there was more bad weather, and the nest with its young was violently rocked again. Through all this the birds emerged unscathed and in a few days were ready to leave the nest.

One day recently I was camping in a tree thicket on the edge of a desert canyon streamlet, and while I sat drinking my morning cup of Indian tea a red-breasted sapsucker flew in and began chiseling an orderly series of small rectangular cuts in the gray bark of a willow sapling. Above and below the spot were fresh cuttings in the bark, and I concluded it was a place he often frequented. The watery sap of the tree was soon collecting in droplets in the rows of small holes he had made. This he sucked up.

A small hummingbird sat quietly on a dead twig nearby, watching him. After the sapsucker had taken up what sap had oozed out, he would then fly away and come back when more sap had collected. As soon as he left, the hummingbird would drop down and begin probing for sap himself. Each time the sapsucker came back, the "hummer" would retire precipitously to its nearby perch to assume a disinterested, innocent attitude and await another opportunity for petty thievery. The behavior of birds is often so human that we are inclined to ascribe to them intelligence of a superior type, especially these gem-like little birds who always provide fresh surprises and arouse fresh admiration with their escapades.

37. *The Hibernating Poorwill*

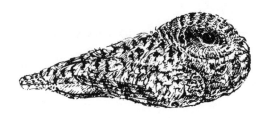

Go out across the broad Southern desert plains almost any warm evening at dusk, and if it is the season of spring, summer, or early autumn you will hear the liquid notes of the Nuttall's poorwill, Western American cousin of the Eastern whippoorwill, or European nightjar. *"Poorwill"* or *"poorwill-up"* it repeats at intervals of two or three seconds, perhaps for hours at a time, with only occasional interruptions. Sometimes the notes are stronger, sometimes fainter, according to the bird ventriloquist's relative position and distance from us. The chances are good that we may actually see in the half-darkness the small, mottled gray, black, and white bird, either as it alights in the dusty road before us or as it flutters upward like a giant moth from its resting place in the sand. It may even be our good fortune to observe it as in irregular, batlike manner it flies close to the earth, snapping up flying insects, particularly moths.

The poorwill's nocturnal call is first heard in late February, and it continues late into October, when suddenly it ceases. Some will confidently tell us that when late autumn arrives the poorwill migrates southward. However, these statements concerning the poorwill's winter life are never confirmed—indeed one can find nothing in the scientific literature, a gap that is significant in itself.

Studies carried on by the author have now cleared up this point. While going through a narrow, high-walled, almost slotlike canyon in the Chuckawalla Mountains of the Colorado Desert of California, on December 29, 1946, two of my students and I by merest chance saw a most unusual sight. On the side wall, about two and a half feet above the sand of the canyon bottom, was a poorwill, resting head upward in a vertical rock-hollow, its gray and black mottled plumage blending so perfectly with the coarse gray granite that we had to look twice to convince ourselves that it was really a poorwill. The shallow crypt, with the deepest part above, was little more than large enough to hold the bird; hence its back was almost flush with the rock surface. When we had observed the poorwill quietly for more than ten minutes without noticing any motion, I reached forward and touched the bird; there was no response. I even stroked the back feathers, but I could see not even the slightest movement. We left the place for a while, then about two hours later returned. The poorwill was still in the same position. I now reached forward and picked it up, freely turning it about in my hands. It seemed to be of unusually light weight, and the feet and eyelids, when touched, felt cold. We made no further attempt to be quiet; we even shouted. I finally returned it to its place in the crypt; but while I was doing this, it slowly opened and shut an eye, the only sign I had that it was a living bird. Unfortunately, we soon afterward had to leave the place and return home without making further observations.

Ten days later at about ten o'clock in the morning I returned with Lloyd Mason Smith, then director of the Palm Springs Desert Museum. To our surprise and satisfaction, the poorwill was still in its rock niche, with every indication that it had not moved. I reached forward and, as before, carefully picked it up. But this time, instead of remaining perfectly quiet, it gave several "puffy" sounds as if expelling air from the lungs, opened an eye, and began to make queer, high-pitched, whining or squeaky mouselike sounds. After some moments it opened its broad mouth widely, as if yawning, and then resumed its quiet. As Mr. Smith further handled it, it again made the whining notes; then suddenly it raised both wings and held them in rigid, fully outstretched, vertical position. The eyes remained closed. After the bird had held the wings stiffly upward for several minutes, we worked together to put them back in normal position; several times we attempted this, but always the wings came quickly back high above the head until the tips almost touched. Some five minutes later, while one of us still held the bird, we tried again, this time more successfully, for we got the wings at least partially in position. We now put the poorwill back in its crypt and left. The morning was cool (42° F.), the sky overcast.

That afternoon, while the sky was still gray with clouds, we returned for further observations. We had put the bird into its crypt in not quite normal position and with feathers somewhat ruffled and wings askew, and so it was now when we found it after an absence of three hours. Mr. Smith picked up the poorwill, hoping to photograph it while I held it. But to our great surprise it whipped open its wings and flew out of his hand in perfectly normal flight, as if it had just become alert to danger. It flew about 40 feet up the canyon into an ironwood tree. We walked toward it and again it flew, alighting this time among the rocks high above us, where we were unable to reach it.

On this day there were fresh coyote tracks directly below the poorwill's roosting site. The position of the footprints indicated that the coyote had stopped and turned toward the bird. There were fresh feces and claw marks in the sand, all indications that he had remained there a number of minutes. Perhaps he even saw or smelled the bird, for it had been perching there on the side of the rock at about the level of

Hibernating Poorwill

Above and below right, the "sleeping" poorwill is measured and weighed
as part of the scientific study carried on during four hibernating seasons.
Below left, the poorwill in a state of torpor in its rock niche.

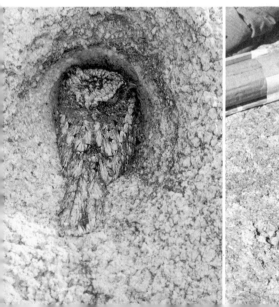

his eye. It is quite possible, though, that during hibernation the poorwill gives off no scent.

These observations on the behavior of this bird led us at once to ask if here we had a bird in a state of hibernation. Winter torpor is known well enough in many other animals, from fish to bears and bats, but it had not been previously observed in birds. Subsequent observations in the three winter seasons of 1947–48, 1948–49, and 1949–50 were to answer this question.

In late November of the 1947–48 season, I again visited the place and to my surprise found the poorwill in the same rock niche in a comatose condition. From this time on it was faithfully visited each week end, excepting two, until February 22, when it was found to have resumed its active state. When picked up, it flew out of the hand as before. To identify the bird accurately I placed a numbered aluminum band around its short lower leg.

Knowing that the true test of hibernation is a low internal temperature, I began to take a series of fortnightly temperature readings covering a period of six weeks. To my surprise, the temperature was even lower than I had suspected—64.4° F.; the normal poorwill temperature is about 106° F.

Other experiments gave additional evidence of complete hibernation. Attempts were made with a stethoscope to listen to the bird's heartbeat, but no sound could be detected. A cold metal mirror was held directly in front of the short tubular nostrils, but no moisture collected; no movement of the chest walls could be noted. One night when we visited our poorwill we found it "sleeping" with one eye wide open. A small fountain-pen type of flashlight was then placed within two inches of the open eye, and a narrow seven-candle-power beam of light was aimed directly into the pupil. The flashlight was held there fully a minute, but to this strong stimulation there was no response, not even an attempt to close the eyelid. A series of weight records showed a gradually diminishing weight. The variation noted from week to week was slight indeed, for the bird was in a very low state of metabolism.

On December 7, 1947, a hard sleet and wind storm occurred in the Chuckawalla Mountain area. It was of such intensity that a crust of mixed sleet and hail was still on the ground in the shade of shrubs 24 hours afterward. To this severe weather the poorwill was exposed, and when on December 8 we visited the bird we noticed that the tail feathers, which were exposed at the bottom of the crypt, were badly battered—so much so that they remained in poor condition the remainder of the season—yet the bird had evidently sat through the storm unaware of its fury.

To my great satisfaction, when I visited the Chuckawalla Mountains in late November of 1948, I found that my banded bird had returned for a third season. It came back to the same place again in November 1949, when we took a series of motion pictures enacting all the scenes of the first discovery and of the experiments we had carried on during three former seasons to learn of its states of winter torpidity. From all this I am led to believe that hibernation is an actuality among certain of our birds.

The Hopi Indians appropriately call the poorwill *hölchko*, "the sleeping one." The Navahos call it *bee' zhee*. Recently, while talking to a Navaho lad about the habits of the poorwill, I asked, "Where do they stay in the winter?" Without any hesitation he answered, "Up in the rocks." It is very natural that pastoral people who wander among the rocks when tending their flocks would occasionally see a poorwill in winter hiding. I take the Indian's reply as a strong corroboration of my belief that poorwills are rock-seeking, hibernating birds in winter. While in the torpid state they are generally so well hidden and camouflaged that they are seldom seen. For about

40 years I have been wandering about in the open and this is the first such bird I have seen in winter. It is doubtful that I shall ever see another.

It may be that availability of food is the controlling factor in the bird's hibernating habits. Sometimes the period of winter lethargy is longer, sometimes shorter. There is also some variation in profoundness of torpor. I believe it will be found that when the season advances to the period when there are no flying insects available, the poorwill goes into its winter sleep, and that the same forces which bring about an abundance of night-flying insects again in spring stimulate the bird's awakening.

Several hibernating poorwills have since been reported. One mentioned in September 1953 by Florence Thorburg, of Tucson, Arizona, was brought in to the Arizona Desert Trailside Museum. It was discovered in January of that year by two young men who were collecting agave in the Silverbell Mountains northwest of Tucson. As a pickaxe was struck into the ground to loosen the plant, the men noticed feathers flying. Investigation revealed a poorwill in a state of stupor under a lower leaf of the agave plant next to the ground. Following is Miss Thorburg's account:

> The men placed the poorwill in the truck cab while they went on with their work of plant collecting for two hours. The warm sun, and perhaps the previous handling, caused the bird to open its eyes and become quite active. During the ride home, which took another hour, the bird was covered with a sweater, and by the time the Museum was reached it was asleep. It did not waken while being observed by several people nor while having its picture taken in the sun.

> For five days it was kept in an unheated adobe building. Nights were cool but days quite warm. The bird would be inert or torpid in the morning, but it showed signs of wakefulness during the warmth of the day. It was then moved outside the building to a box set half underground. Here it again resumed its dormant state.

> On January 25 the poorwill weighed 34.1 grams. On January

29, a cloacal temperature was taken with a quick-recording ther-
mometer, which read 13.2° C. (55.7° F.).

This report was most interesting to me because the behavior of the bird, and the internal temperature and weight
readings, were so similar to those I had previously reported;
they corroborated my earlier findings.

Sam King, superintendent of the Joshua Tree National
Monument, wrote to me in February 1953 of having a poorwill brought into the monument headquarters in a state of
torpidity. It was kept in a cool room for a number of days,
but for reasons unknown the bird died before he was able to
see it.

In July 1953, A. L. McCasland [California] sent me the
following letter:

> Perhaps you will be interested to learn that I found these birds
> hibernating in considerable numbers during the winter of 1931–32
> and 1933–34 along the San Pedro River near Mammoth, Arizona.
> I was collecting dry saguaro and cholla cactus wood to be used
> in the making of rustic furniture and found these birds inside
> hollow saguaro trunks. The saguaro has hard ribs that do not
> rot, while the pulpy interior does, and in some cases it seemed
> that the birds had built a sort of nest or at least had dug in and
> covered themselves with the dry pulp. I met a prospector there
> who knew about these birds and their habits. They caused me
> to pass up some choice timber to avoid destroying their winter
> quarters. I saw evidence that wild animals had torn up some of
> these windfalls and concluded that it had been done to get the
> birds. If you care to visit this district, it is between Winkelman
> and Oracle on the San Pedro River.

I afterwards talked personally with Mr. McCaslund. He
said he thought he had seen between 35 and 40 of the birds
in winter torpor and once had brought in five of them to the
headquarters building of a mine. There he kept them covered over with saguaro sawdust in a box for a period of several weeks. One day he went in to observe them and found
that they had "awakened" and escaped.

In August 1954 William F. Pasivio, a prospector at Riggins, Idaho, reported to the National Geographic Society his experience with a hibernating poorwill.

He wrote that he was prospecting near Wenden, Arizona, in February 1944 when he found a poorwill in a rock cavity in a dormant state. He picked up the bird and found it very light in weight. There was no evidence of breathing, movement, or apparent life. He brushed the bird's feathers, stroked its head, and then laid it in a glove in the warm sunshine. An hour later, while prospecting close by, he saw a bird fly away, and when he went to look for the poorwill it was gone.

In February 1954 Maud A. Minthorn of Northridge, California, wrote:

Your story of the hibernating poorwill was especially interesting to me, because I realized that I had lightly passed over my own experience with one of those little creatures, not knowing at the time how rare hibernation in birds was. It was in the spring of 1909. I went out to teach in a one-family school in Nevada at Wheeler Spring not far from Pioche. My school consisted of the children of one large Mormon family named Wheeler. When I arrived at my tent-schoolhouse sometime in April that first morning there was a bouquet of pink *Ranunculus Andersonii* on my desk, and I greeted the children and showed appreciation of their gift with so much enthusiasm that they took the earliest opportunity to show me another of their nature treasures—a poorwill. I expressed doubt about being able to get near such a shy bird, but they assured me that I could see it at very close range because it was asleep. Sure enough there it was, back in a small hole in a bank. I thought maybe the bird was sick, but they assured me that it slept there every winter, but that it would soon waken and fly away, as spring was coming. Now, as I consider it, I am more surprised than I was then, because it would seem like an excessively long hibernation for such a small creature. I don't know how early the winter snows arrived, but the elevation was over 6,000 feet, and Pioche is far inland. This poorwill must have had nearly seven months of hibernation. Somehow the children had found this bird and were pleased with its odd habit, and went out to look for it each spring when the snow melted. I wish I had known more about birds then; the children would have been so pleased to have their discovery reported to some authority on birds.

The observations of children are often most valuable. Their alert eyes see things that adults never notice. Some of my most interesting correspondents and visitors are children who report to me the unusual things they find on their rambles. They find the first birds' nests and see the spring's earliest flowers. As a wise French savant once said, their queries are the key to philosophy.

38. *Insects and Other Arthropods*

No animals of the desert more readily provoke our curiosity than the slow-moving scorpions. They are handsome creatures, and every movement of the amber-colored, graceful body shows a marvelous adaptation to environment. One evening not long ago I spied a remarkably large scorpion moving with tail aloft toward my bedroll, and I immediately moved up to watch her. It was just about dark; she evidently had just come from hiding beneath a rock and was now hunting for ground-dwelling insects and spiders. As I approached, she sensed my presence immediately with the aid of the special, flaplike, comb-edged sense organs underneath her body. The walking pace was not altered, but the lobsterlike claws were immediately raised menacingly and waved about, perhaps to help her interpret the nature of new danger.

Some moments previously I had caught and imprisoned in a bottle a sun spider. I now turned this loose on the ground immediately in front of the scorpion. Slowly she moved forward a few inches, then suddenly she grasped the creature in her pincerlike claws and, while holding it somewhat aloft, with sudden quickness whipped forward the sting-tipped tail and injected the virulent poison. In a matter of seconds the victim was lifeless. She soon brought the sun spider up to her mouth to make the wounds necessary for the injection of digestive juices. These soon reduced the inner parts of the prey to a juicy pulp. This was necessary, for the scorpion is not adapted to eat solid foods. The partially digested pulpy parts of the victim were slowly sucked up with the aid of the elastic-walled muscular pharynx. Almost half an hour passed before the scorpion cast aside the empty shell of the body of her prey.

The scorpion's daytime dwelling place is easy to identify. A flattish tunnel going into the earth at a slight angle from the horizontal, with a long pile of earth or sand pushed out smoothly in front, betrays its work. The scorpion's hole is seldom more than an inch wide. Once having made itself a burrow, it may occupy it for many days. This I found out under unusual circumstances.

One summer not long ago I went up along a certain side-hill trail every day before sunrise to a small rock-rimmed area where I spent an hour in reading, writing, and meditation. I early noticed that there was one extra-large scorpion burrow right in the middle of my path. When I first saw it I pushed a little earth into it with my foot, plugging the entrance. Next morning it was completely opened up. With a push of my foot I again closed the doorway. Next morning when I ascended the trail there was the scorpion's door open as wide as before. From then on it became a sort of contest: I closed the hole every day; the scorpion persistently opened it up at night. For almost 90 days we played the game, and when I left the scorpion was still in residence in the same tunnel.

Until this experience I had never suspected that these relatives of our spiders were creatures of homing habits. I had always supposed that they were night rovers excavating a new tunnel almost every morning in which to spend the daylight hours. Scorpions are good diggers, and it takes them only a short time to get underneath the earth.

Some of the species which live in desert woodlands of juniper and piñon hide by day under fallen trees, sticks, and stones. I remember coming once into a broad area in south-central Nevada where there seemed to be an unusually large scorpion population; there were perhaps several hundred to the acre. Every piece of dead wood or stone we turned over harbored one or more scorpions. Some of them were large. There were, in addition, many scorpion holes in the earth. We had a difficult time finding what we considered a safe place to camp, being well aware that when night came all these scorpions would be abroad. Finally, after hunting to no avail for scorpion-free territory along some 30 miles of highway, we put our sleeping bags down on a pile of crushed rock left beside the road by some road makers. Our beds were hard, but we felt that we were fairly safe from a scorpion's sting.

What appears to be the tail of a scorpion is not a tail in the proper sense but rather a mere narrow extension of the abdomen with the digestive tube or gut running almost to its end. To the last segment is joined the telson, a bulblike reservoir containing the poison glands. At its terminus is the gracefully curved stinger through which the venom is forced into the wound.

Most of the scorpions we find are practically harmless creatures, and at its worst the sting is not much more severe than that of a bee or wasp—hot and painful at first, then disappearing after an hour or two. There is, however, one species of small scorpion with body not over two inches long, found in southern Arizona and northern Sonora in Mexico, which can inject a poison so virulent that death may come to the victim, if it is a child. The poison is classed as a neurotoxin. The symptoms of distress include difficult breathing, extreme restlessness, and copious flow of saliva. Ice packs and an anti-venin are used in treatment.

The poisonous species possesses a small stiff thorn on the under side of the last tail joint just behind the stinger, a diagnostic structure of no mean importance. I have seen Mexicans light a match and burn off the scorpion's stinger, thinking that the scorpion must starve to death because it is no longer able to kill insects.

The scorpion's eggs develop within the body of the mother. The young, which are quite different in appearance from the parent, are born in the living state. They attach themselves to the mother's back and subsist for several days on the embryonic yolk which fills their mid-gut. They are carried around by the parent until after their first molt; then they drop to the ground and fend for themselves.

MILLEPEDES

One late October morning just after there had been a short, heavy rain, I walked over a big southern Arizona sand dune. As I glanced down I saw literally thousands of small holes from an inch to two inches apart. The punctured sand surface reminded me of the top of a giant pepper shaker. Each hole was almost large enough to admit an ordinary-sized wheat straw and went almost vertically downward. Peculiarly, although the holes seemed deep, there was no sand piled up about the entrance. I began to dig and soon discovered who the hole makers were. In each one was hidden, some three inches below, a small millepede, or thousand-legged worm. Apparently the rain had brought them out during the night, and each had made a fresh burrow. It seems strange to find millepedes on desert sand wastes, for they are thought to be very dependent on humus and other vegetable debris that can retain a more or less permanent supply of moisture. But on dry deserts we have them, and often, after

CENTIPEDE

TUMBLEBUG

SCORPION

rains, in abundance. It is believed that they burrow down to cooler, damper soil during long dry spells.

Most millepedes are harmless and are capable only of slow motion. Some of the tropical species are known to cause severe rashes. The legs are many, two pairs to each segment, except the first few, of the numerous cylindrical body segments. When roughly handled, millepedes coil up and often emit a foul-smelling, protective secretion of dark-brown color. This secretion will stain the hands and the pungent odor will remain for hours. Some of the species are parasitized by flies. Millepedes found on deserts are, for the most part, very small in comparison with some of more humid areas.

CENTIPEDES

Among the small night crawlers that most people fear are the centipedes. Although they are reputed to have a hundred legs, each of which is supposed to sting, the number in most species is less than half a hundred, including the strange posterior pair which look more like antennae than legs. Only the short, first pair found right beside the head is to be feared. These specialized appendages end in sharp claws capable of being pressed into a soft or fragile creature's body. Through them the centipede can inject a poison. It is the centipede's means of overcoming its prey. When the centipede is provoked by pressure or rough handling by human beings, the poison claws with their perforated tips may puncture the flesh and inject a poison which can cause both pain and swelling. I was myself once "bitten" on the foot by a large eight-inch centipede, but I noticed little discomfort other than slight local pain, numbness, and swelling. One of my sympathetic neighbors assured me I might look forward to having my leg rot off, for he had "heard of a man being bitten on the body and having chunks of flesh as big as clenched fists fall from his chest."

The insects, land snails, and other small creatures which

centipedes eat are readily cut up by the strong movable mouth parts just in front of the "poison legs." The last appendages at the end of the body are used as tactile organs, as are the antennae at the fore end. (The sketch on page 252 shows the long-legged centipede.)

If you bring home the next centipede you see and place it in a flat-bottomed container with sand in the bottom, you can watch it eat the insects you bring in to it at night. You will be impressed by the speed with which the centipede cuts up and devours its living prey, and also by how cleverly it can dig U-shaped tunnels in which to lurk while waiting for prey. Into these tunnels it can crawl both frontward and backward.

Centipedes avoid light whenever possible. When brought into the open they seem to be uncomfortable and ceaselessly run about trying to find cover. They prefer a cover that hugs the flattened body from above and below. This is why we most often find them under flat stones or pieces of wood or bark. Such places usually afford not only the darkness they prefer but also moisture, upon the presence of which centipedes are very dependent. If exposed in the open on dry sand, they soon perish.

WHIP SCORPIONS OR VINEGARROONS

Large whip scorpions are quite common in the Arizona, New Mexico, and Texas deserts but are exceedingly rare, or even absent, in California. The long whiplike extension of the abdomen gives them a frightening appearance. This appendage, often taken as a stinging organ, is only a perfectly harmless "tail," probably used as a tactile organ. The pincerlike pedipalpi of the head are very large and powerful, but even these are not to be feared. They may give one a rather painful prick, but nothing more.

Properly, these animals should be called vinegarroons. This name is said to have been coined because these strange creatures have the habit, when roughly handled, of emitting from "stink glands" near the end of the abdomen vinegarodored, gaseous secretions. Whip scorpion is an unsuitable name because they are not scorpions at all, although they are rather closely related to them. Like the true scorpions, they crawl about actively at night and hide by day. You may find one quartered beneath the camp food box or under your sleeping bag in the morning.

The food of vinegarroons is chiefly insects. The eggs are held together in a glutinous mass on the underside of the abdomen of the female. When hatched, the young crawl up on the mother's back, as is also the case with the scorpion, and remain there until they molt at the end of the fifth or sixth day. They then drop to the ground and are ready to take care of themselves.

SOLPUGIDS

The animal popularly referred to in California as a vinegarroon is in reality a solpugid. It bears little resemblance to a true vinegarroon and does not give off a vinegarlike odor. Like the true scorpions and whip scorpions, the solpugids crawl under objects or in crevices to hide by day. I remember having once left a partially closed suitcase out on the ground beside my camp bed and, upon opening it next morning, finding three solpugids hidden among the contents.

These hairy-bodied, spiderlike, tan-colored creatures are active only at night, and then, especially in summer, we find them attracted by lights. They dash about with remarkable speed. On our screen doors and windows we see them darting here and there, snatching up insects. Once caught, the victim is immediately cut up between the parts of the large four-parted, pointed, tooth-edged beak. It is a beak out of all proportion to the size of the abdomen and is reputed by zoologists to be "the most formidable set of jaws in the animal world." Just behind the jaws and appearing much like walking legs are the slender pedipalpi, ending abruptly in cuplike suckers, which assist the animal in climbing vertical surfaces. Behind these are the first walking legs, but instead of aiding in locomotion they function as additional feelers and as such are carried slightly raised and out in front. The entire body is covered with delicate silky hairs, each an exceedingly sensitive organ of touch. Among the extraordinary structures of solpugids are the paired T- or funnel-shaped racquet organs, ten in number, found on the underside of the hind legs. They are thought to be tactile organs but may prove to be specialized structures with other uses.

MUTILLIDS

"Now what do we have here?" said one of my camp companions as he emptied onto the ground from a tin can a strange, hairy insect of considerable size. It looked much like a moving mass of colored fuzz; really more like a big ant covered with a deep cushion of black hair on head and thorax and brick-red hair on the abdomen. It moved fast on its slender black legs and had large black eyes. It was what insect specialists call a mutillid.

To most people it looks like an ant, and often it is called the velvet or buffalo ant. It is not an ant, however, but rather a wasp, and it can give you a sharp sting. We saw it run its long black stinger out—a stinger almost as long as the abdomen itself.

The specimen we had was a female. The males are winged and likely to be much smaller. They are seldom seen. On sunny days the neatly attired female moves ceaselessly. The quick-moving antennae with which she constantly palpates the earth are doubtless valuable tactile organs.

There are several kinds of velvet ants, some with short red hairs all over, some with long red hairs only on the abdomen, like the one my companions discovered, others with many long white or yellowish-white hairs on the upper side. These last are sometimes called "old-man ants" or "white mule-killers" in allusion to the absurd and erroneous belief that their painful sting is fatal even to so strong an animal as the mule.

Because some of the mutillids can make high-pitched, singing notes by forcing air in and out of the breathing tubes located on the sides of the body, the uninformed speak of these insects as singing ants. It is easy to get a female mutillid to "sing" if you put it into a drinking glass or cup and shake it about to make it angry. When you put your ear close, you will hear high-pitched, pulsating, squeaky notes.

The food of adult mutillids is said to be the nectar of flowers. One I held in captivity drank water when deprived of nectar for a few days. She also sipped water in which sugar or honey was dissolved. But where in dry, hot summer days and in autumn do the mutillids get either nectar or water? There certainly are few flowers to supply nectar, and there is little chance to get water even in the form of dew. Never have I seen a mutillid in a flower, even when flowers are plentiful. They are always seen on the ground. Yet hour after hour, day after day, they run rapidly over hot, barren rocks and sand, using up energy and losing water through the process of breathing.

The eggs are laid in the nests of ground-dwelling bees and wasps, and the young mutillid larvae feed on the eggs or larvae of these insects they parasitize.

ELEODES

I always feel that something is missing if, soon after making my desert campfire, I do not have a call from *Eleodes*, the pinacate beetle or tumblebug. Usually he plods along, with deliberate step, unsuspicious of danger. He gradually works his way right up to the zone of warmth near the fire. His scientific name, *Eleodes,* is an apt one. It comes from the Greek and means "like an olive, oily"—of course, like a ripe olive, and that just about describes the appearance of his black, almost olive-shaped body.

Some of our desert Indians think that when, as so often happens, *Eleodes* tips his black abdomen upward and puts his head to the ground, he is listening to learn the will of the gods. This strange way of tipping the body is a fear reaction, a feigning of death. Most often it is induced by strong earth vibrations or by rough handling. It is a protective habit designed to dismay or to deceive the enemy.

Eleodes belongs to a large, widely distributed group of beetles called darkling beetles, since most of them move in the darkness of night or at least avoid the light. Some kinds are found in arid regions the world over, and especially in California, Arizona, northern Mexico, and Africa. The day-roving desert forms with their black or dark-brown bodies must absorb unusual amounts of heat. How they manage to exist through the summer days of heat and dryness will probably long remain a mystery.

Their food consists of dry or decaying vegetation, but green food is not neglected. Our desert forms are fond of fresh fruit, and I find them eating away at the bits of apple or orange pulp I throw down for them. Once I found one eating baked beans from a half-empty tin can.

If on their rambles they come to steep, sandy embankments, they often try for extended periods to surmount the obstacles in their path. They seldom seem discouraged, but try again and again to go up the steep places even though they may many times fall backward far down the slope. Often fearing that they might get trampled as they come crawling into camp, I have picked them up and carried them to some distance, only to find them back in a few minutes.

At times I have seen these beetles digging flattish tunnels in the sand. Once the tunnels are dug, they seldom stay in them. When they are excavating, first all the legs on one side of the body paw at the sand; then these rest and the bank of legs on the other side goes to work. As sand accumulates behind the insect, a reverse motion of the legs pushes the sand toward the tunnel opening.

The rather large, whitish eggs are laid in the sand. The glossy, tough-cuticled, elongate grubs feed underground on vegetable matter. Pupation also takes place in the earth. When the fully formed adults emerge, they leave holes in the ground the diameter of the little finger.

Little is known about the life history of these common insects. They have not received the attention they deserve.

CALIFORNIA PALM BORER

In the late nineteenth century there was a man in San Bernardino, California, who was considered eccentric by his neighbors because he spent most of his time collecting and studying butterflies. This man was W. G. Wright, who in his later years wrote the standard reference book *West Coast Butterflies*. Few copies of this monumental work are in existence because most of the plates and printed pages were destroyed in the San Francisco fire of 1906, before many copies had been offered for sale. (I am the possessor of one of these rare volumes.)

Wright usually went alone on his often lengthy desert journeys, camping out for weeks at a time in places then practically unknown to the average traveler. His neighbors were curious about his strange comings and goings, but learned little from him either about his destinations or discoveries. To their questions of where he had been, they generally got the laconic reply: "Oh, out on the Mohave."

It was after one of his long-drawn-out "Mohave journeys" that he returned with some very valuable beetles, so unbelievably rare and unusual in appearance that he offered them to leading museums for sale and, it is said, got nearly a thousand dollars a pair for them! At least three such sales were made before the price came down: to the British Museum, to the Russian museum at St. Petersburg, and, I believe, to a museum in Paris.

For 11 years the home of this fairly large beetle with dark-brown, cylindrical body and large, rounded head remained known only to Wright, who refused to divulge the "type lo-

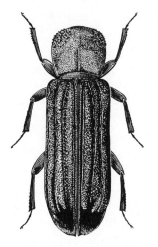

DINAPATE BEETLE

cality," as it is called by entomologists. Many of his collector friends tried to follow him, but he always shook them off his trail.

The beetle was finally classified and given the scientific name of *Dinapate wrightii*, in honor of its discoverer, by a fellow entomologist, G. H. Horn. (*Dinapate* was coined from two Greek words meaning "clever deception," probably in reference to Wright's wily tactics.)

It was quite by accident that someone other than Wright chanced upon one of these "thousand dollar insects." An engineer, or a surveyor, I forget which, happened to be walking down Palm Canyon above Palm Springs, California, one hot September afternoon and came upon, by merest chance, a single wing-cover of this rare insect at the foot of one of the Washingtonia palms. Since this man was also well informed in the field of entomology, he immediately recognized the great scientific import of his discovery. The secret was out— the mysterious beetle lived in the trunk of the desert fan palm! Since that time this curious, hard-to-find beetle has been taken by a number of diligent entomologists and the price on the open market quickly fell, so that today a pair brings only a few dollars. But for a while at least the secret of the California palm-borer, as this beetle is popularly known, was worth as much as a vein of gold to Wright.

What threw most of his followers completely off the track was the roundabout route he took to Palm Canyon, always going out through Cajon Pass to the Mojave Desert and then circling around the San Bernardino Mountains and through Morongo Pass down to the Colorado Desert and Palm Canyon. Wright seldom paused in the village of Palm Springs, but went directly to the canyon without saying a word to anyone. There he hacked open newly fallen palm trunks in quest of his curious insect treasures. Often his searches were fruitless, but sometimes he found the beetles ready to emerge from their labyrinthine tunnels deep inside the prostrate logs.

Perhaps in some of your wanderings among the oases of native palms on our Colorado Desert you have noticed finger-sized holes in brown fallen trunks, holes too small and too deep to be the work of woodpeckers. These openings mark the sites where the adult beetles have emerged. The females lay their eggs in the leaf buds of living palms, and shortly afterward the larvae eat their way into the center of the long trunk. The galleries they make are tightly filled behind them with sawdust-like frass and are gradually made larger by the growing larvae. After several months, these larvae, called grubs, penetrate to the core of the palm, where they complete the life cycle. Later, after boring to the exterior, they emerge as robust adults.

H. G. Hubbard, one of the early collectors of *Dinapate*, regarded the finding of the larvae as one of the most interesting events of his entomological life:

It is hard to realize the enormous extent and dimensions of the Dinapate galleries. If one finds 20 or 30 holes in one of the Washingtonia palms, the interior probably is entirely eaten out from end to end, and one can follow the frass-filled galleries, over one inch in diameter, for 20 feet up and down the trunk following the grain and without diminishing sensibly in size. Then think of the yards and yards of smaller galleries made by the larvae while still young. Such extensive and prodigious borings cannot be made in one or two years, and certainly not in any trunk of moderate size, for it would not yield enough food.

The larval tunnels cross and recross each other in an erratic pattern, practically destroying all the fiber in the region attacked. The feeding grubs may be heard making a sharp *click-click* sound with their mandibles. The sound can be imitated by clicking the nails of the finger and thumb together.

After a dormant period, when the grub is changing into a pupa and then into an adult beetle, the adults emerge one at a time, after dark. Fortunately for other palms, only a few of the larvae live to become full-sized, egg-laying adults, as attested by the small number of holes.

Most of the beetles closely related to the California palm borer are very small; *Dinapate* is the largest of the group. One of the most interesting of its relatives is the long, dark-brown cable borer (*Scobicia declivis*), the adults of which frequently bore into lead-covered telephone cables, permitting water to enter and causing short-circuiting of the wires.

TARANTULAS

Tarantulas, of which there are many species, are, for the most part, harmless creatures. To be sure, they have stout, sharp fangs through which they inject poison, but the venom is as a rule only harmful to such small creatures as grasshoppers, beetles, millepedes, and small spiders upon which they spring. The poison causes only slight swelling, numbness, and itching when injected into the flesh of man. The strong chelicerae are able to produce a painful wound, but the chances of being "bitten" are so few that one need have no worry. People often pick up these large, slow-moving, hairy spiders and let them walk over their hands and arms. They even may make pets of them.

It is usually in autumn when tarantulas are seen in numbers. This is the time when the males are hunting mates. Sometimes so many are crossing the highways that it looks like a mass migration. The females are much less often seen; they mostly stay in their deep burrows in sand or gravel.

One rather warm April, while visiting the thorn forest of acacias and cacti on the southern plains of Sonora, three of us made our evening campfire in a barren flat and were soon visited by a number of tarantulas, which seemed to be attracted by the firelight. They rapidly approached the fire, then suddenly about-faced when they felt the heat. Time and again they returned, only to repeat the withdrawal. Since it was not the time of mating, we were surprised to see so many of them around.

In time one becomes quite adept in locating tarantula burrows. A loose bit of webbing at the entrance of the burrow shows that it is being used. When winter comes, the tarantula may actually make a plug of leaves, sand, and silk to shore up the entrance. The occupant can be induced to come forth from its underground retreat by pouring water down the hole. Once on top of the ground it can readily be picked up for examination.

These spiders are deliberate walkers, picking their steps with greatest grace and caution. In spite of their loitering gait they cover considerable ground in a day's time. Their bodies are so light in weight that they seldom leave track marks except on the finest powdery sands and clays. Many persons believe that these large, hairy creatures are great jumpers; actually they can only leap a few inches.

Like other spiders, tarantulas at least partially digest their solid food outside their bodies. When prey is captured, large or small, a wound is made, and into this is poured buccal digestive juices, which soon reduce any food to a condition where it is soft enough to be sucked up with the aid of muscles attached to the stomach. Later it is absorbed in the mid-gut, with its series of large branching sacs and their glandular extensions within the cephalothorax.

When it comes time for egg-laying, the female spins a large sheet of webbing and upon this she deposits numerous large, round, pearly-white eggs. A second sheet of webbing is placed over them and its edges bound together with silken threads. This flattened egg sac or cocoon is watched over for six or seven weeks until the eggs are hatched.

The small tarantulas generally remain within the burrow for some days, after which they disperse and establish holes of their own.

Tarantulas are normally long-lived creatures. The period of time necessary to arrive at sexual maturity is long—perhaps up to ten years. During this time they undergo a number of molts, and until the last one takes place it is quite impossible to distinguish males from females. The mature male is dark-colored, even black, while the female is brownish, the degree of coloring varying with the species. The adult males now abandon their burrows and go forth to seek mates. This is generally in late summer or early autumn.

After mating, many of the males live only a short time. Some die a natural death; others are eaten by the females at the time of courtship or just after copulation. Some females have a life span of 20 to 25 years. However, long life is rare: there are too many enemies, among these are spider-eating birds, lizards, and snakes; also parasitic flies and wasps. *Pepsis*, the large metallic blue, green, and red wasp, often called the tarantula hawk, is among all enemies the fiercest and most dreaded. Once it has met, stung, and paralyzed the spider, it drags it to a prepared burrow, deposits its egg on the abdomen, and seals the victim in. Upon escaping from the egg, the larval wasp feeds on the paralyzed tarantula.

The tarantula is a useful member of the desert fauna and should not be persecuted or killed. If its presence is not desired, it can readily be placed in a container and transported to some area where it can continue to live unmolested its useful life.

39. *Desert Mollusks*

One early spring evening long ago, while the earth was still damp from a recent rain, I walked from the Cahuilla Indian Village at Palm Springs, California, to my hillside shanty perched among the rocks. On the rough, steep mountainside above me I saw a slowly moving light. Sometimes the yellow glow remained stationary; sometimes it moved erratically back and forth. For more than an hour it was in view. Unquestionably it was the light of a kerosene lantern.

Next morning when I walked the half-mile footpath to the village store, I learned that other persons had seen the moving light too. The following night we saw the same strange light again.

The puzzle was solved the following morning when a professional-looking man with well-trimmed beard stopped at my small board-and-shake house, "just," as he said, "to have a chat about snails." He introduced himself as Dr. Emmet Rixford of San Francisco.

"I've been out for two nights with a lantern trying to collect some live land snails. There is a rather rare one hereabouts. At night it comes out from beneath the boulders to find green plants on which to feed.

"I have here in this little box several dozen of the banded shells and all with living animals inside. The California Academy of Sciences, knowing that I was going to Palm Springs, asked me to collect some live ones. To have live ones is very important, for only by making a dissection of the internal organs is it possible to make an exact identification."

To me that visit with Dr. Rixford was momentous, for it opened up a wholly new interest in a phase of natural history I had long neglected. At once I decided that I too must explore the mountain slopes and rocky hills of the desert for land mollusks.

My first snail hunt led me into the arid Spring Mountains of southern Nevada, a limestone range of scenic grandeur. It was at a time when Las Vegas was still a small village and the mouintains were unused by summer vacationists. Our camps were at the ends of roads wholly impassable to any vehicle except Model T Fords and trucks. Our closest companions were the chipmunks, nesting robins, occasional Townsend Solitaires, and Ruby-crowned Kinglets. It was a paradise for the collector-naturalist, for the lime rocks abounded in fossil echinoderms, corals, and lamp shells (brachiopods). The plants and animals of this region had been little studied.

When I began delving into the rock slides for snails, my efforts were at once rewarded by finding a number of small ones, some so tiny that they were just visible to the naked eye. I wore my fingernails to the quick digging among the small rocks for the tiny mollusks. As I worked my way along and threw stones to one side, I literally made trenches, some as much as three feet deep and ten feet long. After all the intervening years these sizable excavations are still discernible. They must puzzle people who find them. The results of these early labors were wholly satisfactory, for they yielded at least three different kinds of snails, one of which proved to be a new one to science.

My success in the limestone mountains of southern Nevada led me to believe that if I could find similar terrain westward across the California-Nevada border I could turn up some exciting new mollusk territory in the California deserts. The arid limestone slopes of Clark Mountain, 7,903 feet high, seemed a good place for successful prospecting. I knew of no trails to the mountain's summit, so I ascended the narrow and exceedingly steep, slotlike gorge on its west side. It was a most difficult climb and consumed half a day.

When I reached the top, there was not much left of my shoes, shirt, trousers, or strength. But of enthusiasm for discovery there was plenty. In spite of a close watch, I had found no land snails on the way up, but within a few feet of the topmost ridge, I dug into some plant debris under some white fir trees and at once found a whole handful of dime-sized snails, the first of their kind ever taken.

The snail specimens were later described under the name of *Oreohelix californica,* the only species of that genus on the mainland of California. There is an *Oreohelix* found far to the west on Santa Catalina Island off the California coast, and only full knowledge of the geographical past can explain the relationship between the two species.

Some years later a small group of fellow naturalists and I made a spring journey to the Death Valley area. Included in the party was the eminent mollusk specialist, Dr. S. Stillman Berry, of Redlands, California, and William H. Thorpe (of Jesus College, Cambridge University), a well-known zoologist and authority on animal behavior.

A number of important zoological discoveries were made by us, including that of some unique insects which Dr. Thorpe took from the saline pools on the valley floor. Unfortunately we missed a discovery of great scientific importance when we failed to heed Dr. Thorpe's repeated and urgent request to visit Bad Water, the lowest point in the Western Hemisphere. Only a few months later Allyn Smith of Berkeley, California, skimmed those Bad Water pools and came up with the world's only known soft-bodied invertebrate animal in saturated salt water. It was small as snails go, but of great scientific interest. It was given the euphonious scientific name of *Assiminea infirma*.

This water snail may have attained its ability to survive in these salt-laden waters by a gradual physiological and structural evolution over the many years that elapsed while the brackish-water lake (Lake Manly), which once occupied the troughlike depression of Death Valley, gradually diminished in size and notably increased in the amount of its mineral constituents. When, because of increasing aridity, the lake finally dried up, small remaining populations of aquatic animals, ranging in diversity from small cyprinodont minnows to insects and this snail, persisted in such places as Bad Water and Saratoga Springs. It is even possible that representatives of the snail genus *Assiminea* were introduced into Death Valley on the feet or feathers of aquatic or shore-loving birds which were flying eastward from coastal California, where snails of this genus are now found living in brackish waters.

As one travels down the black-top highway to the Mexican fishing pueblo of San Felipe on the Gulf of California, one sees to the west the high, precipitous Sierra San Pedro Mártir, which culminates in the granite peak known to the Mexicans as La Providencia, El Encantado, or Picacho del Diablo (10,136 feet high).

During this past year I have twice visited the steep-walled, picturesque canyons which spew their debris of rock and sand out over the low desert plain below. Upon entering the main canyons we found seemingly numberless small canyons which drain into them and carry the waters of the infrequent rains. It is a very rough country made beautiful not only by the often grotesquely shaped and intricately banded granitic rocks but also by numerous giant tree cacti (*Pachycereus Pringlei*), agaves, two kinds of elephant trees, and other strange vegetation found only in this hot southern extension of the Colorado Desert.

Searching here for land snails, we soon came upon numerous empty, banded shells. We were aware that never before had land snails been collected in mountains facing the Gulf of California. We were disappointed in not finding live snails; we probably should have looked for them under the dried leaves of the numerous agaves or century plants which are so common there.

As a rule, the collector of land snails does not expect to find these small, soft-bodied animals in the desert's piñon and juniper country, but recently the author and his student assistant found among huge granite rocks in just such country in northern Baja California a land snail with brown-banded shell of the genus *Helminthoglypta.* This marked a new southern limit of distribution for this genus so well represented in more arid environments in Southern California mountains.

The first land snail collected in the Sonoran Desert was found in 1865 by an explorer and traveler named Frick, who was going over the Old Yuma Trail to California. It was in southwestern Arizona in the barren but beautiful Gila Mountains. In 1894 Dr. Edgar A. Mearns, while on the U.S.–Mexican Boundary Survey, took specimens of this snail near the same area. The only other collection of this mollusk was made by two of my students and me in the vicinity of the famous Tinajas Altas along the historic Camino del Diablo. This was in 1934 and was considered a very important rediscovery. This land mollusk was described under the name *Micrarionta Rowelli.*

People often wonder how new plants and animals get their scientific names. A good way to illustrate this is to tell of a snail I collected in Black Canyon in the mid-Mohave Desert in 1928. It is an area deeply covered by black volcanic rocks. My snail specimens were sent to Dr. S. Stillman Berry.

Because this snail is found around black rocks at the entrance to the canyon, he described it under the specific name of *melanopylon* (Greek *melanos*, black; *pylon*, gate, entrance). To a snail I discovered in the Eagle Mountains of the Colorado Desert he gave the specific name *aëtotes* (Greek, of the eagles). A snail first found on Sidewinder Mountain (named after the prevalent rattlesnake of the region) was named *crotalina* (New Latin *crotalinus*, pertaining to a rattle [snake]; Greek *krotalon*, rattle). The stem *krotal* also occurs in the generic name *Crotalus*, a name chosen by the Swedish naturalist, Linnaeus, for the rattlesnakes.

The hilly and mountainous country of the area where Arizona, New Mexico, and the Mexican states of Chihuahua and Sonora meet is said to be richest in representation of species of land snails of any place in the Southwest. Often a single arid mountain canyon will have a number of species, and almost every somewhat isolated rocky hill may boast of its own snail candidate for scientific fame. Much of it is limestone country where the genera *Sonorella* and *Oreohelix* are in ascendency, especially in the lower canyon rockslides. Much of it is unexplored snail territory and rich rewards await the patient, intelligent collector.

The desert floor of southern Arizona, as is often true of other flat areas, is poor snail country, but the surrounding low mountains and even the low, isolated conical hills are often good land snail territory. But those mollusks may be hard to find, since one may have to dig four or five feet to locate them. When the hills are made of volcanic rocks millenniums old, collecting is generally disappointing, the region having been too recently burned out. The still older cinder may yield most interesting material, however.

40. Lizards

The best time to learn about lizards is during the late spring and early summer months; but midsummer and autumn days are not to be shunned. It is in March, April, and May that these creatures are most active in feeding and engaging in all of their marvelous mating antics. The sunny morning hours between eight and ten o'clock are most rewarding when collecting them for study. Going out with a few small muslin sacks for carrying the lizards, a crowbar with which to pry up rocks, and a six-foot bamboo pole fitted with a horsehair or string noose, I begin my stalking. When it is warm, lizards are unusually alert, and it is necessary to adopt special tricks to get close to them. One of these tricks is to get someone to wave a hand or a small object to attract and hold the reptile's attention while I approach slowly from another direction with the noosed pole. By this diversion, it is quite easy to slip up on lizards and even to take them by hand. The use of pole and noose, instead of the hand, is best because it guards against breaking off tails or otherwise injuring them. Once I get the reptiles home, I put them for a few days in screened observation boxes where I can watch them closely. Studies so made must, however, be supplemented by many observations in the open.

On clear days the big scaly lizards (*Sceloporus magister*) may be encountered running around the rocks or basking on warm rock surfaces, especially in the early morning, turning this way and that to warm themselves. They tend to reside among bushes, including the spiny yuccas and the many species of tall, branching cacti known as *opuntias,* whose needle-like spines don't seem to bother them. At our approach, they either flatten themselves against the trunk of the shrub or scuttle swiftly down and around the back of the stem to reach a hole where they can get out of sight. Small beetles and ants are their chief food.

Race runners or whiptailed lizards (*Cnemidophorus*) are among the more abundant saurians of the lowland plains where there are thickets of creosote bush, cactus, and ocotillo. They are creatures of slender form, long snouts, long tails, and slithering gait. The legs, though long, are comparatively weak, and body movements are relied upon to aid in carrying the animal over the ground. When hunting, this lizard bobs its head up and down, proceeding with its belly close to or actually on the ground. Progress forward is accomplished by a series of jerking, forward movements with frequent pauses. The most common species is *C. tigris,* often called the tiger whiptail. It is found over much of the arid Great Basin region. It is among the most difficult lizards to get into the noose. When slinking along on the dunes, these lizards drag their tails behind them, leaving a characteristic trail. When alarmed, they skim over the ground with great speed. They make their own burrows in the sand, excavating the material by alternate strokes of the front feet, reminding one of the way a dog digs. The body color is a metallic brownish-gray above, with the lower surfaces creamy-white, suffused with gray.

The ocellated sand lizard (*Uma notata*) is rather large for a lizard and a swift runner. We find it on the sands, especially those of dunes, a habitat to which it is particularly adapted because of the fringes of elongate scales on the toes. The foot, thus fitted, becomes an especially efficient organ for burrowing as well as for running rapidly over the loose sands. Its special nasal valves and its shovel-like snout enable it to swiftly work its way completely out of sight into the sand by a sort of wriggling motion. The burial is usually quite shallow.

Other sand-inhabiting lizards of this genus are *Uma inornata* of the upper Coachella Valley and *Uma scorparia* of the Mohave Desert area.

The large crested lizard (*Dipsosaurus*) is usually found among the sparse growths of creosote bush, mesquite, and ironwood trees. When alarmed, it quietly takes refuge in burrows made by rodents or other small animals in the sand mounds found about the bases of bushes. If one has enough patience to wait until it comes out again, one can easily slip a noose over its head and bag it.

These lizards are often spoken of as brown-spotted, white lizards. As we see them against a background of sand, even very light-colored sand, the body appears to be of an almost glaring white. It is when we get near them that the numerous brown spots and bands become apparent. These round-nosed lizards are late-rising and timid creatures. They are almost exclusively plant feeders and sometimes are seen about the bases of low shrubs, nipping off flowers and green leaves. Like the chuckawalla, they may inflate their bodies and make it difficult to pull them from their burrows.

The *Dipsosaurus* can really take the heat; temperatures up to 115° F. are not adverse to its comfort and activity. I believe there are none of our lizards that are its equal in this respect. When really frightened it may raise the whole forepart of the body and run with great speed on its strong hind limbs.

Lizards of the genus *Uta* take their name from the Ute Indians, in whose territory the first scientifically described specimens were collected. Nearly all of them are handsome creatures, but of small size. The tail in some is short, in others exceedingly long. They are very active lizards, many of them being seen even on cloudy or cool days. One of the most common desert species is *U. stansburiana elegans*, the brown-shouldered *Uta*, named after Howard Stansbury, who in 1850 made the famous Exploration and Survey of the Valley of the Great Salt Lake of Utah. When molested, these lizards often disappear in holes. Some of the holes they dig themselves by using their front feet and working the head from side to side. They are adept stalkers and snatchers of flies, and sometimes if two flies are near and directly in line in front of them they will leap forward rapidly and snap up both insects at the same time. This small *Uta* is found in the desert regions of Arizona, California, New Mexico, Texas, and Sonora. It is one of the few lizards of the Colorado Desert that are active all winter during the warmer parts of the day.

The long-tailed brush lizard (*Uta graciosa*) often climbs into low bushes, and it is then very difficult to see because it lines up its body, long tail, and legs closely with the limb it is resting on; moreover, it often is of the same color as the bark. Mearn's rock lizard (*Uta mearnisi*), of the western Colorado Desert, is an exceedingly handsome creature almost wholly confined to rocky canyons, where it runs with remarkable speed over the almost vertical walls of rock while hunting insects. It has a blackish collar usually noticeably bordered behind with white. It is sometimes mistaken for the true collared lizard (*Crotaphytus collaris*), which has two transverse collar bars.

The leopard lizard (*Crotophytus wislizeni*), although closely related to the collared lizard, is without the broad collar of double transverse black bars. Over its gray body and back are numerous dusky spots and very noticeable

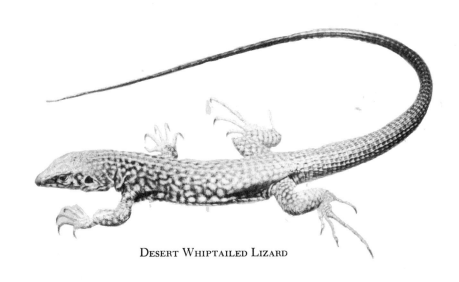

DESERT WHIPTAILED LIZARD

ERT GRIDIRON-TAILED LIZARD

DESERT IGUANA

ERT SPINY LIZARD

COLORADO DESERT FRINGE-FOOTED SAND LIZARD

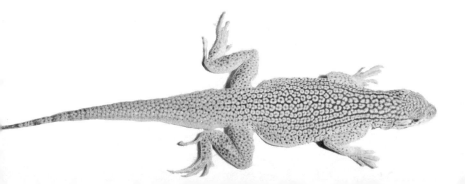

whitish cross bars. They eat not only other lizards but even their own kind. They are very fast and exceedingly wary, so they are difficult to approach, even more so to catch by hand or by noose. The black throat lining is revealed when the mouth is opened threateningly.

The gridiron-tailed or zebra-tailed lizards (*Callisaurus*) take their common name from the parallel-placed, blackish bands on the underside of the tail. These are often prominently displayed as the animal runs. Several kinds are found in the deserts of California, Arizona, and southern New Mexico. With tail coiled over the back, they run with such amazing swiftness that it is almost impossible for the eye to follow them; this is true especially if they are running along the line of sight. They then appear, indeed, as mere streaks on the silver sands. They are further aided in eluding us by their near-sand colors and by their habit of abruptly stopping or of slipping under bushes. Study of motion pictures taken of these lizards reveals that when fully alarmed they may rush forward in semierect position, running only on their two hind feet. The hotter the day, the stronger the sun, the better they seem to like it. Often their presence cannot be detected until suddenly, "like a ball shot from a cannon," they leap forward on the white sands and dash away.

When they are pursued, they run straight away or move in wide circles. When finally they stop in the open, they elevate the body on the slender forelegs and curl and uncurl the tail in excitement or lash it defiantly from side to side. At times, these lively creatures seek safety by entering holes. At dusk, gridiron-tailed lizards bury themselves in the heated sand. In burrowing, they move the head from side to side and push the body forward with the hind feet; the forefeet are held limply pressed to the body.

The males have conspicuous blue and black markings set diagonally on the sides. During the mating season they sometimes display a throat fan. These lizards eat smaller lizards and insects which they catch on the run. Some green plants are eaten to vary the diet.

This is the saurian that fares best in Death Valley's torrid summer. But when the day temperatures run up to 120–130° F. it is seen only in the early morning and late afternoon hours. When these creatures become too warm a kind of paralysis sets in.

The horned toads (*Phrynosoma*) are not toads in any sense, but true lizards. Horned lizard is the correct name for them. There are several desert species, and the habits of these are, in general, similar. They are friendly, docile creatures and are seldom mistreated by human captors. It is well to remember that the so-called horns or spines of the head have bony cores connected with the skull and are not movable. The size, form, and arrangement of these head adornments differ from species to species and are valuable aids in identification. All horned lizards are fond of ants, and these in many cases are their chief fare. The tiny young are active feeders even when but the size of a dime. Their ability to scramble quickly for cover and their close resemblance to the coarse soil or sand on which they crawl aid in avoiding detection by enemies. Some of the horned lizards are viviparous; others lay eggs.

These horned lizards are great lovers of the sun. When night comes, they quickly dig themselves into the warm, sandy soil, using a sort of swimming motion. The burial is shallow, and sometimes the head spines remain jutting out above the sand surface. The nostrils are provided with closely fitting valves to prevent sand from getting in.

Chuckawallas (*Sauromalus obesus**), though widely distributed throughout the desert regions of southern Utah, southern Nevada, western Arizona, and eastern California,

---

* The generic name, *Sauromalus*, literally means "flat lizard"; *obesus*, the specific name, means "fat."

CHUCKAWALI

DESERT BANDED GECKO

YUCCA NIGHT LIZARD

DESERT HORNED TOAD

are always found in rocky areas. When alarmed, they take refuge in rock crevices or underneath rocks, so one needs a crowbar to get at them readily. They are great sun bathers and spend many hours, especially in the morning, in "napping" and from time to time slipping over and among the rocks. Often we see them waddling along, then suddenly leaping from rock to rock. In spite of their ungainly appearance, they move about with great speed—in contrast to their profound patience while lying still. One that I found eating flowers in an encelia bush suddenly dropped down and took refuge in a rock crevice. It was more than an hour before it came forth and began feeding again. A full-grown chuckawalla may be 20 inches long. (See pp. 275 and 282.)

This vegetarian lizard was always a great favorite in the diet of the desert Indians. The strong limbs and tail contain a considerable amount of meat. One day long ago, while traveling through the southern Nevada deserts, I came upon three Paiute Indians camping in a rocky gorge. It was late afternoon, and they were sitting around a fire cooking a half-dozen large chuckawallas in an iron kettle. They had not taken the trouble either to behead or to skin the creatures, and as I looked into the boiling pot I had only a feeling of repugnance for food. The Indians said they would remove the skin when they ate the lizards.

The Gila monster (*Heloderma suspectum*) of Arizona, New Mexico, and extreme southwestern Utah is a clumsy, thick-tailed lizard with upper skin covered with rounded beadlike scales and spotted or banded with orange or yellow on a dark ground. The underparts are covered with flat scales.

It is peculiar among lizards in having fanglike, grooved teeth which communicate with poison glands in the lower jaw. The secretions ooze out between the teeth and lower lip. This is a very sluggish creature, as awkward as it is revolting in appearance. "It will snap and bite," says Dr. Charles T. Vorhies, "when irritated, and will cling like a bulldog when it gets hold." I have always contended that any-one who is persistent enough in his rough handling of the patient animal to cause it to bite deserves to be bitten.

The Gila monster's food consists of such things as centi-pedes, insects, and lizard eggs. During the hottest days of summer, they spend their time in a kind of stupor called estivation.

Among many cowhands and superstitious people of the country districts there exists the absurd notion that these lizards have no anus and that they are poisonous because the body waste accumulates in the digestive tract and must be voided through the mouth.

During the day we find the little branded gecko (*Cole-onyx variagatus*) under pieces of wood or rocks. This is a crepuscular or nocturnal species and comes out to feed shortly after sundown. It takes the name "gecko" from the fact that it may utter a faint, squeaking note such as *gĕ'-ko* or *yĕ'-ko,* said to be produced by clicking the tongue against the roof of the mouth. Banded geckos found on the low deserts often show spots of dull brown on a light, pinkish-tan, soft, granu-lar skin, whereas those found at higher elevations usually have bar or bandlike markings. The plump, cross-barred tail has odd fleshy spurs on either side near the base.

Food consists of small insects, both crawling and flying, and these they get by slowly creeping up on them. When about near enough to take their prey, they slightly raise the tail to give them balance and make a short forward pounce, seizing the insect with a quick snap. After swallowing their food they have a peculiar way of thrusting out the tongue, licking their jaws, and opening the mouth as if to yawn. "Re-minds me of a helpless, sleepy, day-old puppy," said Johnny Deems, my prospector friend, when I showed him his first banded gecko.

The small night lizards (*Xantusia vigilis*), like the geckos, are night feeders, and if we wish to see them during the day we must seek them in their favorite hiding places in the rotted trunks of tree and shrub yuccas. Their presence there is easily explained by the fact that one of their chief foods is termites. They also feed on aphids, ants, flies, ticks, and even spiders. These shy, dark-scaled lizards, when suddenly exposed to the bright light, may seem for a moment to be sluggish, but soon they blink their eyes, hold up their heads, and show other signs of considerable alertness; hence the specific name *vigilis*. The warmer the weather, the darker the scale-covered skin appears; cool weather induces paleness.

Dr. Storer tells us that "the egg membrane is torn by the female when the leathery-skinned egg first protrudes and that the young lizard is aided in its escape from the egg by its own wriggling motions, sometimes encouraged by a nip from the mother." The one, two, or three young are born during the months of autumn.

It was once thought that this lizard was to be found only in tree yucca country, but now we know that it may be observed in the thatch and weathered stems of other yuccas and even under other shrubs of the yucca belt. I recently took several under bushes of desert rue (*Thamnosma*). Once supposed to be occasional, it is now quite commonly seen in suitable places from the Death Valley area to near-mile-high places in the Mohave Desert mountains; I have never seen it in the Colorado Desert. Other kinds of night lizards are known from Lower California and Arizona; the latter (*Xantusia arizonae*) is found under large flakes of granite that have broken loose from sizable boulders.

Many of the desert lizards have the internal body cavity lined with membranes of deep black. The question arises concerning to what extent this velvet-black pigmented surface reacts to keep out heat waves of certain parts of the solar spectrum. We know that transmission of ultra violet rays through the dark skin of several desert lizards is absolutely nil and that protection of the underlying tissues by the horny part of the skin against any type of solar radiation is most efficient.

41. Desert Snakes

For the most part, desert snakes are night crawlers, and it is only by looking for them after dark that we can make a fair census of them or learn how many different kinds there are. Many snakes formerly thought to be rare are now known to be quite common. Illustrating this statement, we may cite the history of the leaf-nosed snakes. Between the time of their discovery, shortly after Civil War days, and 1922, only 11 specimens were known to the museums of the world. In 1922, Laurence M. Klauber, of San Diego, driving his auto over lonely desert highways at night, found that these snakes were in no way rare. Indeed, he often collected in a single night more specimens than had been collected in all the preceding years.

Of the 20 or more snakes which live in the deserts of New Mexico, Arizona, Nevada, Utah, and California, only a few, such as the rattlesnakes, gopher snakes, red racers, and king snakes, are known to most desert travelers and residents. Names such as worm snake, patch-nosed snake, leaf-nosed snake, spotted night snake, lyre snake, and glossy snake are wholly unfamiliar to them; yet snakes bearing these names

DESERT GLOSSY SNAKE

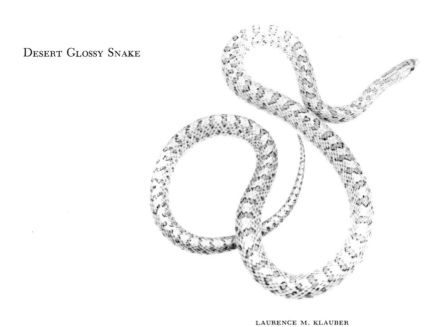

LAURENCE M. KLAUBER

DESERT LONG-NOSED SNAKE

LAURENCE M. KLAUBER

are always about in fair numbers and are known well enough to the serious students and collectors of reptiles.

Most of the habits of the "rattlers" and other commonly seen arid-area snakes are matters of common knowledge, but concerning the ways of most of the others only fragments of information are yet available.

"If you wish to have some of the weirdest desert experiences you have ever had in all your life, tomorrow night come around and we will go hunt snakes and other night creatures on the dunes and in mesquite thickets." So said Charlie, my cowboy friend on the Arroyo Seca, one warm summer evening not long ago.

And so out we went, Charlie leading the way; for I must confess, it looked like nasty, frightening business, calling on rattlesnakes at night. We each carried low to the ground a Coleman gas lantern, with high illuminating power. The deep shadows cast in the hollows of the tracks of snakes, lizards, wild mice, scorpions, and insects made fascinating designs and showed up the tracks more plainly than in the bright sunlight. We saw where large snakes such as the tiger or pallid "rattlers" left their broad, fattish, crooked tracks in the sand. We observed how the little gray, horn-eyed rattlesnake, known better as the sidewinder, left his series of unconnected, parallel, J-like markings trailing diagonally across the sands. By noting the length of these J's, we could make a good estimate of the length of the snake. Mingled among the rattlesnake trails were the sinuous markings left by the harmless, shovel-nosed snake and the dainty tread-patterns of scorpions, centipedes, and ground-crawling beetles such as *Eleodes*. We started out at eight o'clock and did not get home until after midnight, but it will always be one of my most unforgettable nights.

Most of our snakes are wholly harmless creatures; many with vivid colors and strange scale patterns. Only the rattle-

Mohave Desert Shovel-nosed Snake

Western Worm Snake

Chaparral Patch-nosed Snake

Desert Leaf-nosed Snake

San Diegan Spotted Night Snake

PHOTOGRAPHS BY LAURENCE M. KLAUBER

snakes and lyre snakes are definitely poisonous; they alone have habits which make them, to many people, dreaded creatures. The lyre snake found on the deserts of Arizona is an especially hot-tempered reptile and puts on a most frightening aspect when writhing and coiling and repeatedly striking in a fierce manner. This snake has, instead of a rattle, a long, pointed tail, but it has a broad head much as the rattlesnake has and otherwise simulates the fight behavior of the latter. This show of ferocity is mostly bluff, however, and there is little to fear. No lyre snake is dangerously venomous. The small poison fangs are far back on the jaws, and the only way this snake can possibly poison you is to "swallow" your finger. Few specimens are large enough for that!

In the early spring, rattlesnakes are out in the open during sunny hours, either crawling about or basking on rocks; but when summer comes they avoid the bright sun and seek the daytime shelter of bushes, trees, or rocks. Soon after sunset they become night rovers. This leads us to take the precaution of not placing our sleeping bags on the ground in summer; nor do we walk about, especially when barefooted, without use of a flashlight or lantern. Even then, since rattlesnakes so often simulate in color the soils on which they crawl, one may, if not unusually cautious, occasionally step on one. I have had this experience several times.

During the day, sidewinders may often be found in the shade of bushes or buried in the sand with only the flat, spade-shaped head protruding. On summer nights they often may be found lying alongside railroad rails, taking advantage of the warmth they retain. Usually when resting at night they are coiled wholly on the sand surface. Frequently one may see in the sand the saucerlike imprints left by such coiled sidewinders.

Not much can be recorded in detail about the habits of the lesser-known Southwestern desert snakes. The following is an abbreviated list of desert species.

Desert worm snake, *Leptotyplops humilis cahuilae*
Desert patch-nosed snake, *Salvadora hexalepis hexalepis*
Mohave Desert patch-nosed snake, *Salvadora hexalepis mohavensis*
Desert leaf-nosed snake, *Phyllorhynchus decurtatus perkinsi*
West Mohave glossy snake, *Arizona elegans candida*
Desert glossy snake, *Arizona elegans erburnata*
Painted Desert glossy snake, *Arizona elegans philipi*
Desert long-nosed snake, *Rhinocheilus lecontei clarus*
Mohave Desert shovel-nosed snake, *Chionactis occipitalis occipitalis*
Colorado Desert shovel-nosed snake, *Chionactis occipitalis annulata*
Desert spotted night snake, *Hypsiglena torquata deserticola*
Arizona lyre snake, *Trimorphodon lambda*
Desert black-headed snake, *Tantilla eisini transmontana*
Mohave Desert sidewinder, *Crotalus cerastes cerastes*
Colorado Desert sidewinder, *Crotalus cerastes laterorepens*
Panamint rattlesnake, *Crotalus mitchelli stephensi*
Mohave rattlesnake, *Crotalus scutulatus scutulatus*
Tiger rattlesnake, *Crotalus tigris*

42. The Desert Tortoise

It was one of those pleasantly warm mid-mornings in late August. The night before it had rained, and the air was still pungent with the odor of creosote bush. Basking in the sun in front of a hole in the west side of a steep arroyo bank was a desert tortoise. Just inside the burrow entrance, but in the sun, was another, probably her mate, with outstretched neck and blinking, yellow-irised eyes. He, too, had been activated by the coolness accompanying the night's heavy shower.

As I approached the tortoise which was well out of its den, she evidently sensed danger, for she hurried back into the opening, pushing her slow-moving companion before her. He had no time to turn around or even protest. She kept on pushing with her strong limbs until both tortoises were fully three feet back in the obliquely descending burrow.

Seldom are desert tortoises found, as these were, out in the daytime in midsummer. During the warm hours they are, as a rule, hidden under bushes or "holed up," as the prospectors say, to avoid the heat to which they are sensitive. Their principal period of daytime activity is during sunny days in March, April, and May, when the temperatures are moderate and the green vegetation on which they largely subsist is abundant. As the growing season of annual plants comes to an end, they eat sparingly of dry grasses and herbs.

Spring is the time for finding their mates. The males then engage in strange bouts. As they approach one another, each stretches out its long neck and begins a series of peculiar head bobbings. Usually one tortoise is more aggressive than the other and clumsily circles round and round, attempting to bite the legs or head of his rival. Failing in this, he makes repeated forward lunges, trying to bump or ram the other with his gular horn, the strange, bifid, forward-pointing extension of the lower body shell-plate or plastron. Sometimes, he may actually turn over his antagonist, leaving the poor creature to struggle, perhaps for hours, to right himself by means of outthrust head and strong legs. If he cannot throw himself back to normal position, he may die, either because of congestion of blood in the lungs or through suffocation. The thin, flat lungs are broadly spread out just beneath the back shell or carapace, and when the reptile is on its back all the weight of the other internal organs rests upon the lungs, making normal breathing impossible.

Some of the males seem much more pugnacious than others and engage in jousts with females as well as with other males. Bouts between tortoises may occur at any time during their season of activity and are not necessarily related to mating or to sexual rivalry.

Mating may take place any time from March to August— earlier, of course, in the Southern deserts. The peak of egg-laying time appears to be in June, and the time of most frequent hatching, September. When preparing to lay her eggs, the female uses one of her strong, elephant-footed, hind legs to dig a hole three or four inches deep in sand or other loose soil. In this she deposits her eggs, three to five of them, and then covers them up, probably employing the same hind limb. The hard-shelled eggs are nearly round, and when first laid, sufficiently transluscent to show a small gas bubble inside. The yolk is cream-colored and surrounded by a watery albumen. The newly hatched young are tiny replicas of the parent and have dull mustard-yellow or brown shells with all the tiny scales beautifully marked. Even after two months' growth they are scarcely larger than a silver dollar. Growth is slow, and when we see a large tortoise with a shell measuring 12 or 13 inches in length, we may conclude it is very old, perhaps 20 or 25 years or more. It can be definitely stated that there is no way to determine the exact age. Certainly it cannot be done by counting the "rings" on their broad scales, or by comparing the length of the tails, as is sometimes suggested.

The chief activities of tortoises are sun-basking, sleeping, traveling, eating, and digging. That they have considerable ability to climb the steeps is attested by the fact that we often find them or their large, fusiform, fecal droppings high up among hillside rocks. They move with considerable deliberation, but their persistence makes it possible for them to cover fair distances, perhaps up to several hundred yards, in an hour's time. Careful studies made by Angus W. Woodbury and Dr. Ross Hardy tend to show that tortoises do not travel over the country at random but, instead, tend to remain in rather restricted areas, generally of only a few acres' extent.

Sometimes, when quickly approached, a tortoise will withdraw into its shell with a distinct "hiss." Except for the "grunts" of males when courting or engaging in copulation, this is the only sound desert tortoises make. After withdrawing within their shell, they generally remain motionless for some time. When picked up, a tortoise occasionally keeps the head and limbs out and kicks in what might be termed a protest. When placed on the ground, it may even make immediate efforts to escape, but this is unusual.

Practically the only water these creatures get is from eating succulent plant tissues or is manufactured by synthesis within their own bodies. They will drink freely from shallow, rain-water pools in natural rock basins when they can, but such opportunities, in a land as dry as theirs usually is, are few. The scale-covered shell and horny skin, which are practically waterproof, reduce evaporation from the body surface to an almost zero minimum. The bladder holds considerable amounts of water, but this water probably cannot be utilized and serves only as a fluid to hold the white, insoluble, uric-acid wastes. When picked up, tortoises often quickly void this bladder-stored water, probably as a defensive measure. As long ago as 1881, E. T. Cox, of Tucson, Arizona, reported finding within the body of a tortoise a pair of large membranous sacs filled with clear water; he concluded, probably correctly, that these were reservoirs for water storage, useful in time of extreme drought.

Examination of tortoise shells shows evidence that they are quite frequently menaced by the attacks of predators such as coyotes and wildcats. Toothmarks about the edges of the shell are often numerous. Occasionally I find empty shells of adults which indicate that the victims met death through violence; the shells are badly broken and all the internal parts have been cleaned out. The young tortoises face the greatest peril. Their shells are soft and incompletely ossified, and their small size makes them a tempting mouthful to a carnivore.

Our desert tortoises have two kinds of underground shelters—the shallow, individual, summer holes and the more extensive, communal, winter ones, perhaps inhabited by as many as a dozen hibernating individuals. Tunnels, especially those made in the open desert in gravelly soils, have half-moon-shaped entrances conforming to the tortoise's body. They descend into the earth obliquely, generally at an angle of about 30 degrees to the horizontal. The lengthier ones may go straight in six or seven feet, then curve and branch,

Desert Tortoise

Den of a Desert Tortoise

ultimately to reach a length of 20 or even 30 feet. Such long burrows are probably to be found only in the most northern parts of the tortoise's range, where it is necessary to go deep to find equitable winter temperatures. The winter dens are often used year after year.

Digging is done by the forefeet. When the amount of earth excavated begins to interfere with further progress, the tortoise turns about, and, pushing with the strong hind limbs, makes of itself a sort of animated bulldozer and shoves the accumulated earth outward in front of it.

The habitat and distribution of desert tortoises is largely determined by soil types. As pointed out by Dr. Hardy, the soil must be sufficiently free from rocks to permit digging, and at the same time compact enough to maintain a strong archway over the hole after it is dug. This readily explains why these reptiles are absent from dune areas and also from places where stony, volcanic soils are prevalent.

In suitable places, desert tortoises are found inhabiting the more arid areas of extreme southern Utah, southern Nevada (mostly in Clark County), the California deserts, and deserts of southern and western Arizona and northern Sonora in Mexico.

These slow-moving creatures of the desert are properly called tortoises, not "turtles," as we so often hear. In general, the word "turtle" should be used to distinguish the sea-dwelling paddle-limbed chelonians in which the digits are closely united to form a "flipper" or "swim paddle." In both the freshwater and true, or land, tortoises the ends of the digits are free and terminate in curved, horny claws. Their limbs are often adapted for walking on land. To this group belongs our desert tortoise, as well as all the box tortoises with hinged plaston. These all have high, vaulted shells, and the upper and lower shell parts are completely welded together into an ovoid box. The pond tortoises are set apart because of their aquatic habits and their depressed and shelving upper shells.

The terrapins are distinguished from the land tortoises by having the digits furnished with webs, or at least rudiments of them. This segregation agrees with the point of view of British students of reptiles. It is thoroughly scientific, and there is much to say in its favor. In the United States, as pointed out by Clifford H. Pope, there is a tendency to think of all chelonians as "turtles," and to call all fresh-water species with market value "terrapins"; strictly land forms, with high, vaulted backs and stump-shaped hind limbs, we call "tortoises."

The tortoise's worst enemy is man, who so often thinks he must either kill or take home alive to show to his children at least one of these inoffensive, shy creatures. The chances are that only a few weeks or months pass until all interest is lost, and the poor tortoise either dies of neglect or is killed on city streets by a fast-moving vehicle. I have made many special trips to the desert hinterland to return to their native environment wandering tortoises that I have picked up on city streets.

Says Angus W. Woodbury:

One of the most sinister dangers comes from service station operators in the tortoise country who gather up tortoises and give or sell them to travelers. By this means, tortoises have been dispersed widely over the country. Few cities, especially in the west, have been without tortoises in somebody's back yard. This is the end of the line for them. Many of them invariably escape and wander around the neighborhood. They may find new homes or they may wander into the countryside and get lost where they may live out the rest of their lives in solitude. There is practically no chance that they will ever find a mate and perpetuate their kind or found a colony in a new place. In cold climates, there is little chance that they will survive a winter.

The only hope of salvation for the desert tortoise appears to be stopping the raids on its natural population at its source. Educate people to the fact that excessive removal of tortoises from a given area threatens depletion of the population to the vanishing point. Its long life, its sparse population and its low rate of reproduction make it especially vulnerable to continual removal of small numbers of tortoises successively over a considerable period of time. It should become common knowledge that taking just one tortoise for a pet by each of large numbers of people makes in aggregate a serious threat. We should foster the idea that everyone should be alert to the danger and spread the public opinion that would frown upon anyone taking a tortoise or running over one.

Selected References

Arnold, Edward A. *Bird Life*. London: Lindsay Drummond, Ltd., 1949.

Bailey, Florence Merriam. *Birds of New Mexico*. New Mexico Department of Fish and Game, 1928.

Bailey, Vernon. *Harmful and Beneficial Mammals of the Arid Interior*. Washington, D.C.: U.S. Department of Agriculture, Farmers Bulletin, No. 335, 1908.

―――. "Mammals of New Mexico," *North American Fauna, No. 53*. Washington, D.C.: U.S. Department of Agriculture, Bureau of Biological Survey, 1931.

―――. "Life Zones and Crop Zone of New Mexico," *North American Fauna, No. 35*, Washington, D.C.: U.S. Department of Agriculture, Bureau of Biological Survey, 1913.

Bent, Arthur Cleveland. *Life Histories of North American Diving Birds*. Washington, D.C.: Government Printing Office, 1919.

Blake, Emmet Reid. *Birds of Mexico*. Chicago: University of Chicago Press, 1953.

Burt, W. H., and R. P. Grossenheider. *A Field Guide to the Mammals*. Boston: Houghton Mifflin Company, 1952.

Buxton, P. A. *Animal Life in Deserts*. London: Edward Arnold & Co., 1923.

Cahalane, Victor H. *Mammals of North America*. New York: The Macmillan Company, 1947.

Coues, Elliott. *Fur-Bearing Animals: A Monograph of North American Mustellidae*. U.S. Department of Interior, Geological Survey, Misc. Publ. No. 8. Washington, D.C.: Government Printing Office, 1877.

Davis, William B. *The Mammals of Texas*. Austin, Texas: Fish & Game Commission, Bulletin 41, 1960.

Essig, E. O. *Insects and Mites of Western North America*. 2d ed. New York: The Macmillan Company, 1958.

Grinnell, Joseph. *An Account of the Mammals and Birds of the Lower Colorado Valley*. University of California Publications in Zoology, Vol. XV, 1914.

Grinnell, Joseph, Joseph S. Dixon, and Jean M. Linsdale. *Fur-Bearing Mammals of California*. Berkeley: University of California Press, 1937.

Hall, E. Raymond. *Mammals of Nevada*. Berkeley: University of California Press, 1946.

Hausman, Leon Augustus. *The Illustrated Encyclopedia of American Birds*. New York: Halcyon House, 1944.

Hoffmann, Ralph. *Birds of the Pacific States*. Boston: Houghton Mifflin Company, 1927.

Hornaday, W. T. *Camp-fires on Desert and Lava*. New York: Charles Scribner's Sons, 1908.

Ingles, Lloyd Glenn. *Mammals of California and Its Coastal Waters*. Stanford: Stanford University Press. 1954.

Jaeger, Edmund C. *The California Deserts*. 3d ed. Stanford: Stanford University Press, 1955.

———. *Denizens of the Desert*. Boston: Houghton Mifflin Company, 1922.

———. *A Naturalist's Death Valley*. Palm Desert: Desert Magazine Press, 1961.

———. *The North American Deserts*. Stanford: Stanford University Press, 1957.

Johnson, David H., Monroe D. Bryant, and Alden H. Miller. *Vertebrate Animals of the Providence Mountains Area of California*. Berkeley and Los Angeles: University of California Press, 1948.

Klauber, Laurence M. "A Key to the Rattlesnakes with Summary of Characteristics," *Transactions of the San Diego Society of Natural History*, Vol. VIII (1936), No. 20.

———. *Rattlesnakes*. Berkeley and Los Angeles: University of California Press, 1956.

Leopold, A. Starker. *Wildlife of Mexico*. Berkeley and Los Angeles: University of California Press, 1959.

Ligon, J. S. *Wild Life of New Mexico, Its Conservation and Management*. New Mexico State Game Commission, 1927.

Lumholtz, Karl. *New Trails in Mexico*. New York: Charles Scribner's Sons, 1912.

Lydekker, Richard. *The Royal Natural History*. London: Frederick Warne & Co., 1894.

Mearns, Edgar Alexander. *Mammals of the Mexican Boundary of the United States, Part I*. Washington, D.C.: Government Printing Office, 1907.

Merriam, J. C. "Extinct Faunas of the Mohave Desert," *Popular Science*, LXXXVI (1915), 245–64.

Miller, Loye Holmes. "Notes on the Desert Tortoise," *Transactions of the San Diego Society of Natural History*, Vol. VII (1932), No. 18.

Mosauer, Walter. "The Reptiles of a Sand Dune Area and Its Surroundings in the Colorado Desert," *Ecology*, Vol. XVI (1935), No. 1.

Murie, O. J. *A Field Guide to Animal Tracks*. Boston: Houghton Mifflin Company, 1954.

Murphy, Robert Cushman. "Natural History Observations from the Mexican Portion of the Colorado Desert," *Abstract of the Proceedings*, The Linnean Society of New York, 1917, Nos. 24–25.

Nelson, E. W. "The Larger North American Mammals," and "The Smaller North American Mammals," *National Geographic Magazine*, 1916, 1918.

Olin, George. *Animals of the Southwest Deserts*. Globe, Ariz.: Southwestern Monuments Association, 1954.

Peterson, Roger Tory. *A Field Guide to Western Birds*. Boston: Houghton Mifflin Company, 1961.

Seton, E. T. *Lives of Game Animals*. Garden City, N.Y.: Doubleday Doran & Company, 1925–28.

Stebbins, Robert C. *Amphibians and Reptiles of Western North America*. New York: McGraw-Hill Book Company, Inc., 1954.

Sumner, F. B. "Some Biological Problems of Our Southwestern Deserts," *Ecology*, VI (1925), 352–71.

Vorhies, C. T. *Poisonous Animals of the Desert*. University of Arizona Agricultural Experiment Station Bulletin, No. 83, 1917.

Wyman, Luther E., and Elizabeth F. Burnell. *Field Book of Birds of the Southwestern United States*. Boston: Houghton Mifflin Company, 1925.

Index